THE
ADVERSARY
ECONOMY

THE ADVERSARY ECONOMY

Business Responses to Changing Government Requirements

Alfred A. Marcus

Q

Quorum Books
Westport, Connecticut • London, England

Library of Congress Cataloging in Publication Data

Marcus, Alfred Allen, 1950–
    The adversary economy.

    Bibliography: p.
    Includes index.
    1. Industry and state—United States.   2. Industrial
management—United States.   I. Title.
HD3616.U46M28   1984   338.973   83-17674
ISBN 0-89930-055-3 (lib. bdg.)

Library of Congress Catalog Card Number: 83-17674
ISBN: 0-89930-055-3

First published in 1984 by Quorum Books

Greenwood Press
A division of Congressional Information Service, Inc.
88 Post Road West, Westport, Connecticut 06881

Printed in the United States of America

10 9 8 7 6 5 4 3 2 1

To the memory of my daughter, Rachel Rebecca

Contents

Tables

Preface

This book is addressed to managers in the public and private sectors; students and teachers of public and business administration; lawyers, engineers, accountants, and other professional groups, including public relations specialists who are engaged in managing regulation; and those in the general public who are interested in the topic of regulation and concerned about the state of the American economy. It provides perspective on the context of the business system, a subject that is very important given the current national economic conditions of slumping industries, high unemployment, and limited growth. For those in the public sector, it offers insight about how to structure regulation to achieve public ends. For those in the private sector, it gives guidance on how to cope with regulation in a responsible manner.

By and large, relationships between business and government in the United States are adversarial in nature. The contrast is striking between this situation and the dominant European and Japanese approach, which is a partnership, or at least close cooperation, between business and government. Adversary relations between government and business in the United States have profound consequences for the way the firm is managed. Business executives, in addition to performing traditional functions such as accounting, finance, and marketing, also play the role of political strategists.

Rapid changes in government requirements in recent years have made businesses increasingly subject to the uncertain outcomes of government political and organizational processes. Businesses are subject to external political and organizational processes that may be as manageable as their efforts to deal with competitors, stockholders, creditors, suppliers, and customers and to secure new markets, develop new techniques, or acquire additional capital.

Governments provide incentives to conducting certain business activities and erect barriers to performing other activities. A strategic approach to the regulatory process is therefore as important to firms as a focus on traditional decision variables such as price, entry, or innovation. Together these elements play a key role in determining the success and viability of the business enterprise.

This book develops a strategic approach to regulatory management. The first four chapters trace important changes in government regulations and their consequences for the firm. The remaining chapters focus on the strategies managers have adopted to cope with these changes.

Chapters 5-10 trace business responses to two types of regulation—the "old economic" and the "new social" regulation—at three points in the policy-making process. Old economic regulation refers to agencies such as the Federal Communications Commission, the Interstate Commerce Commission, and the Civil Aeronautics Board, which control entry, rate, and quality of service. New social regulation refers to agencies such as the Environmental Protection Agency, the Occupational Safety and Health Administration, and the Consumer Product Safety Commission, which control the processes of production and the character of goods produced. Businesses respond to these types of regulation when (1) new agencies are created and regulatory legislation passed, (2) regulatory programs are implemented and the firm must make decisions about compliance, and (3) regulatory programs are evaluated and suggestions for reform made.

The strategies that managers have used at these stages in the policy cycle are examined. This book is based on conceptual models which are supplemented extensively by case materials and applications to current issue areas. It uses research I have carried out over the past six years in various capacities. Some of the research has been published previously and has appeared in other forms in books, journals, or government reports.

Acknowledgments

Many of my early thoughts about regulatory management were inspired by Barry Mitnick. My colleagues at the Battelle Human Affairs Research Centers also provided a stimulating environment for formulating and developing the ideas in this book. C. Richard Schuller introduced me to the area of synfuel politics and provided continuing insights; Rollie Cole taught me about the concept of incentives and constraints; and Fred Morris contributed insights about the strategic approach, institutional and legal analysis, and implementation. I also would like to thank Paul Sommers and Herb Edelhertz for discussions about compliance, and Richard Shikiar and Richard Osborn for sharing their knowledge of organizational theory and behavior.

James Post, Joseph Raelin, Roger Noll, Daniel Bell, Mel Dubnick, Perri Arnold, Ted Harpham, Alan Stone, Irving Leonard Markovitz, Paul Hammond, Richard Tobin, John Brigham, Don Brown, Bob Mikki, Mark Nadel, Dean Mann, Steve Linder, J. Clarence Davies, and others commented on parts of this book in draft form and provided assistance in other ways. The Department of Energy, Nuclear Regulatory Commission, and the General Electric Foundation gave support for carrying out parts of the research. The views expressed are entirely my own. Individuals at the Environmental Protection Agency also kindly consented to be interviewed for parts of the research.

I would like to express my gratitude to Kenneth Walters and R. Joseph Monsen of the University of Washington School of Business, who gave me the opportunity to teach a course where the ideas expressed here were presented to students. In addition, I owe lasting intellectual debts to James Q. Wilson, Professor of Government at Harvard University, and to John Steinbruner of the Brookings Foundation.

Finally, I would like to thank my wife, Judy, who read early drafts and helped prepare the notes; the secretaries at the Battelle Science and Government Study Center (Kathy Feaster, Kathy Katterman, Pat Davis, and Sandy Smith), who patiently assisted with the word processing; the Battelle librarians, Brenna Louzin and Carla Ginnis, for helping prepare the bibliography; and the director of the Science and Government Study Center, A. Henry Schilling, who, in the last days, when my energies were waning, allowed me to finish the book.

The Rabbis, who wrote the teachings found in the "Ethics of the Fathers," were a constant inspiration. If this book has a motto, it comes from their writings: "If I am not for myself, who will be for me; if I am only for myself, what am I; and, if not now, when?"

THE
ADVERSARY
ECONOMY

1 | The Strategic Approach to Regulation

Companies can transform what appear to be regulatory constraints into opportunities for gain. In the case of small cars and the controversy over safety and reliability, American manufacturers were subject to numerous recalls and prolonged public questioning, while Japanese manufacturers avoided major incidents. Rather than appearing reactive, crisis-driven, and defensive, as did American manufacturers, the Japanese appeared to be anticipatory and crisis-avoiding. They preserved their image and achieved market dominance at least partly because of their ability to take advantage of regulatory changes.

John Mahon and Edwin Murray argue that a firm's ability to manage its relationships with regulatory agencies can be an important strategic advantage.[1] Under the constraints of regulation, negotiating skills as well as traditional marketing and financial competencies are necessary. However, John Meyer questions these assumptions about the importance of business/government interactions and holds that confrontation on regulatory issues tends to distract the firm from focusing on substantive economic issues.[2] Similarly, Mahon and Murray express doubts about whether technical skills developed to meet regulatory constraints can have a positive impact on traditional strategic variables such as pricing and marketing.[3]

The aim of the firm with a strategic orientation should be to identify the relevant competitive impacts of alternative regulatory policies. For example, regulations have different effects on the firms in an industry. In some cases, the largest and most efficient firms have lower costs because of factors such as economies of scale. In other cases, smaller and more recent entrants into the market have lower costs because of more rapid progress on the "learning curve." In either instance, lower costs provide opportunities for gain.[4] Competitors have to comply at a later time with more bother, greater expense, and a tarnished image.

Firms have a strategic interest in preserving regulations governing areas where they have relatively lower costs and in eliminating those where their relative costs of compliance are higher. To develop a strategic approach, management needs to take into account both economic and political factors. It not only has to improve forecasting and correctly perceive the competitive consequences of government regulation, but it also has to show political acumen. The firm should use political and communication skills to persuade politicians and government officials, but before lobbying or making political or technical presentations it has to assess costs, efficiency, and the competitive implications of alternative regulatory policies. To achieve its ends, it needs to appreciate the complexity of overlapping political concerns. However, political skills entail more than public relations or lobbying. They require a strong economic and technical base, direct interactions with the staffs of regulatory agencies, and the ability to form broad coalitions and make public interest arguments.

In responding to regulation, businesses have strategic choices. They can "fight all the way" and "do only what is required," or "be progressive," and "lead the industry." Their responses have been characterized as "reaction and defense" and/or "accommodation and proaction." Most generally, the responses fall into three broad categories: stonewalling, opportunism, and mixed strategies. In this chapter, strategies, organizations, and tactics that firms use in responding to regulatory requirements are discussed.

Stonewalling is the use of public relations and legal and administrative processes to buffer the corporation from the uncertainties of regulatory change. Keith Davis and Robert Blomstrom refer to it as a public relations, legal, bargaining approach.[5] A corporation may resort to such tactics for protection against costly and unnecessary changes. In an uncertain environment, stonewalling can promise a measure of predictability.

The response of Reserve Mining Corporation to water pollution regulations is an illustration of an effort to resist the tide by responding slowly to government expectations (see chapter 9.)[6] The company steadfastly adhered to legal procedure to delay the implementation of a ban on direct dumping of taconite wastes, an iron ore by-product that may cause cancer. Reserve's strategy was to dispute the precise nature of the discharge, its biological effects, and the eventual destination of the discharged wastes. Similarly, Firestone Tire questioned a government report that its 500 series of steel-belted radials was prone to blowouts, tread separations, and other "dangerous deformities."[7] It chose to lay the blame on drivers and refused to cooperate with government agencies. Its strategy was to fight all the way and to do only what was required.[8]

Stonewalling firms usually respond to political pressure and legal compulsion with a series of short-term actions based on precedent and standard operating procedure.[9] Division managers or their subordinates usually take the lead. Their work involves specific technical functions such as finance, marketing, engineering, or research and development. They believe that the core of a corporation is its technical operations, which define what it does. These managers relate to the specific problems that affect their technical areas, and in responding to regulation receive advice and support from the firm's public relations and legal staffs. Top-level management is less likely to be immediately involved, or if it is, will be involved in a minor way. A broad perspective on how the requirement affects of the firm as a whole is likely to be absent.

Opportunism is the effort to transform regulatory constraints into opportunities for gain. For example, a firm can benefit from economic regulation in at least four ways. It can (1) exclude competitors, (2) guarantee prices and profits, (3) control complements and substitutes, and (4) obtain subsidies (see chapter 5). Deregulation gives firms the opportunity to enter markets or increase market share (see chapter 7). United Airlines, an established firm in the aviation industry, saw the opportunity for gain from deregulation, as did other small and aggressive new entrants such as People Express, which staked their future on taking advantage of the competitive implications of regulatory change.

Opportunism emphasizes overall managerial initiative and leadership in responding to regulatory developments.[10] The chief executive and his or her staff have to recognize the issue and make a commitment to do something about it. They must appoint specialists to coordinate activities, generate information, and develop and institutionalize a policy. A classic example is the initial response of the Dow Chemical Company to environmental pollution requirements (see chapter 9). Herbert Doan, former president of Dow Chemical, has called pollution control "an opportunity to profit."[11] In his opinion, "the chemical industry is in the best position of anyone to profit by environmental cleanup. Fundamentally we have the best opportunity to turn reduction of wastes into increases in yields."[12] Dow tried in various ways to make pollution control profitable. Other firms made similar efforts to profit from these requirements. Armco Steel helped formulate EPA's "bubble" policy, which allowed pollutors to replace stack-by-stack requirements with overall cost-effective methods (see chapter 10). As a consequence, it achieved a more competitive cost structure.

The opportunistic firm may be willing to put up with more regulatory constraints because of the opportunities for profit. Like Dow and Armco,

Three M (Minnesota Mining and Manufacturing Company) tried to use pollution control requirements as an opportunity for profit.[13] Its growth and survival were dependent on effective regulatory management. The company's policies rested on a corporate-wide recognition of the importance of technological innovation in achieving regulatory goals, after which it delegated responsibility and initiative to lower operating levels and rewarded lower-level personnel for cost savings.

The Three M program was coordinated from company headquarters. The vice president for environmental engineering and pollution control maintained direct contact with specific managers in the corporation's plants and divisions. At the plant and division levels, special committees were created to deal with particular problems. These pollution control committees were usually composed of plant superintendents; the engineering, manufacturing, and maintenance department heads; and a staff person. They concentrated on eliminating waste in industrial processes and selling or converting residual wastes to useful products. Moreover, the company created a division to produce pollution control equipment and provide engineering assistance to other firms. Starting in 1976, it expanded production and at the same time significantly reduced pollution. The cleanup resulted in cost savings of over $2 million a year. Its success was largely attributable to a strategic orientation that was institutionalized as part of the company's reward and allocation systems.[14]

The four stages in a strategic response are awareness, commitment, policy selection, and implementation.[15] Strategic behavior involves issue identification, analysis and priority setting, and action and evaluation. Information systems that are capable of identifying relevant data and trends and presenting them for management use are needed.[16] Like Three M, the organization has to become aware of an issue, develop a commitment to a response strategy, select specific actions, and see that they are implemented. Action, then, is taken not only to meet legal requirements or to change public expectations, but to positively adjust the organization to the new situation in order to reap economic rewards, if available, and avoid penalties, if they threaten.

Opportunism is a thought-out, longer-term strategy that needs to be made part of overall business practice.[17] In contrast to stonewalling, it is not pressure-driven. An opportunistic firm follows up its awareness of the competitive implications of regulatory changes with the formation of separate units to deal with the political aspects of regulatory policy, but it does so only after it has a thorough understanding of the competitive and economic implications of regulatory changes. Moreover, it expects the political affairs unit to do more than just "fight fires." This unit should also anticipate how an issue will develop, help plan responses to expected events, and consider unlikely contingencies.

MIXED STRATEGIES

Opportunism emphasizes organizational action to promote change, while stonewalling relies more on adaption to external events. The firm's responses to regulatory challenges, however, are rarely as consistent as this discussion has so far indicated. Most firms move from stonewalling to opportunism, or from opportunism to stonewalling, or adopt elements of both strategies at the same or different times. General Motors and Union Carbide, like Reserve Mining, began to stonewall when confronted with the new social regulations (see chapter 9). They looked for legal remedies and refused to comply, based on their belief that the regulations would be of no permanent significance. Over time, however, these two firms adjusted their response and moved from a stonewalling approach to opportunism.

Another example of a mixed strategy is Dupont's response to the fluorocarbon issue.[18] The largest manufacturer of fluorocarbons, with about 50 percent of the market, the company initially disputed reports about depletion of the atmosphere's ozone, arguing that the reports were sensational and premature. Concerned about the economic damage that might ensue if production were curtailed, Dupont began a publicity campaign to convince the public that the controversy was subjective and unscientific. It used various organizations to act on its behalf—the Manufacturing Chemists Association, the Aerosol Education Board, and the Council on Atmospheric Sciences. Dupont argued that it would take years to complete research on the subject, that immediate ozone damage was not major, and that regulation was not justified.

Other firms responded differently to the threat of curtailed fluorocarbon production. Johnson Wax Company immediately removed all fluorocarbon propellants from its product lines, while Gillette formed a task force that planned an orderly transition to alternative propellants. Even Dupont did not respond in a purely defensive manner. Its initial stonewalling was subsequently tempered with the recognition that the company had to conduct serious research to find suitable replacements. Indeed, in 1979, when the Environmental Protection Agency (EPA), the Food and Drug Administration (FDA), and the Consumer Product Safety Commission (CPSC) jointly announced a ban on fluorocarbon propellants, Robert Abplanalp, inventor of the first workable aerosol valve, announced a new design, and alternative products that were cheaper and potentially as effective became readily available.

Because opportunism and stonewalling both have pitfalls, firms move from strategy to strategy. Despite the possible psychological satisfaction of fighting seemingly unjust regulation, stonewalling absorbs time, trouble, and money that might be better spent on corporate activities with a more direct promise of gain. Indeed, there is some evidence that many firms needlessly stonewall, apparently for organizational or psychological reasons, when opportunism would be cheaper and make more sense from a business perspective.[19]

Stonewalling can damage a company's image, which can affect markets, especially if the company is selling to the general public. Stonewalling is a particularly dangerous strategy for firms selling products to individual consumers. Ford's delay and inability to perceive the threat from reports that the Pinto was prone to accidents resulted in a gigantic loss of market (see chapter 9). Ultimately, it discontinued a very profitable product line.

Stonewalling can erode public confidence. It can also sour relations with a regulatory agency, making it difficult to influence future regulation and to deal with the agency on routine matters. Pure opportunism, however, also is hazardous. The principal danger is speculating wrongly on the future of regulatory requirements. A classic example is Eaton, which planned to manufacture and sell automobile air bags (see chapter 9). Like Dow, it was trying to take advantage of government regulations to achieve corporate profits. Its opportunism, however, ran into trouble because of the uncertainties of the political process and the "untidiness" of democratic decision making.[20] Eaton never had the chance to sell air bags because of unforeseen changes in government policy. Policy uncertainty also hurt the infant synfuels industry (see chapter 4). Uncertainty, in fact, has been a major deterrent to economic development.

Stonewalling, therefore, may be combined with opportunism to develop an appropriate strategy for an uncertain environment. Elizabeth Gatewood and Archie Carroll give the example of Procter and Gamble and the toxic shock syndrome (TSS).[21] At first, the company assembled a panel of scientific experts and was prepared to "fight . . . to keep an important brand (Rely Tampons) from being hurt by insufficient data in the hands of a bureaucracy."[22] The company challenged toxic shock news coverage and "quibbled" with studies that showed risk.[23] However, "in about four months" it moved "along the continuum from a defensive response to one that was quite positive—indeed quite progressive."[24] Procter and Gamble took Rely off the market in spite of having invested $75 million and twenty years of market preparation; agreed to buy back any unused product the customer had; pledged research support for the Center for Disease Control; and directed a large educational program about TSS. The advantages were a rapid change in attitude about the company and a recapturing of image after initial negative publicity.

Mixed strategies, as these examples indicate, are interactive; that is, they involve simultaneous changes in the corporation and its environment.[25] As environmental conditions change from relatively stable and placid to relatively unstable and turbulent, firms must alter their strategies. In a placid environment in which impacts are random or predictable, they are likely to respond in an ad hoc fashion with no conscious concept of strategy. Learning is based on trial and error and precedent. In a disturbed environment with multiple processes of interaction and greater uncertainty, companies make internal and external organizational changes to reduce uncertainty. In still more turbulent environments, they try to become proactive—to change the environment, the organization, and the interfaces between them to promote stability and reduce conflict.

ORGANIZING FOR ACTION

Lee S. Sproull holds that corporations do not base their responses to regulation on economic calculations alone: organizational factors play an important role.[26] Basic organizational elements that need attention are the processes by which attention is captured, meaning about external stimuli constructed, alternatives evaluated, choices made, and guides for actions communicated from headquarters to departments.

Most would agree that to avoid "knee-jerk" stonewalling reactions, a company needs to centrally coordinate its effort. Top management should be involved in continuously scanning public affairs and planning policy. Indeed, a survey of large American corporations by *Business Week* showed that corporate executives spent more than 25 percent of their time on public affairs.[27] However, CEO activism has its limits. Peter Drucker argues that traditionally top managers focused on managing the internal affairs of the business, but that today, with less of their time available for this job, they tend to spread themselves too thin.[28] In the end, they slight both public affairs and strategic decisions (see chapter 11).

Public affairs are not peripheral concerns. They should be integrated into marketing and other operational aspects of a business. According to J. P. Kotter, a firm can reduce external pressure by "decoupling or decentralizing . . . to be more . . . responsive to external pressures."[29] Jeffrey Pfeffer and Gerald Salancik also argue for "loosening resource dependencies through greater decentralization."[30]

Firms are composed of technical, administrative, and institutional subsystems with varying amounts of power: the technical subsystem defines the productive competence; the administrative subsystem provides management support and coordination; and the institutional subsystem negotiates and obtains from society the "right" to operate.[31] A dominant coalition (see chapter 2) shapes the corporate response to regulatory challenges. Depending on which subsystem has power, the corporation may respond in different ways to different regulations.

Issue perception often is dependent on the organizational position of key officials.[32] Chief executives, legal staff, public relations specialists, lobbyists, technical people, and operating managers have different viewpoints depending on their positions, professional training, personal inclination, and other factors. Each of these officials interacts with different external groups in ways that differ in their formality and emotional intensity. CEOs, for example, are likely to make pronouncements of corporate ideology and intentions to the general public. Company lawyers, on the other hand, will show concern about precedent and abstract principles that play a role in judicial settings. While public relations officers relate to the media and try to influence public opinion, other executives will focus directly on lobbying, confronting opposing groups and forming alliances with sympathetic ones, and presenting position papers to legislative officials. Operating engineers are likely to be those most directly affected by regulatory changes. They need a clear understanding of the technical requirements of regulatory changes and interact directly with the regulatory agency's technical engineers. Operating managers seek quick resolution of issues so that they can meet their cost schedules and production deadlines.

A corporation, then, is influenced by a broad group of executives with different interests. Issues are likely to be monitored by a variety of key officials with different stakes in the outcomes. Moreover, issues have phases, and during each phase a different group of managers may have dominance.[33] For example, after public expectations change political controversy usually ensues, followed by legislation and litigation. Primary responsibility for issue management passes from one group of officials to another depending on the stage in the political cycle.

The existence of broad and changing coalitions and different groups handling an issue is appropriate to unstable governmental conditions. It is a check on the distorted viewpoints and limited judgmental capabilities of the few top managers who otherwise might make the decisions. According to Jeffrey Sonnenfeld, the number of "windows on the world" should be increased to limit "perceptual distortion" and open the corporation to different concepts.[34] Sonnenfeld maintains that an organization's foresight and receptiveness are determined by structural sensitivity to external perceptions.[35]

Sonnenfeld advocates setting up a special "sensory mechanism" for detecting, acquiring, and interpreting outside information, and yet maintaining the diversity that exists.[36] Likewise, J. D. Thompson calls for "specialized anticipatory scanning" units, which are created to deal with particular issues.[37] These units can buffer the corporation from excessive change and identify opportunities for strategic advantage.[38]

Flexibility in structure to allow for differentiation in the face of diverse environmental stimuli is important. Three organizational mechanisms that may be useful are (1) ad hoc, temporary task forces; (2) permanent top echelon committees; and (3) separate full-time departments. Indeed, many studies have shown that public affairs positions and units are proliferating in the modern corporation (see chapters 3 and 11). In a survey of *Fortune* 500 firms, S. L. Holmes found a movement toward greater formalization among these units.[39] Formalization is linked to the effort to make environmental scanning more sophisticated.

However, with new organizational units come issues of internal power, influence, and coordination. How are the units to be integrated into the existing corporate structure? People in the corporation may consider the new units a nuisance. They may view them as "narrow flack-catchers" created in the wake of external challenges and not useful to the enterprise's major concerns.[40] Analyses and understandings provided by the new units may be ignored because of such suspicions. The units may not be valued because they are not perceived as central to the organization's purpose, and may be recognized as important only if a crisis arises that needs immediate attention.

An organizational subunit which serves as a "sensory mechanism" must be given formal powers by chief executives and corporate boards of directors. Chief executives need to "approve and endorse the work of public affairs units" by giving them attention, involving them in performance appraisals and planning by other units, and providing public affairs officials with an adequate career path.[41] The public affairs function also must be linked to other staff functions, such as legal affairs and public relations; and it must be tied to technical experts in line operations. As Sonnenfeld notes, insight into issues and their implications is often more fully available in production and operation departments.[42]

The power of new units ultimately depends on personal expertise, not formal authority, coercion, or control of resources.[43] Nonetheless the chief executive officer can give more stature to these units by showing that he or she regards them as central components for carrying out the strategic approach. The political clout of these units can also be enhanced if the individuals in them have stature, and if the individuals who choose to sponsor and lead them have prominence and recognized abilities. However, if they are to have a lasting influence the units must demonstrate their worth by showing the firm how to take advantage of its strategic opportunities.

Each unit in the firm must be in a position to take action regardless of its impact on other units. Pfeffer and Salancik argue that there is no need to completely rationalize the relationships between the scanning unit and the rest of the organization.[44] While "mechanistic" and rigid managerial systems are most appropriate for stable environmental conditions, looser "organic" systems with more informal communications systems are more appropriate for rapidly changing environments.[45] Changing regulatory environments require flexibility.

STRATEGIC ANALYSIS

As a general rule, an anticipatory strategy is preferable to a reactive strategy. The organization that anticipates public expectations will have more options. A company can improve its competitive position and increase public and political support while meeting profit and performance goals more expeditiously than otherwise would be the case. However, there may be specific instances where footdragging or stonewalling is reasonable. Therefore, strategic analysis is needed.

Effective strategic analysis consists of at least the following three elements.[46] The first is a recognition that the impacts of regulation are felt at operating levels. They influence decisions about innovation, equipment selection, product development, marketing, finance, and personnel, and apply regardless of the social merits of a particular government requirement (see chapter 9). Second, regulations affect institutional relations and influence the kinds of skills that managers need (see chapter 2). Third, they may offer strategic advantages.

Different firms need different strategies, depending on the type of industry, the size of the company, and other factors. Some companies are more affected by regulation. An Arthur Andersen study for the Business Roundtable found that the electric, gas, chemical, primary metals, and transportation equipment industries were most severely impacted by EPA requirements.[47] Similarly, Arthur Gerstenfeld found that safety regulations had the most impact on the textile, shoe, and wood products industries.[48] In fact, corporations can be categorized by the extent of regulatory impact. Some firms face *limited* economic and health and safety regulation (for example, companies in the electronics and entertainment industries). Others face *maximum* health and safety and economic regulation (for example, companies in the utility and transportation industries). Still others face *maximum* health and safety regulation, but *limited* economic regulation (for example, companies in the steel, chemical, and paper industries). Finally, others face *maximum* economic regulation, but *limited* health and safety regulation (for example, companies in the broadcasting industry).

Firms with maximum economic regulation but limited health and safety regulation are likely to show stable but not spectacular economic performance largely because of this regulatory configuration. Similarly, firms in which economic regulation is dominant over social regulation will do better than firms in which social regulation dominates. The firms that perform worst are likely to be those where social regulation dominates and economic regulation is minimal or nonexistent.

Of course, which firms perform best is an empirical question that requires further investigation. The argument made here is based on the premise that the tendency of economic regulation is to create stability, while the tendency of social regulation is to constrain profits in the industry as a whole. There is a trade-off between stability, on the one hand, and profits, on the other. Further discussion of the different goals of the firm and the different effects of the two types of regulation is found in later chapters.

Another point is that the critical problems facing a corporation may vary with size. For example, it has been suggested that small firms tend to face problems at the core of their existence, such as in technical areas of financing or production. Medium size firms are likely to face these problems in purchasing and marketing, while for large firms the critical problems may be regulatory in nature.

Regulation tends to create concentration in an industry. Murray Weidenbaum and Barry Mitnick maintain that dominant firms have an advantage in responding to government requirements earlier because they have a larger resource base and can take advantage of economies of scale.[49] They can more easily afford the capital costs to pay for required equipment. It is also easier for them to absorb paperwork and reporting costs and the expense of the trained officials needed to file reports. However, Joseph Raelin and Betty Sokol have pointed out that the unstructured nature of the small firm puts it "in a good position for initiating innovative responses to regulatory constraints."[50] Raelin has found that independent companies, as opposed to divisional or subsidiary entities, tend to "react favorably to regulations."[51] They are less constrained by the need to obtain headquarters approval and therefore are more flexible.

In a survey of forty firms representing a wide variety of industries, Raelin found that concentration on market share and productivity contributed to regulatory opportunism, whereas stress on return on investment and profitability contributed to reactive responses.[52] The opportunistic firms traded off short-term profitability for long-term growth. A respondent in a proactive firm commented that to increase market share it was necessary "to take advantage of regulation."[53] In contrast, Raelin found that officials in companies with high technical expertise and profitability often felt that regulatory agencies were "meddling in their affairs."[54]

TACTICS

In periods of rapid regulatory change, it may be hard for firms to take advantage of regulatory opportunities. Instead, they may be pushed into a defensive posture, where the objective is simply to prevent negative consequences. Strategic retreat implies that under changing political circumstances and rapid regulatory innovation, regulated firms may have to give up some ground to new technologies and claimants for power.

However, they should embark on retreat gradually and under carefully controlled circumstances. An example of controlled retreat is the response of the established broadcast industry to a series of innovations in broadcasting regulation in the 1960s and 1970s (see chapter 6).[55] A number of tactics were used by the industry. To avoid worse defeat on the issue of ultrahigh frequency (UHF) channels, it agreed to a compromise. Conceding a lesser point to avoid greater evil is a tactic that can be used to support strategic retreat. In addition, in the case of threatened curtailment of advertising time, the industry formulated its own standards. If some standards are inevitable, standards formulated, developed, and applied by industry are preferable to those imposed by a regulatory agency. Furthermore, in the case of citizen's band (CB) radio, the industry simply resigned itself to an innovation that it could not control. There was little that either the established broadcasting industry, or the Federal Communications Commission (FCC) for that matter, could do to police this technology and prevent its introduction. The situation called for resignation, as long as resignation did not result in permanent damage to the industry. Other tactics used in support of strategic retreat are insisting on case-by-case rulemaking and general policy statements rather than specific rules; appealing to other decision-making bodies; controlling the damage done by developing economic interests in competing technologies; and making symbolic gestures of accommodation.

Frontal attack, on the other hand, is the simultaneous resistance of numerous business and professional groups to an agency's policies. The Federal Trade Commission (FTC) was attacked forcefully for policies that were opposed by numerous business interests including funeral directors, used car dealers, and organized physicians and optometrists. The Chamber of Commerce led a group of thirty to forty business associations and companies in a coalition that proposed a legislative veto which would apply to all FTC actions. When faced with frontal attack from such formidable opposition, a regulatory agency has little choice but to retreat. The legislative veto, however, was not long lasting, as it was overturned by a Supreme Court ruling. Another lesson to learn is the shortness and inconsequence of some hard-won regulatory victories.

Additional Tactics

Good strategies are long-term in nature. They imply coherence among a set of actions which are purposeful and consistent. Tactics, on the other hand, are short-term and designed for immediate impact. In formulating a strategy, a variety of tactics is available.

Rely on the production and distribution of information to influence regulatory decision making. The flow of information to regulatory agencies is a crucial element in affecting their decisions. Robert Leone reports that Weyerhaeuser in its relations with the government attempts to "seize the data base. . . . thus instead of seeking public relations or lobbying solutions to its problems, Weyerhaeuser actively encourages the direct interaction of its technical staff with the technical staff of . . . regulatory agencies."[56] Weyerhaeuser's presumption is that "a properly informed regulatory agency" produces less burdensome regulations.[57]

Use outside experts. Because government policy is increasingly influenced by academic and other technical experts, it makes sense to use experts. Bruce Owen and Ronald Braeutigam mention the case of American Telephone and Telegraph (AT&T), which made it a policy to hire some of the best Ph.D.s in economics produced by elite educational institutions.[58] AT&T also sponsored a major journal in economics, the *Bell Journal*. According to Owen and Braeutigam, it was not "entirely accidental" that the *Journal* "produced a formidable new theory of multi-product natural monopoly" that served as a "powerful argument in favor of barriers to entry and the exclusion of competitors from AT&T markets."[59]

Use litigation. On occasion, litigation costs are small in comparison with the stakes an established firm or industry has in a regulatory decision. In a number of cases, lawyers have convinced the courts to reinterpret the "environment" to include social and economic aspects.[60] As a result, companies have sometimes managed to escape certain regulations. For example, in Los Angeles utility companies successfully argued that peak hour pricing would adversely affect the lives of employees who had to work night shifts, and they thereby prevented the imposition of this practice.

Take advantage of jurisdictional conflicts to play off one government agency against another. Sometimes a regulated entity can choose among more than one regulator. For example, banking regulations sometimes allow financial institutions to choose between federal and state requirements.[61] Therefore, a number of banks may choose state regulation over federal regulation to avoid the more stringent federal requirements.

Use innovation. The output of inventions can be controlled for strategic purposes. Owen and Braeutigam argue that when faced with rate-of-return regulation, high profits can be maintained by encouraging a "steady stream of cost producing innovation."[62] Technological fixes can be used to deal with regulatory decisions that threaten to go against regulated firms.

Organize to achieve political ends. To cope effectively with regulation, corporations have developed new administrative patterns (see chapter 3). An analysis of public affairs issues is now often included in established decision-making processes and functions. Major regulatory controversies have involved "platoons of intermediaries." New business organizations have developed: for example, the Business Roundtable has encouraged direct lobbying by chief executive officers, and political action committees (PACs) have solicited funds from employees to be used for political purposes.

Develop a partnership with regulators. Obviously, companies must be licensed to perform some activities and must act in accordance with regulatory standards to carry out others. Thus, companies need agencies to respond positively to their requests. At the same time, agencies cannot avoid responding to companies if they are to carry out their mandates. This relationship of mutual dependence affords a major opportunity for companies and regulators to forge a working partnership. Agreement on basic methods for licensing and enforcing regulations through extensive sharing of information, frequent informal contacts, and the use of other tactics can ease the burden of regulation.

Mix public considerations with self-interest. B. Peter Pashigian argues that the non-deterioration sections of the 1977 Clean Air Act amendments were motivated by "regional competition and the desire of the industrially developed areas to protect their self-interest."[63] Members of Congress from northern states overwhelmingly favored the law, while members from southern states overwhelmingly opposed it. The amendments were, in effect, an attack by northern business interests against Sun Belt industry. The nature of most political activities requires the use of broad arguments to attract a constituency. As is argued in chapter 5, the factors that ultimately affect a business's success in influencing politicians include the ability to build coalitions within the context of broad social and political movements. The influence that a business exerts at any given time is largely a function of its ability to fuse its demands with a program that has wider appeal. Beliefs are as important as interests in politics; positions must be justified in terms other than mere self-interest; and appeals to broad constituencies are important.

While the strategy of opportunism pays major dividends, stonewalling creates the impression of irresponsibility. Perhaps the greatest disadvantage of stonewalling is loss of decision-making discretion. Unless a regulatory requirement is so obviously impossible to meet that failing to challenge it could result in extreme difficulties later, companies are well advised to avoid stonewalling.

Tactics make sense only when they are applied from a strategic perspective. They are means, not ends, and depend first and foremost on an organization's goals (growth, short-term profit, market share, return on investment). They rely on what the organization is capable of achieving, given its organizational configuration (centralized, decentralized, dominant coalitions, special monitoring and scanning units). Some corporations have the organizational flexibility to be opportunistic, that is, to stress growth and market share over short-term profit and return on investment. Other corporations have limited flexibility and have to be concerned with the latter to the exclusion of the former.

Moreover, there is no absolute correlation between proactive and cooperative responses and reactive and uncooperative responses. A firm may be proactive and at the same time refuse to cooperate with the government. It may be anticipatory and at the same time rely on stonewalling tactics; and it may be reactive and give the appearance of cooperating with regulators. Firms may respond by changing internal structures or processes or by adopting external tactics, such as product diversification or trade association membership. Finally, any of these actions can have positive, negative, or mixed results in terms of impact on the regulated party and the regulator.

Depending on these factors, firms make different responses to regulations and use different tactics to achieve strategic goals. In their strategies and tactics, most firms steer between the extremes of stonewalling and opportunism. They move from one set of strategies, tactics, and organizations to another depending on the issue, the power of the key participants, and the competitive implications.

2 Adversary Relations

In an adversary economy, representatives of business and government are opponents that approach each other as trial lawyers do when they are preparing a court struggle, or as lobbyists do when they are preparing for legislative hearings.[1] A business advocate decribes his role as a "hired gun" in this way: "Ours is an adversarial system. . . . My opponents were doing an effective job of pointing out the imperfections in my client, and I was responsible for countering with the positive aspects of our positions."[2] Advocates present their "best case," not all they know, for they are interested in doing well in the struggle.[3] They bring in experts to make a point, not to enlighten. Character assassination may be common, and motives and inclinations are open to question. If the advocates cannot win, they at least seek to prevent major harm.

The relations between business and government have been compared to war. The trained advocate for either side is like a "military commander." He or she may "prey upon" the "enemy" in an effort to "annihilate it." He or she may bend the "powers" of intellect and the "resources" of knowledge to "deceive, . . . surprise, [and] . . . overwhelm."[4] One's gain is perceived to be the other's loss, but many conflicts are as long and drawn out as the Vietnam or Arab-Israeli wars and the outcomes are as uncertain. The adversary economy is often a stalemate economy with decisive business or government "victories" being infrequent and harm to the public interest being common.

ROOTS OF THE ADVERSARY SYSTEM

Recent concern with the adversary system may be found in federal investigations and congressional hearings of the 1960s and 1970s that resulted in new laws in areas such as environmental controls, noise reduction, workplace safety, and discrimination. People in the business community felt that they had been subjected to a "massive" imposition of federal legislative and regulatory controls over many phases of their operations.[5] The growth in the number of pages in the *Federal Register*, according to business leaders, was "phenomenal" (from 2,411 pages in 1946 to over 60,000 pages in 1977).[6] They pointed out that the steel industry alone was subject to control by twenty-seven different agencies.[7]

Many business leaders felt as if they were "drowning in law."[8] They argued that regulations contributed to a decline in productivity and innovation, increased inflation and unemployment, and created a capital shortage. Claims such as the following were made by business leaders:

- It cost Caterpillar Tractor over $65 million to comply with government regulations in 1976, of which over 90 percent was for compliance with the dictates of two agencies—the EPA and the Occupational Safety and Health Administration (OSHA).[9] Caterpillar argued that its costs for compliance were higher than those of any of its foreign competitors, that a large share of the money it could invest in innovation was being diverted from this productive activity, and that its competitiveness in international markets was being reduced because of increasing government requirements.
- In 1973, OSHA singled out the foundry industry because of a high incidence of occupational injury. Industry spokesmen suggested a program based on the foundries with the poorest safety records, but OSHA insisted on inspecting foundries with the best records, and cited them for numerous violations.[10] The industry argued that the end result of OSHA intervention was an increase in the number of injuries.
- Spokesmen in the foundry industry also blamed regulation for a shortage of capital. The industry forecast capital requirements over a five-year period of $10 billion, but it maintained that 18 percent would have to come from unknown sources or was not available.[11]

These perceptions of unfair regulatory requirements led to political activity. Management began to speak out on the issues. It created grass roots political action organizations among employees and stockholders and "public interest" law firms to represent it. Businesses took many other actions, as managers tried to determine the conditions of the struggle and define the issues as well as secure favorable outcomes.

Critics, however, continued to maintain that business involvement was primarily reactive, and that its purpose was to block passage of major new legislation without offering constructive alternatives.[12] Business leadership, in particular, was often divided, and it confronted agencies in highly contested issues without always having an adequate understanding of the forces involved.

Different Business-Government Perceptions

Government leaders who have worked in business and scholars who have studied both sectors point out that corporate and government personnel have different backgrounds, approach issues with different time frames, view the press and media differently, and have different values and objectives.[13] As institutions, business and government matured at different time periods, for different reasons. The people involved have conflicting attitudes, perspectives, work orientations, and subcultures. It is quite understandable that they find it difficult to communicate and agree about issues.

One obvious difference is that business executives operate according to financial targets that are quantifiable and discrete. They understand share of market, profit, and return on investment, while power and the elusive notion of balancing competing interests are the staples of political debate.[14] The politician's world view and the executive's world view are often in conflict.

George Schultz, the current secretary of state, has served in both business and government. He calls the relationship between the two sectors "the abrasive interface."[15] Businesses as a rule value efficiency, while governments value equity. Businesses are likely to have a "pyramidal structure," while governments, reflecting the checks and balances in the Constitution, are more likely to have a "flat" organization.[16] Shultz believes that the business organization rewards people who get things done, while the government rewards those who formulate policy and maneuver legislative compromise. The two organizatons, in Shultz's opinion, are different, because one is a "doing" and the other a "debating" organization.[17]

The consequences of the conflict between them, according to Mancur Olson, are stagflation and falloff in growth and productivity in advanced industrial nations like the United States and Great Britain.[18] The United States and Great Britain make decisions more slowly than their international competitors, the Japanese and the Germans. Japan and Germany had totalitarian governments before World War II which destroyed most of their organizations for collective action. As a result, these countries have fewer drawn-out and difficult to resolve distributional controversies and are capable of more rapid growth.

The same phenomenon explains the more rapid growth of the American Sun Belt in comparison with the older industrial heartland.[19] The Sun Belt is burdened by fewer special interests and less distributional conflict.

Industries there can take prompt action to exploit new business opportunities. In contrast, older industrial areas like Great Britain and the North Central states of the United States are in certain respects "ungovernable" because of their "crowded governmental agendas" and "overloaded bargaining tables."[20] They do not have the ability to make the prompt decisions needed for rapid industrial and commercial progress.

For example, in 1975 Standard Oil of Ohio (SOHIO) began the effort to secure the necessary permits to move oil inland from California by pipeline. By 1979, when it decided to abandon this project, it had secured only 250 of the 700 permits required, had spent over $50 million, and was spending over $1 million per month on the approval process.[21] In the words of Irving Shapiro, former chairman of the board and chief operating officer of Dupont, in cases like this government and business are like "gladiators in combat, blocking and parrying each other's moves."[22] The end result is that no action is taken in spite of major efforts.

The true costs and benefits of this waste have not been calculated, but many economists and business leaders can show specific instances where adversary relations have done great harm. It is not that people in business and government simply misunderstand each other; rather, they have real conflicts of interest. Adversary relations are often caused by scarcity of resources as well as by genuine policy differences. The resources available are not sufficient to meet the demands of both the public and private sectors, and the economy is affected by the resulting feelings of tension and hostility. Government and business try to thwart one another, and conflict occurs in a series of seemingly unrelated incidents, each of which leaves in its wake negative consequences that make future relations that much more difficult.

The increased tension between the two sectors is a challenge to managers. According to Shapiro, it brings to the forefront a "new breed of manager" who has to be versed in the intricacies of both the business firm and the government agency.[23]

THE BUSINESS FIRM

Even those who assume that businesses have goals other than profit assume that these goals ultimately have to be subservient to profit. Thorsten Veblen, for example, held that other goals at best acted as a "constraint on pecuniary advantage."[24] They did not constitute an "abrogation."[25] The firm that ended up serving its customers and the community to the exclusion of profit faced ultimate failure.

The assumption that the search for profit motivates business firms, regarded by some as the foundation for the success and survival of capitalist society, has made possible major advances in economic theory and methods. Most economic theories of the firm leave little question that companies are influenced by the profit motive.[26] The possibility of profit directs the enterprise in many ways:

1. It is "a necessary condition for bringing a firm into being."[27]
2. It is a factor in the ability of the firm to attract new capital.
3. It may lead to reorganization or change, or if the absence of profit is apparent, it may result in the firm's demise.

Profit is the basic criterion by which subunits of large corporations and the managers of these subunits are judged. The business organization provides "goods and services to society" under the incentive of profit, which is its "reason for being."[28] It tries to produce products of unique qualities that capture a market because they cannot be duplicated by competitors.

Writers such as M. H. Spencer and L. Siegelman argue that under certain circumstances managers may sacrifice profit for prestige, stability, and liquidity.[29] Short-run revenue opportunities may be less important than long-run efforts to gain competitive advantage. J. Chamberlain argues that the objective of business is not necessarily profit maximization, but "rate of return on net worth, total assets, or sales" in comparison with other firms in the industry and based on historical performance.[30] R. Marris maintains that the incentives that influence managerial behavior—salary, power, status, profits, share of market, and public image—are correlated with size.[31] Firms do not try to maximize or "satisfice" profit but growth. According to H. A. Simon, the search for "satisfactory" financial success takes precedence over simple profit maximization.[32]

Even if they are not strict profit maximizers, business leaders are likely to have targets for achieving overall financial well-being. Given a particular regulatory setting, it is likely that the long-run behavior of firms will be consistent with efforts to achieve certain financial targets. However, short-run behavior may depend to a large extent on the firm's specific pattern of decision making.[33] The pattern of decision making often is neglected in discussions by economists. Conventional economic concepts, which portray decision making as the rational pursuit of predetermined objectives (whether they be profit, growth, or competitive advantage), are not "descriptively accurate."[34] The view of conventional economics, which assumes that "corporate management has considerable discretion, is analytical and rational, and can plan comprehensively," is too narrow.[35]

The behavioral theory of R. M. Cyert and J. G. March, on the other hand, assumes that firms have multiple centers of power.[36] Groups from within and without (such as managers, workers, stockholders, suppliers, bankers, customers, lawyers, accountants, and regulatory officials) have different subgoals which they pursue simultaneously. At least five internal subgoals (production, inventory, sales, market share, and profit) and sometimes many more are involved. The actual goals of the organization as a whole are likely to be ambiguous and to reflect the bargaining among various internal units as well as pressures from society.

In a large corporate organization, there may be hundreds of groups of participants, each having a different status, job assignment, geographic location, educational background, career aspiration, attitude toward the firm, and expectations. Boards of directors may have the direct authority, but most analyses of their actual role show that they have limited power. In American companies, where ownership of stock is widely dispersed, the role that shareholders play in companies they nominally own is small. Corporate executives often have sizable but not controlling stock holdings in the firms they manage.

At Exxon, the board of directors is a large group that meets relatively infrequently and is a forum for the exchange of information, not an arena for challenging the decisions of internal management.[37] The company is run by a management committee composed of the more than ten presidents of operating companies and more than fifteen vice presidents of staff departments. In simplified terms, the presidents of the affiliate companies compete for a greater share of the organization's resources, while the staff vice presidents have in mind broad corporate goals. The chief executive officer, who has ultimate day-to-day responsibility for operations, usually plays a role in maintaining the company's public image, appearing on radio and television talk shows and participating in a lobbying group for corporate chief executive officers.[38]

The corporation experiences a variety of pressures stemming from the existence of different coalitions of interests in its internal and external environments. Jerry McAfee, a Gulf Oil Corporation executive believes that "the nature of modern industry is such that management clearly and properly is responsible to at least three groups: the stockholders, the employees, and the community. The inherently different interests of these groups lead to a diversity of sometimes opposing forces and pressures which seek to influence managerial decisions."[39] John Kenneth Galbraith points out that "the decisive power" is exerted "not by capital but by . . . organization, not by the capitalist, but by the industrial bureaucrat."[40] Owners may be interested in maximum return on investment, while managers are interested in the stable returns and steady growth that produce high salaries. Managers may be averse to taking risks and slow to innovate. Once certain financial constraints are met, they may be responsive to external constituencies.

Pressures from society are likely to come from customers, suppliers, and regulatory agencies. For the firm's survival, the search for customers is critical. A major reason for business failures is inattention to markets. From suppliers the firm must obtain labor, materials, and equipment. They are important because they influence costs and prices. Regulatory agencies impose constraints by legal action or by the implied threat of legal action, but they also provide opportunities for competitive advantage and improving public image. As E. A. Grefe comments: "If the chief executive officer's attention is focused solely on share of the market, the market itself could vanish or be severely restricted by regulation. Witness the experience of any number of industries: nuclear power, tobacco, candy, cereal, bottling, chemical, paper, oil, to name but a few."[41]

Pfeffer and Salancik view business organizations as structures of coordinated behavior which need to attract necessary environmental support for survival.[42] The department within the corporation that is most likely to be influential at any given time is the one which is best able to meet external contingencies. At the turn of the century, critical resource exchanges were negotiated by the production and finance departments. As time passed, personnel and industrial relations departments played a more prominent role. Recently, public relations and political affairs have taken on greater significance as the critical challenges to the firm have shifted from effective resource exchanges with customers and suppliers to effective exchanges with government agencies.

Firms alter their purposes and direction as changes take place in the external environment. Because external relations play such a key role in a firm's viability, managers are constantly striving for greater external stability—by trying to attract customers and encourage competition among suppliers, and by exerting pressure to influence regulatory actions.

Some writers have treated firms as essentially political entities. Although most companies are not major articulators of society's values, they are very powerful in some regions and circumstances. They provide jobs, income, and status, and determine what is produced and how much. A possible approach to corporate decision making that stems from studies of political leadership and the exertion of power by key executives is in the tradition of the organizational process approach of Cyert and March.[43] This approach must be distinguished from the rational actor approach of traditional economics.

Moreover, Charles Lindblom has described the process in both public and private organizations that he calls muddling through, in which managers make incremental changes to avoid potential disasters, rather than attaining specific objectives.[44] Likewise Henry Mintzberg and associates, after carefully observing the behavior of business managers, suggest that managerial decision making generally is characterized by "novelty, complexity, and open endedness"; by the fact that organizations rarely begin "with full understanding of the decision situation" they face or "the need to find a solution," and have only "a vague idea of what that solution might be or how it will be evaluated when it is developed."[45] The corporation gropes "through a recursive, discontinuous process involving many difficult steps and a host of dynamic factors over a considerable period of time."[46]

Although ultimately motivated by profits and other indicators of financial success, firm behavior in the short run is complex. Stockholders, employees, and the community play a role; internal and external coalitions with different interests and goals affect outcomes; and leadership may make a difference. The firm is, in a sense, a political entity, as decision making involves groping for solutions gradually over a considerable period of time, and avoiding pitfalls without radically changing policies. "Bounded rationality, conflicting goals, and limited information" are likely to be the norm.[47]

REGULATORY AGENCIES

The behavior of regulatory agencies similarly is complex. Many theories of agency behavior exist. In some ways, they parallel the theories of corporate decision making. The organizational process and political leadership theories of managerial decision making, for example, apply equally to any large-scale organization, whether government bureaucracy or business firm.

Significant differences in the behavior of government agencies and private corporations should, however, be noted (see Table 2.1). Even the most

Table 2.1
Ways That Public Bureaucracies Differ from Private Corporations

---

1. Less market exposure
   a. Fewer incentives to cost reduction and operating efficiency
   b. Lower allocational efficiency, reflection of consumer preferences, and proportioning of supply to demand
2. Proliferation of formal specifications and controls from the legislative and judicial branches
   a. Constraints on procedures and spheres of operation
3. Diversity of bureaucratic perspectives
4. External political influences
   a. Diversity and intensity of external sources of influence
   b. Fragmentation of external sources of influence
   c. Need for support
   d. Bargaining
5. Public scrutiny
   a. Public expectations
   b. Multiplicity, diversity, vagueness, and intangibility of objectives

---

Adapted from Hal Rainey, Robert Backoff, and Charles Levine, "Comparing Public and Private Organizations," *Public Administration Review* 36 (March/April 1976): 233-43.

hard-nosed economist would not hold that government agencies are rational actors that maximize, strive for efficiency, or routinely attempt to achieve low-cost solutions. They generally do not strive to achieve financial indicators of success in either the long or the short term. Officials are more likely to strive for organizational preservation or expansion, which depend critically on the attitudes of voters and legislators.

James Q. Wilson, for example, holds that the "tasks an agency performs," "the constitutional framework," and the "preferences and attitudes of citizens and legislatures" are critically important to an agency's performance.[48] This stress on the need for support from external constituencies parallels the stress that Jerry McAfee places on the firm's need for external support. Citizens and legislatures, however, are more important to regulatory agencies, while stockholders are more important to regulated firms. Stockholders expect a profit that can be transformed into return on investment. The expectations of citizens and legislatures, on the other hand, are harder to determine and may be affected by the behavior and attitudes of regulatory officials.

Like corporate executives, agency officials have a variety of motivations. In every agency, there are cautious civil servants, aspiring politicians, and professionals.[49] For civil servants, survival and stability are likely to be the most important considerations. Political appointees, on the other hand, may use their position as "a stepping stone to higher office." Agency members whose loyalty is to professional groups (such as lawyers, public health specialists, economists, accountants) are primarily conditioned by "professional norms outside the agency."[50] Officials with different aspirations play a role in determining policy. Nonetheless, they are only one factor. The constraints imposed by statutes, the administrative process, and court precedent are equally important.[51] According to Paul Joskow, regulatory agencies "seek to minimize conflict and criticism appearing as signals from the economic and social environment in which they operate, subject to binding legal and procedural constraints imposed by the legislature and the courts."[52]

Because of their dependence on statutes, administrative processes, and precedents, regulatory behavior presents challenges for the analyst. For one thing, regulatory statutes may be quite vague.[53] "Legislatures," Joskow notes, "rarely specify the regulatory instruments and procedures that administrative agencies must follow, but rather leave it up to the administrative agencies themselves to determine what instruments to use and how they should be applied."[54] As a consequence, regulatory agencies may have substantial discretion in deciding how to interpret and implement statutes which bind them. In addition, although the courts require that agencies adhere to due process procedures inherent in common law and statutory law, no reasonable interpretation of statutes and court decisions implies that an agency should provide a particular set of opportunities for a business firm or impose a particular set of constraints. Vague statutes and judicial requirements make regulatory agency behavior very uncertain and difficult to predict.

Regulatory Choice and Implementation

Agencies are not rational actors that systematically pursue objectives and achieve results. Their actions may lead to unexpected outcomes, and their decisions may produce unintended results. A goal-maximizing agency would (1) clarify and rank goals; (2) collect all relevant options for achieving goals; (3) predict the consequences of each option and assess the extent to which each option would achieve intended outcomes; and (4) select alternatives that come closest to maximizing objectives.[55] However, actual government agencies have neither the time nor the information to carry out these steps, and they usually rely on simplistic decision rules. The ideal model of rational behavior does not reflect reality, due to lack of information for calculating maximal goals; the neglect of important alternatives; inability to predict consequences; and selection based on agreement, not on the best option.[56]

Policymakers cannot take everything into account. There are limits to their intellectual capabilities and to the available information. They therefore tend to ignore some of the signficant alternatives. The alternatives they select may tend to differ in relatively small degrees from the policies already in effect. Specifically, marginal or incremental comparisons may be made between policy A and policy B based on which policy accomplishes slightly more of objectives x and y. One policy may provide slightly more of value x; the other policy may give slightly more of value y. Policy choice typically starts with means and proceeds to ends, where choices are made between a little more of x or a little more of y.

Theory that would be helpful in predicting outcomes can be constructed only after the collection of many observations and, even so, may be imprecise in application.[57] Without a theory that is precise enough to predict consequences, it is necessary to rely heavily on the record of past experiences and to take small steps so as to avoid major mistakes.

According to incremental theory, policymaking is often based on a series of limited comparisons carried out over time, and is not rational as defined here. The test of good policy made by public officials is not that it is the most appropriate means to a desired end. Rather, the test is that relevant officials and their constituencies agree and are willing to accept it. Political actors with interests and ambitions seek to convince others of the correctness of their views. Comprehensive rationality probably "assumes intellectual capacities and sources of information that humans do not possess."[58] It may be an "absurd approach," because time and money are always limited. Reaching agreement on a policy, however, may be a poor substitute for testing it against its objectives.

To test a policy against its objectives it is necessary to be sensitive to institutional feasibility and implementation issues: to know if the regulatory agency will receive policy instructions without distortion; adhere closely to these instructions, deviating from them only to improve performance; and show predictability in outcome.[59] Actual implementation is likely to contradict these notions because of such problems as distortion, discretion, and the complexity of joint action.

Government officials receive instructions from different branches of government, and have legitimate grounds to interpret the instructions in different ways. Also, they are creatures of custom and habit and are concerned with how they can cope with the stress and complexity of their immediate tasks. They therefore often oppose efforts to change their operating procedures, and screen out instructions they do not wish to pursue.[60] Moreover, they must take into account conflicting imperatives: legal imperatives to do what is legally defensible; professional imperatives to do what is prestigious in the eyes of professional colleagues; and consensual imperatives to do what is agreeable to the conflicting parties with a stake in the outcome. The roles they play are rarely so clearly defined by rules and procedures as to preclude discretion. Many participants, numerous decisions, many steps, and many attempts to secure agreement from the participants also mean that policies that seem simple and straightforward when established often become complex and convoluted when implemented.[61]

BUSINESS-GOVERNMENT INTERACTION

The interaction between regulatory agencies and regulatory firms may be viewed as a complex system, the parts of which interact in intricate ways.[62] The labyrinthine character of the interactions prevents the achievement of stated objectives and the carrying out of expected outcomes. The basic characteristic of the system is its unpredictability. Theories of the firm and of the agency indicate that there are many interacting parts in the regulatory system. From theories of the firm, business participants such as the following may be derived: stockholders, bankers, employees, top executives, managers, suppliers, and customers. From theories of agency behavior, participants such as the following may be derived: agency officials, congressional staff, politicians, judges, lawyers, White House executives, scientists, economists, and citizen group representatives. The components are different in composition, form, and behavior, and all may contribute to regulatory outcomes. The interaction of components may be described with a full matrix, which implies complete interdependence among parts.[63] In cases of such interdependence outcomes are not predictable. The system as a whole does not have orderly properties that can be described through probability analysis.[64] The system is not like gas molecules under pressure, voters in general elections, or other aggregates of randomly interacting elements that can be adequately described with statistical techniques.

Outcomes

Outcomes of business-government interaction often depend on a group of processes such as (1) agenda building; (2) establishing the "rules of the game"; and (3) administrative politics and policy-making.

Agenda building. The collection of social problems facing a society is not a static quantity, although many problems persist for a long time and become part of the basic structure of public life. From time to time, specific problems rise to the surface, gain widespread visibility, and are translated into public policy.[65] These issues rarely emerge spontaneously. Political culture, public opinion, the social and economic systems, and particularly noteworthy events and crises may offer policymakers opportunities to try new approaches. In many important cases, however, issues are generated by conscious political efforts. Individuals known as policy entrepreneurs put issues on the agenda.[66] The media play an important role. At any given time, a different number of specific entrepreneurs will be involved in agenda building. Coming from within the government and from outside it, they may include elected officials, appointed executives, career civil servants, leaders of interest groups, corporations, the media, and experts. Priorities and perceptions stemming from organizational affiliations, the general culture, and self-interest often determine the reasons that a participant promotes an issue.

Rules of the game. Laws, custom, and bureaucratic routines establish rules of the game for political bargaining.[67] They are a regularized means of reaching a decision or taking action on a specific issue.[68] Rules determine the specific range of issues subject to bargaining. They permit entry to the bargainers. They sanction some moves—such as persuasion, bluff, and threat—while prohibiting others as inappropriate on legal, moral, or sportsmanlike grounds.

For major categories of decisions and actions, formal rules of the game are well established—for example, the annual budgetary process. For others, formal rules are less well established; informal rules prevail. The *iron triangle*, a well-known decision path, refers to close relations developed over time among regulated industries, government agencies, and congressional committees with jurisdiction over these agencies. The members of this triangle have an interest in regulation that is intense and direct, whereas the interest of the general public is weak, diffuse, and less well represented. The strength of the triangle, however, may vary over time, over the subject matter of regulation, and over the specific issues involved. Rules may change; for example, a participant excluded from an issue may enter at a later point when the rules are different.

Administrative politics and policymaking. Officials who implement policy must foster, develop, and maintain support, because widespread acceptance is generally necessary to implement the policy. Support is needed from at least three groups—*key constituencies, active allies,* and *passive collaborators.*[69] Key constituencies are critical for carrying out the policy; active allies have the power to help implement or block various aspects of the policy; and passive collaborators have to agree with the policy or be neutral about it before it can be implemented. Coalition building requires gathering together networks of supporters to press for the policy's implementation.

Conflicts between members of diverse coalitions, however, dilute their effectiveness. Eugene Bardach argues that "tokenism" and "massive resistance" are some of the political reasons that administrators cannot assemble needed support.[70] Some participants appear to contribute to the program publicly, but privately concede only small or token support. Massive resistance, on the other hand, occurs when the participants refuse to comply and overwhelm the capacity of the agency to enforce sanctions for noncompliance. Overcoming tokenism or massive resistance requires the existence of effective control mechanisms that often are not available to administrators.[71] Frequently, well-intentioned officials who seek to faithfully carry out a policy are unable to assemble the elements required to achieve their original policy goals.

Ultimate decisions result from the power and influence of the key participants.[72] Values neglected by one party are likely to be important concerns for another party.[73] Almost every important interest group will try to have a watchdog to redress the damage done by others or to head off injury before it occurs. A participant's influence on government decisions and actions depends on its bargaining advantages and its skill and ability in using bargaining tactics. The tactics firms use to influence government behavior, for example, are important.

Firms may try to manage the flow of information, co-opt the experts, take advantage of jurisdictional conflicts to play off one government agency against another, and make strategic use of innovations (see chapter 1). Individuals who exert power sit at key leverage points. A process of mutual adjustment, negotiation, and concession prevails in the decisions that are actually reached. Many decisions, however, are never made, and policy stalemate may persist for long periods of time. As Steinbruner argues,

Bargaining implies a willingness and capacity on the part of actors to adjust their conflicting objectives in a process of reaching an accommodation—a clear form of value integration. It is natural to suppose, by contrast, that actors will not display the same degree of deliberate accommodation, will act more independently, and will by-pass bargains which under analytic assumptions would appear to be obvious. The limited outcome calculations, the single-value focus, and the dependence on selected feedback channels should all retard the process of accommodation. If, because of the peculiarities of a given decision problem, conflict among the separate actors is relatively intense, then the overall decision process should display less coherence than that produced by mutual accommodations among analytic actors.[74]

An adversary economy is often a stalemate economy.

Confrontation and polarization retard the pace of decision making. In an adversary economy, when business officials and government representatives perceive that the situation is "either-or," for or against, they fight, attack, and counterattack in a zero- or constant-sum game. Outcomes depend on bargaining rules and action channels as well as on the participants involved, their stance on the issues, and their skill and resources in influencing others.[75] Many issues, however, are never resolved successfully to the pleasure of any of the parties.

STRATEGIC IMPLICATIONS

The complexity and uncertainty of business-government interactions in an adversary economy make strategic behavior necessary. Firms have reason to try to mold regulatory agencies, change regulatory situations, and create opportunities for gain. The strategic approach goes against the school of thought that supposes that regulation's only major impact is the imposition of burdens; that it imposes costly requirements, increases paperwork, and decreases innovation; that it means a loss of power for management and a general decline in managerial discretion.[76] It also goes against the school of thought that views agencies as always and inevitably liable to business "capture." Businesses are not always able to use regulations for their own ends, and the meaning of regulation is not simple business domination of the regulatory process.[77]

Regulation as imposition of burdens and as capture are views of predictable business/government relations. The adversary economy, in contrast, has no predetermined outcomes. When agencies regulate and firms respond, firms can "win" or "lose," agencies can "win" or "lose," and both parties as well as other interests in society may gain or suffer setbacks. The adversary economy is notable for its emphasis on the potential for gain and loss by all the participants.

Because the regulatory process is unpredictable, the adversary economy implies a need for a more active role by business in government affairs. The creation of political action committees, the increase in business planning to meet regulatory challenges, and the added employees whose task it is to oversee regulation are signs that an activist approach has now become a much more common part of business practice. In their public statements, however, many managers continue to equate regulation with red tape and the high costs of doing business.[78] They hold it responsible for a "wide assortment of ills," such as "loss of business, layoffs, rising prices, substantial compliance costs, and retarded innovation."[79] The list of alleged regulatory "misdeeds" is very long. However, if the regulatory process is open-ended, then there are strategies and tactics that firms can use, and have been using, in their dealings with regulatory agencies (see chapter 1).

Businesses have some power to arrange regulatory situations to their benefit. Managers, therefore, need to carefully track and monitor the development and implementation of policy to prevent negative outcomes. This means maintaining at least one full-time person (depending on the size of the firm and the complexity of its regulatory environment) as an expert in these matters.[80] This person may act alone, as part of a committee, or as head of a department. He or she may be aided by trade associations, registered lobbyists, or consulting organizations, or may carry out the task with little additional assistance. The responsibilities of a government liaison officer would include understanding agendas and participants, building coalitions, and exercising power.

Understanding agendas and participants. The government affairs officer should keep track of legislation being considered by Congress. It is important to know which subcommittee is hearing the legislative proposal, which interest groups are involved, and the stance of executives, public officials, and others who participate in decision making. Congressional hearings should be attended when necessary; reports and other relevant documents should be read; and contacts should be maintained with members of relevant oversight and appropriation committees and subcommittees and their staffs. Voting records should be scrutinized.

The response officer must keep track of the *people* at the agencies, the Executive Office of the President, the courts, and other institutions that play a role in implementation. The liaison officer should visit the implementing agency and get to know mid-level career officials in order to clarify features of their programs such as target groups, evaluation criteria, and intergovernmental considerations. Communication should be maintained with the group of reporters that covers the issue for trade journals.

Building coalitions and exercising power. Following the development and implementation of policy, however, is not enough. Being an effective participant is as important as being a knowledgeable one. To exercise power, the corporate liaison officer must obtain support from Congress and bureaucratic officials and must form coalitions. The surest way to become part of the policy-determining structure is to be factually informed, to be reasonably objective in presentation, and to take the broader public interest into account. When a company is confronted with unsatisfactory regulatory outcomes, a basic approach is to create and propose alternative policies. Additionally, a response officer may want to propose different procedures or organizational arrangements.

Proposing a different policy, however, is somewhat risky. Redefining an issue may mean that those whom industry wished to exclude may become involved. Moving programs from one decision-making or implementation arena to another may create additional constituencies and change existing coalitions. An awareness of the political implications of proposed changes is therefore necessary.

The business aim should be to overcome the stalemate effects of the adversary economy and to improve outcomes by offering constructive proposals. Still, it is necessary to realize that business expectations about government cannot be the same as its expectations about economic institutions, such as other firms that are motivated by similar financial rewards. Because conflicting actors and goals are so important in government outcomes, the government cannot be a rational or predictable actor governed by the systematic pursuit of objectives. It is necessary to conclude with a note of caution. How a firm should respond to the constraints and opportunities of an adversary economy is rarely obvious. Decisions must be made under considerable uncertainty.

3 | Measuring and Analyzing Regulatory Changes

Discussions about regulatory changes involve fundamental questions about the power of the federal government and its relation to the private sector. An increase in federal authority over business and a reassertion of business power are among the most notable changes in business-government relations in recent years.

To date, analyses of regulatory changes have often been limited to obvious indicators—readily available statistics on the number of employees and the budgets of regulatory agencies, the cost of regulation to the private sector, and the number of agencies and regulatory enactments. The usefulness of these measures, however, is limited in considering governmental activity and its impacts, as many of the crucial and interesting questions are political in nature. This chapter criticizes conventional measures and develops a political viewpoint on the topic of regulatory changes.

CONVENTIONAL MEASURES

There is no doubt that regulatory agencies have more employees now than in the past. EPA, which had under 4,000 employees in 1970, had over 11,000 a decade later; OSHA's staff increased from over 1,500 positions in 1972 to nearly 3,000 in 1980; and the Interstate Commerce Commission (ICC), which had over 1,000 positions in 1951, had more than 2,000 in 1980.[1]

The Center for the Study of American Business (CSAB), under the leadership of the former chairman of the Reagan administration's Council of Economic Advisers, Murray Weidenbaum, annually surveys the growth of federal regulation. According to the CSAB, federal regulatory agencies employed about 28,000 people in 1969, while by 1979 this number had increased to about 88,000.[2] During the 1970s, annual increases in the number of employees in regulatory agencies ranged from 87 percent in 1972 to 1 percent in 1980.[3] (See Table 3.1.)

The years with the largest increases in regulatory staffing were 1972 and 1973, during the Nixon administration. The rest of the 1970s saw more moderate (4-6 percent) growth rates in regulatory employment. In 1979, the annual growth rate plummeted to 2 percent, and in 1980, the last year of the Carter administration, the growth rate was 1 percent. The Reagan administration continued this trend and achieved an actual decrease in regulatory staffing in 1981 and 1982.[4] The year 1982 was the most radical in terms of declines in staffing, with estimated decreases after that year much more modest and regulatory staffing remaining constant at about 77,000.

Nonetheless, it should be noted that although regulatory staffing expanded in the 1970s, the percentage of employees engaged in the regulatory function in comparison with total federal employment never exceeded 3 percent. Undeniably, over the years, there has been substantial growth in total federal employment. In 1790, the federal government functioned with approximately 1,000 employees. By 1979, the executive branch employed over 2.8 million civil servants. But much of this growth is attributable to wars and defense needs, not regulation. A. T. Peacock and J. Wiseman show that the relative growth may be attributed to "an awakening of social awareness caused by war and its aftermath."[5] According to Bruce Porter, from 1916 to 1976 the government experienced four rapid and intensive growth spurts, coinciding respectively with World War I, World War II, the Korean War, and the war in Vietnam.[6]

Another indicator of regulatory changes, growing budgets for regulatory agencies, is also susceptible to varying interpretations. According to the CSAB, in 1969 major regulatory agencies spent $50 million; by 1979, they spent nearly $5 billion; and federal spending for regulation peaked under the Reagan administration at a level of $6.6 billion in 1981.[7] There is no doubt that between 1970 and 1981 the budgets of major regulatory agencies increased, but again it must be pointed out that the proportion of total federal spending for regulation, even according to CSAB figures, was small in comparison with total spending for other purposes. The budget of all regulatory agencies in 1975, after the very rapid spending increases of the early 1970s, was only $4.7 billion, in comparison with a total federal budget of $235 billion.[8] This means that only 2 percent of the total budget was earmarked for regulation.[9]

Table 3.1
Staffing and Expenditures for Federal Regulatory Activities

Year	Annual Percentage Increase in Staffing	Annual Real (adjusted for inflation) Percentage Increase in Expenditures
1971	5	34
1972	87	56
1973	23	9
1974	6	13
1975	5	5
1976	4	5
1977	6	7
1978	5	13
1979	2	3
1980	1	8
1981	−4	1
1982	−8	−1

Adapted from Ronald J. Penoyer, *Directory of Federal Regulatory Agencies—1981 Update* (St. Louis: Center for the Study of American Business, 1981), pp. 1-30.

It is clear that during the last twenty years most of the items that have increased in proportion to the total budget have been for purposes other than regulation—welfare payments, grants and aid to states and localities, and interest paid on the federal debt.[10] And much of the increase in outlays has been caused by inflation. For instance, in fiscal 1980 the increase in outlays for regulatory agencies was 18 percent; however, when adjusted for inflation, the rate of growth was 8 percent.[11] Growth in government generally and the growth caused by regulation should not be confused.

COSTS TO THE PRIVATE SECTOR

Nonetheless, it is argued that regulatory growth has significance beyond the number of employees and the size of the budget. Costs to the private sector, for example, are not reflected in federal staffing or budget statistics.[12] According to the General Accounting Office (GAO) and the Office of Management and Budget (OMB), paperwork requirements of regulatory agencies added 75 million man-hours, or $850 million, to business expenses in 1976.[13] In 1976, CSAB calculated that the budget of major regulatory agencies was $3.2 billion, and that the agencies imposed compliance costs of $62.9 billion—a ratio of 20 to 1. In 1979 it calculated regulatory budgets of $4.8 billion, and multiplied by twenty to reach an estimate of $100 billion in compliance costs.[14]

Though the estimate is large, such studies should be put into perspective.[15] Environmentalists and public interest advocates argue that these studies are sponsored by business groups. An examination of one of the most influential business studies suggests that costs are localized in specific industries, come predominately from a single agency, and are less substantial than many other business costs. The Business Roundtable, a group of chief executives from nearly 200 major corporations, has shown that the regulatory policies of six agencies (including EPA, the Equal Employment Opportunity Commission [EEOC], OSHA, the Department of Energy [DOE], and the FTC) cost forty-eight major corporations in more than twenty industries a total of $2.6 billion in 1977.[16] Manufacturing industries were the hardest hit by the additional costs of regulation ($2.3 billion of the $2.6 billion total), and a single agency—EPA—imposed over three-quarters of the total costs. Furthermore, when costs were compared with outlays for other purposes, the following was true. Compared with capital expenditures by these companies ($25.8 billion), research and development costs ($6 billion), and net income after taxes ($15.6 billion), the $2.6 billion spent on regulation was less consequential.[17]

Moreover, a recent study indicates that cost increases due to pollution regulation started to decline in the late 1970s.[18] According to the Commerce Department's Bureau of Economic Analysis, real spending for pollution abatement and control increased by only 1.5 percent in 1979, after an increase of 5 percent in 1978 and annual average increases of 6 percent from 1972 to 1978. According to the Commerce Department, the last large increase in spending occurred in 1975; increases after 1975 were "moderate" or "small."[19]

Cost studies also are suspect because they ignore benefits. Few studies have analyzed the benefits of regulation, and fewer still have compared costs with benefits. EPA estimates the cumulative costs of its regulations to the public and private sectors at more than $360 billion between 1977 and 1986; however, the agency acknowledges that it "has never applied comprehensive benefit estimation methodologies to a contemplated regulatory decision."[20] A group of academics working for EPA indicated that air pollution deaths cost the nation $5 billion to $16 billion a year and that air pollution diseases cost it about $36 billion a year.[21] Many benefits, including aesthetic ones, are viewed "as intangible and therefore nonmeasurable." Despite difficulties in quantifying benefits, a study issued by Ralph Nader's Corporate Accountability Research Group estimates that five agencies that imposed costs of $31.4 billion in 1978 produced benefits of $36 billion in the same year.[22] The study also estimates that these benefits will increase to $80.6 billion by 1985.

Methodological and ethical issues have complicated efforts to undertake needed cost-benefit comparisons. Benefit studies frequently ascribe a monetary sum to the value of a human life. However, a strikingly broad range of values is currently used by economists in estimating the value of a life. Some economists rely on the present discounted value of future earnings, which amounts to about $63,000 for the average person; while other economists use a willingness-to-pay criterion, which can amount to $1.5 million for the life of an individual.[23]

Estimates of the number of lives that can be saved by a given pollution reduction measure also vary. For example, the low estimate of the lives that can be saved annually from a 1 percent reduction in sulfur oxides emissions is 114, while the high estimate is 1,330.[24] Using different measures of the value of a human life, the benefits of reducing sulfate emissions by 1 percent vary from $7.2 million to $1,995 million, enough variation to justify almost any argument about the appropriate level of abatement.

Moreover, agencies differ in the amount of money they appear to be willing to spend to save a life. Some agencies, such as the National Highway Traffic Safety Commission (NHTSC), it has been calculated, have passed up opportunities for saving lives at costs below $50,000 per life, and have not been able to spend much above $200,000; while other agencies, such as the EPA and the Nuclear Regulatory Commission (NRC), have spent sums calculated to be in excess of $500,000.[25] Such inconsistencies in benefit valuation make cost comparisons a very uncertain tool.

AGENCIES AND LAWS

The existence of federal agencies as counterparts to diversified business operations is considered to be another indicator of regulatory change. According to Weidenbaum, over fifty regulatory agencies act as the counterparts of business activities.[26] He connects specific agencies to business functions (finance, personnel, marketing, manufacturing, purchasing, and R&D), and argues that no major function of the modern business enterprise is immune from interference by numerous agencies. Weidenbaum, though, does not define regulation precisely. His list of regulatory agencies shows the presence of agencies and bureaus that may have regulatory functions, but are not regulatory in character—the Department of Defense, the Department of Health and Human Services, and even Congress.

The CSAB asserts that there were fifty-seven major regulatory agencies in 1981, an increase of more than twenty in ten years; but by what standard can it justify including the Copyright Office, the Bureau of Customs, the Coast Guard, the Drug Enforcement Administration, and the Secret Service?[27] Likewise, Lilley and Miller may have an inflated view of regulatory enactments.[28] In a list of significant regulatory legislation in the 1970 to 1975 period, they include the Flood Disaster Protection and Housing and Community Development Acts.

To assert that there has been significant growth in the number of regulatory agencies it is necessary to define regulation precisely.[29] Robert Cushman's definition of regulation as "government *control* or *discipline* over private conduct" is too general.[30] Similarly, Mitnick's definition of regulation—"policing, according to a rule, of a subject's choice of activity" by a public administrative agent—is too broad.[31] A useful definition of regulation needs to distinguish between regulation and other activities. For example, Theodore Lowi distinguishes between regulatory policies and redistributive and distributive policies.[32] Regulatory policy involves conflict among a limited number of interest groups with a direct stake in the issue, while redistributive policy involves conflict among broad categories of social classes, and distributive policy involves allocation to a single group without broad conflict.

A useful definition should also distinguish between regulatory functions. Alfred Kahn's typology of regulatory functions includes (1) the control of market entry; (2) price fixing; and (3) prescription of quality standards and the conditions of service.[33] He is concerned with the *old economic regulation*: (1) public utility regulation that places controls over industries where competition may be inappropriate or destructive; and (2) programs to promote conditions that increase the effectiveness of a free and open marketplace (for example, antitrust laws). Harold D. Koontz adds agencies that control financial and exchange institutions. These agencies are designed to protect the integrity of the fiduciary relations between such institutions and the public.[34]

Examples of old economic agencies include industry-oriented bodies created at the request of private parties for the purpose of stabilizing or promoting a sector of the economy (such as trucking or commercial aviation), or programs to balance relations between contending groups (for example, labor and management, or securities dealers and investors).

Roger Noll mentions another regulatory function—the imposition of product and process controls.[35] He is suggesting a different type of regulation, involving programs in the areas of health and safety, employment opportunity, and energy and the environment, that came into being more recently than the industry-serving and competition-promoting regulation of the past. These programs often deal with "externalities"—social causes and effects not normally taken into account during private transactions. They fit into the category that has been called the *new social regulation*.

THE EXPANSION AND CONTRACTION OF REGULATORY POWERS

Regulation may be defined as the functions of government agencies that are engaged in directing corporate behavior. As Aharoni observes: "In all countries of the world today . . . the government has significant powers to curb and circumscribe the discretion of private entrepreneurs. Governments often constitute the single most important decision making body for a private businessman to take into account."[36] Government powers that define regulation are derived from English common law and involve traditional government authority to establish and disestablish economic activity.[37]

Two types of control are involved: government control over the number of participants in a given branch of economic activity, the conditions of participation, and prices; and government control over the character of production and the quality of goods and services produced. If regulation is viewed in these terms, two periods of regulatory growth stand out: from 1887 to 1948, when regulation primarily involved control over participants, conditions of participation, and prices (see Table 3.2); and from 1948 to 1978, when it was more often designed to control production and the quality of goods and services (see Table 3.3).[38] Fourteen federal agencies came into being before 1948, and are considered the old economic agencies. Fourteen are post-1948 creations, and represent the new social regulation.

Types of Control Historically Considered

The first major regulatory body at the federal level, the Interstate Commerce Commission (ICC), was not created until 1887. In the pre-1887 period, regulation was carried out, if at all, by state and local governments. From 1790 to 1870, the federal government's activities were predominantly promotional in regard to business. During the nineteenth century, the country's major enterprise was westward expansion, and the action of the central government set the framework for this expansion. The opening and development of the frontier required the assurance of claims and titles and a strong army. Land was the basic commodity, and the federal government was often engaged in land auctions, open sales, public grants, and the provision of land to homesteaders.

Precedents for federal regulation first had to be established in the courts. The Justice Department's Antitrust Division—created in 1890—and the Federal Trade Commission—created in 1914—handled, under federal auspices, business conflicts that had been private and local. These agencies had broadly delegated but narrowly defined powers to impose solutions in cases of disputes among competing interests (such as small business versus big business, or consumers versus producers).

Starting in the 1920s the federal government extended its licensing and ratemaking powers to new forms of transportation and communication. Laws to control hydroelectric development, distribute wavelengths among broadcasters, and control aviation were passed. So-called government-sponsored cartels—price-fixing and market-sharing rings that tried to

Table 3.2

The Old Economic Regulation: Control over Participants, Conditions of Participation, and Rates

Agency	Budget ($ Millions)		Employment	
	1970	1981	1970	1981
Interstate Commerce Commission (1887)	27	66	1,907	1,836
Antitrust Division (Justice Department) (1890)	9	49	595	939
Federal Trade Commission (1914)	20	70	1,385	1,587
Federal Power Commission (1920)[a]	18	70	1,162	1,607
Commodity Exchange Authority (1922)[b]	–	18	–	550
Food and Drug Administration (1931)	68	337	4,152	7,521
Federal Home Loan Bank Board (1932)	21	60	933	1,440
Farm Credit Administration (1933)	4	13	225	267
Federal Deposit Insurance Corporation (1933)	39	124	2,669	3,554
Federal Communications Commission (1934)	24	81	1,637	2,004
Securities and Exchange Commission (1934)	22	78	1,432	1,928
National Labor Relations Board (1935)	38	114	2,281	3,313
Federal Maritime Commission (1936)	4	12	250	306
Civil Aeronautics Board 1938)	48	147	685	650
Totals	342	1,239	19,313	27,502

Adapted from Ronald J. Penoyer, *Director of Federal Regulatory Agencies—1981 Update* (St. Louis: Center for the Study of American Business, 1981), pp. 34-42.

[a]Became Federal Energy Regulatory Commission in 1975.

[b]Became Commodity Futures Trading Commission in 1974.

Table 3.3
The New Social Regulation: Control over Production
and Quality of Goods and Services

Agency	Budget ($ Millions)		Employment	
	1970	1981	1970	1981
Federal Aviation Administration (1948)	–	269	–	–
Equal Employment Opportunity Commission (1964)	12	134	780	3,412
National Transportation Safety Board (1966)	5	18	275	359
Federal Railroad Administration (1966)	4	29	246	431
Council on Environmental Quality (1969)	–	3	–	16
Environmental Protection Agency (1970)	71	1,360	–	9,799
National Highway Traffic Safety Administration (1970)	32	125	518	797
Occupational Safety and Health Administration (1970)	–	195	–	3,009
Occupational Safety and Health Review Commission (1970)	–	8	–	160
Consumer Product Safety Commission (1972)	–	41	–	812
Federal Energy Administration (1973)[a]	–	132	–	1,400
Nuclear Regulatory Commission (1973)[b]	12	417	–	3,029
Mining Enforcement and Safety Administration (1973)[c]	–	131	–	1,036
Totals	136	2,862	1,819	24,260

Adapted from Ronald J. Penoyer, *Directory of Federal Regulatory Agencies—1981 Update* (St. Louis: Center for the Study of American Business, 1981), pp. 34-42.

[a]Became the Economic Regulatory Administration in 1977.

[b]Prior to 1973 was part of the Atomic Energy Commission.

[c]Became the Mine Safety and Health Administration in 1977.

enhance the profits of regulated firms—developed. Supported by iron triangles—made up of persons from the regulatory agency, the congressional committee with jurisdiction, and the regulated industry—the regulatory authorities that developed during the 1930s Depression generally did not threaten business. The explicit mandate of many agencies was to stimulate business development and to promote the revival of a depressed economy.

After 1948, a new type of regulation, far less acceptable to business because it often involved government control over production and the quality of goods and services, came into being. The new regulation differed from earlier regulation in two additional respects.[39] First, the new agencies often had lengthy, specific laws rather than vague statutes. The EPA, for example, had precise pollution reduction targets and timetables which allowed little room for discretion.[40] In contrast, the Federal Trade Commission, which had no specific timetable for eliminating unfair methods of competition, had great latitude for discretionary behavior. In addition, the new agencies were in many cases organized along functional lines. The EPA, for example, regulated the pollution of all firms, unlike the FCC or the ICC, which were limited to a particular industry. The new agencies, as a result, were more resistant to domination by forces within a single industry.

According to Weidenbaum, these changes signified a "second managerial revolution." The first revolution involved a shift in decision-making power from the formal owners of business corporations to professional managers. The second revolution, it was asserted, shifted power from corporate management to "government planners and regulators," who influenced and controlled key managerial tasks.[41] Weidenbaum argues that the second managerial revolution was responsible for a "fundamental change" in the nature of society, with the distinction between private power and public power "becoming increasingly blurred."[42]

In our view, the shift in power from corporate managers to government planners and regulators did not involve such a fundamental change in society. Instead, under the regulation created after 1948, agencies and businesses were frequently adversaries, not allies. Iron triangles to protect regulated firms did not develop. The more appropriate image of the policy process became that of an *elastic net*, as the politics of regulation became broader and more complicated.[43] While iron triangles connote "stable relations among a limited number of participants in a relatively closed policy area," elastic nets involve fragmented, open, complex, and ill-structured relations. Elastic nets make it difficult to resolve conflicts and reach authoritative decisions. They are the opposites of hierarchy, discipline, command, and stability, the opposites of a simple shift in power to government planners and regulators. "The set of participants," writes A. Grant Jordan, "is unlimited and unpredictable."[44] A. L. Fritschler, in his study of the politics of smoking finds radical policy changes in the years between 1968 and 1975, as a small group in Congress, the federal agencies, and the tobacco industry expanded, and additional entities took part in the policy struggle.[45] Elastic nets suggest the pluralist notion that nobody dominates. Nets are imprecise and unpredictable. There is a bias against agreement and a reward for intransigence, an absence of final decision-making authority, and a tendency toward policy drift.

Government Growth

As emphasized, regulatory growth must not be confused with growth in government generally. The trend of government growth is undeniable and today is perceived to be a major public policy problem. In 1929, for example, there were 68,000 civilian federal employees in Washington, and 500,000 federal civil servants in the nation, of whom 300,000 worked for the Post Office. Nonetheless, the federal government was smaller than companies such as United States Steel, General Motors, and Standard Oil. By 1940, however, there were a million federal employees, and by 1970 nearly three million.[46] The government far surpassed most corporations in number of employees.

A political perspective must be applied to this growth. Some have argued that government bureaucrats have advanced a concept of the public interest that is "apart from and opposed to the marketplace." Paul Weaver asserts that the values and world view of bureaucrats and their allies are that of a "distinctive class" which has a "peculiar culture [and] . . . relationship to the means of production." The intent of this class is "to define, dominate, and rule." It has brought distinctive values, including an "inclination to oppose widespread consumption," to bear on policy questions.[47]

The "new class" has not been the main determinant of government growth. In addition to wars and the needs of defense, growth in government has some of the following determinants:

Economic development. In developing nations, taxes and social security contributions typically account for a much lower percentage of gross national product (GNP) than in developed nations. Wagner's "law of increasing state activity" attributes growth in government to the complex social changes associated with industrialization.[48]

Party politics. According to D. R. Cameron, whether a nation's government is controlled by left-wing or right-wing parties provides a strong key to the relative degree of change in government spending.[49] He also finds a strong positive correlation between the size of increases in the public sector and measures of economic equality.

Voting. Alexis de Tocqueville, in his classic formulation, attributes the expansion of government expenditures to the spread of the franchise and an increase in economic equality.[50] According to Allan Meltzer and Scott

Richard, as the franchise is extended, the income of the median voter declines.[51] The median voter, then, has the ability to take income from the rich and redistribute it.

The supply of revenues. Economic development, party politics, and voting are *demand-side theories.* Other theories focus on the *supply side.*[52] They explain government growth in terms of the public revenues that can be sustained through taxation. The *bracket creep* explanation of government growth, for example, holds that a progressive income tax, with inflation and unindexed brackets, moves taxpayers into higher marginal brackets, and leads to increased revenues and a real increase in public expenditures.[53] James Kau and Paul Rubin similarly argue that decreases in self-employment lead to increases in taxable earnings, as employees are less able to underreport income than are the self-employed.[54]

Legislative decision making. Other explanations for increased government expenditures focus on institutions. For example, in a simplified world, legislators are likely to favor all bills benefitting their own districts.[55] When the costs of such bills are allocated across all districts, legislators will agree to pass all these bills, provided passage of the bills benefitting their own districts is guaranteed.

Bureaucratic process. Another theory is that the size and structure of the budget are the inadvertent result of bureaucratic drift.[56] How bureaucrats solve year-to-year problems influences the problems and sets of solutions available in subsequent years. Short-sighted yearly decisions lead to cumulative long-terms problems.

The size and scope of governments in countries with different systems vary a great deal. As can be seen from Table 3.4, the United States is behind many other countries in total taxes as a percentage of gross national product. The relative size of the government sector is lower in the United States than in any other major developed country except Japan. Federal civilian employment, which peaked at 2.7 million in 1969, has been virtually unchanged since then.[57] More important, no theory provides guidance about what the size and scope of government should be in countries with various social, political, and cultural systems.

Regulatory Contraction and Decline

Regulatory growth halted in the late 1970s. In 1976, support for regulation from a Democratic president, a liberal Congress, and a sympathetic bureaucracy appeared very high. The next year, however, the House of Representatives voted against establishing a consumer protection agency. Shortly thereafter, the Carter administration supported establishment of the Energy Mobilization Board, which would have had broad powers to override environmental requirements in the name of energy development. The administration established a Regulatory Analysis and Reform Group

Table 3.4
Tax Revenues in Relation to GNP in Selected Countries

Country	Total Taxes as Percent of Gross National Project	
	1966	1976
Spain	15.0	20.3
Japan	17.6	20.9
Turkey	17.0	24.9
United States	26.9	29.3
Canada	27.6	32.9
United Kingdom	32.2	36.7
Federal Republic of Germany	32.2	36.7
France	34.8	39.5
Denmark	32.6	44.7
Netherlands	37.0	46.2
Sweden	36.4	50.9

Adapted from Patrick Larkey, Chandler Stolp, and Mark Winer, "Theorizing about the Growth of Government: A Research Assessment," *Journal of Public Policy* 1, pt. 2 (May 1981): 162.

in the White House, had regulatory agencies in the executive branch do economic analyses of proposed rules, and gave the Council on Wage and Price Stability the right to file dissenting opinions on agencies' rulemaking proceedings.[58]

Congress made changes in statutes, which included passage of the following reforms:[59]

• Deregulation of the commercial air transport industry by the Civil Aeronautics Board (CAB) proceeded under the Airline Deregulation Act of 1978. In addition, the International Air Transportation Competition Act of 1979 promoted competition among foreign and domestic carriers in the international market.

• The Federal Trade Commission Improvement Act of 1980 provided for congressional review and veto power of FTC actions. It also required detailed analyses of rules, including cost-benefit studies.

After 1978, support for regulation waned. Business failures increased dramatically, and the government began to subsidize ailing industries to increase the competitiveness of U.S. industry in world markets. Major shifts in the direction of economic and tax policy accompanied a backlash against regulation.[60] Reforming taxes and stimulating private savings, corporate investment, and innovation replaced regulation as areas of major government initiative.

Since that time, President Reagan has appointed agency heads and commission chairmen who are often opposed to the very programs they are supposed to administer (for example, Thorne Auchter at OSHA). After taking office, the president issued an executive order that required agencies to list alternatives to specific regulations, and their costs and benefits. These actions were combined with a freeze on the regulations issued in the final days of the Carter administration and the appointment of a cabinet-level Task Force on Regulatory Relief.[61]

The Reagan administration proposed:

- Extensive restructuring of the Department of Energy and review of all of its regulatory activities, including accelerated phasing out of natural gas pricing regulations and relaxed requirements for coal conversions.
- Streamlining of nuclear power plant licensing.
- Review of the Delaney Amendment, by which the Food and Drug Administration prohibits cancer-causing additives in foods no matter how small the amount.
- Review of EPA "cradle to grave" regulations on the generation, handling, and disposal of hazardous waste.
- Easing of restrictions under the Clean Air Act of 1970.

In 1981, the administration announced the following accomplishments:

- Decontrol of domestic price and allocation controls on domestic oil and gasoline production and distribution.
- Withdrawal of Department of Energy proposed efficiency standards for air conditioners, refrigerators, and other household appliances.
- Elimination of proposed OSHA chemical labeling requirements.[62]

The administration also proposed to rescind or revise thirty-four regulations for automobiles, ranging from specifications on bumper strength to exhaust emission standards and certification procedures.

The size, scope, budget, and continued existence of numerous regulatory agencies was affected.[63] In 1982, regulatory staffing decreased by 8 percent. The CSAB estimates that under the Reagan program, the budgets of social regulatory agencies will have been cut by 15 percent in real terms in 1982 and 1983. As a consequence, many agencies have removed initiatives from their agendas, including passive restraints for autos (NHTSA), the children's advertising case (FTC), the IBM case (Antitrust Division), and public transportation access requirements for the handicapped (Department of Transportation).[64] Moreover, many agencies also have decreased the volume of their enforcement activities, with EPA bringing fewer pollutors to court, CPSC recalling fewer products, and NHTSA detecting fewer violations.[65]

Nonetheless, criticisms were made that the Reagan programs did not go far enough. Marvin Kosters and Jeffrey Eisenbach say that the "momentum" has been "lost," and that what appeared to be "a clear sense of direction" has given "way to a disappointing drift."[66] Robert Crandall believes that Mr. Reagan's "supporters . . . cannot be counted on to encourage the substitution of market forces for government regulation and protection."[67]

As evidence of the "disappointing drift" in regulatory reform, Kosters and Eisenbach point out that only about a third of the 8,000 proposed regulations that were published in the Federal Register went through OMB review, and that of the more than 2,700 regulations that OMB reviewed in 1981, almost all were approved as submitted.[68] Moreover, the administration's legislative program was generally conceded to be weak. No coherent proposals for modifying the clean air and clean water acts were presented to Congress. The administration failed to strongly support an omnibus regulatory reform proposal. It did not advance a bill that would accelerate deregulation of natural gas, and it failed to continue Carter administration progress in trucking deregulation.

THE POWER OF AFFECTED INTERESTS

As the rush to regulate lost momentum, relationships between business and government began to change. Opposition to regulation came primarily from affected businesses, which had to pay the costs of additional government requirements. Businesses reasserted themselves in a variety of ways, including the following:

A "BOOM" IN CORPORATE LEGAL STAFF

The Conference Board, in an examination of the impact of government regulations on corporate decision making in U.S. companies, found "explosive growth in corporate legal departments." A surprising 21 percent of the firms surveyed created their first legal departments during the 1970s. On the average, the size of legal staffs more than doubled during the decade. Many firms developed what amounted to a "corporate civil service" to deal with regulation.[69]

A PROLIFERATION OF BUSINESS-GOVERNMENT INTERMEDIARIES

In 1970, it was estimated that 80 percent of the 1,000 largest U.S. corporations had representatives in Washington.[70] By 1980, no major firm was likely to be without a lobbyist. About a dozen new corporate offices located in Washington, D.C., each year. Companies that did not have their own offices secured representation from law firms or public relations firms. Moreover, more than 1,500 trade associations also had Washington headquarters. Perhaps the largest was the American Petroleum Institute, with a budget of $40 million and a staff of over 375 people. The American Bankers Association had a budget of $20 million, and the American Iron and Steel Institute had a budget of $10 million.[71]

Regulatory controversies involved "platoons" of intermediaries, including Washington-based lawyers who represented business before regulatory agencies in the federal courts; lobbyists who represented businesses before Congress; trade association personnel who kept up with pending regulations and legislation; public relations specialists who briefed executives on corporate image; specialized journalists who reported on government developments; and consultants who provided other information.[72] The proliferation of intermediaries was supposed to make it easier for businesses to deal with regulatory phenomena.

THE LINKING OF CORPORATE PLANNING AND GOVERNMENT AFFAIRS

In order to cope effectively with government requirements, corporations developed new administrative patterns. An analysis of public affairs issues was often included in established decision-making processes and functions. Issues became linked to the overall corporate planning process. The future effects of societal and political changes were analyzed in corporate plans, and efforts were made to have line managers internalize the lessons of analysis and provide for them in planning and capital budgeting. Internally, the corporation became more political.[73]

DIRECT LOBBYING BY CORPORATE CHIEF EXECUTIVES

In the past, the chief executive officers of major corporations considered that their task was "to make profits, and to keep stockholders happy," not to engage in politics.[74] The traditional attitude of executives, however, began to shift in the 1970s. The Business Roundtable, a corporate lobbying organization created in 1972, was composed of the chief executive officers of 131 of the 500 largest American corporations. Similarly, the American Business Conference, formed in 1981, brought together 100 chief executives in firms that had grown by at least 15 percent in each of the last five years. These organizations had top corporate officers meet more regularly with members of Congress, the executive branch, and the higher levels of the bureaucracy.

THE DEVELOPMENT OF CORPORATE POLITICAL ACTION COMMITTEES

Federal, state, and local candidates received millions of dollars in campaign contributions from corporate political action committees (PACs). Middle and senior managers often felt pressured to contribute.[75] In 1971, the Federal Election Campaign Act permitted corporations to use corporate treasury funds to establish, administer, and solicit money to be utilized for political purposes.[76] The 1975 Federal Election Commission's ruling in a case involving Sun Oil Company set the ground rules for fund raising by giving corporate committees the right to solicit voluntary contributions from stockholders and management supervisory personnel. Corporate funds could be used to administer the committee, and payroll deduction or check-off plans were permissible. By 1978, the number of corporate political action committees had doubled. They contributed $9.8 million to federal candidates—$4 million more than in 1976.[77] In 1980, their reported receipts were larger than those of labor.[78] Their number had grown from 89 in 1974 to 1,127, and they contributed more than $35 million to House and Senate candidates.[79]

No overall limit has been placed on the amount of money a candidate may receive from PACs. Money, almost without exception, is a critical factor in Congressional races. Only when a challenger outspends an incumbent is it likely that an incumbent will lose. Also, in the 1978 Supreme Court case *First National Bank of Boston* vs. *Bellotti*, the Court ruled that states could not restrict the amount of corporate money spent in initiative campaigns.[80] It argued that corporations could claim protection from laws limiting or prohibiting their spending under the First Amendment right of free speech. This decision also expanded the possible scope of business politics.

BUSINESS COALITIONS

For years, separate business associations fought for specific provisions to aid particular industries. Recently, however, businesses have had more success in uniting their efforts.[81] Lobbyists have cooperated to avoid overlapping and confusing positions and to press for laws that would help businesses generally. By working in effective coalitions, businesses have won a number of important legislative victories. In the battle against the establishment of a federal consumer advocacy agency, for example, businesses formed a coalition and won. They also united in 1980 to cut back the authority of the Federal Trade Commission, and another coalition won support for a bill that would streamline federal regulatory procedures. Their purpose has been to present a united front to lawmakers, to combine in seeking supporters in local districts who will influence their representatives, and to deluge legislators with mail.

THE RESURGENCE OF THE CHAMBER OF COMMERCE

In 1980, the Chamber of Commerce spent $58 million, more than three times its budget six years earlier. In 1981, it was projected to spend around $87 million, an increase over the previous year approaching the entire budget of the AFL-CIO. (This figure is for the national Chamber only, as state and local chapters spend many additional dollars.) Between 1976 and 1980, membership and revenues in the Chamber increased by 100 percent. A nationwide grass roots network, which organized around congressional action committees, saw the number of committees increase from 1,400 in 1975 to 2,700 in 1980. Over 76,000 individuals began to participate in

Chamber activities through a subsidiary organization, Citizens' Choice, which started in 1977. The Chamber also had 600 full-time salaried salespeople selling memberships at a rate of 10,000 a month. By 1983, its membership was expected to reach one-half million.[82]

ADVOCACY ADVERTISING

Since 1975, business has increased its spending for publicity campaigns in major media communications such as the *New York Times*, the *Wall Street Journal*, and national television networks. The purpose of advocacy advertising has been to influence the public in areas where businesses feel they have a major stake. Corporations and their representatives spent $429 million on institutional advertising in 1980, an increase of more than 100 percent over 1975. Mobil has been a leader in the use of this type of publicity. It spent $312 million for articles on energy deregulation on the op-ed pages of major newspapers.[83] Other firms, such as International Telephone and Telegraph (ITT), Texaco, and Gulf, have been involved. Issues addressed include pollution control, consumerism, energy, economics, and regulation in general.

THE DECLINE OF PUBLIC INTEREST ASSOCIATIONS

In contrast to the increased activities of business, many environmental, consumer, and other public interest groups formed in the early 1970s were fighting to keep their memberships and budgets stable.[84] Direct mailings no longer were as effective, as citizens responded less frequently during the recession. Large foundations also began to withdraw support. The Ford Foundation, which had spent large sums of money, was retreating.[85] Common Cause declined from a peak membership of 325,000 to 225,000 members. The various Nader organizations also expected to raise less money than previously. Marginal public interest associations folded.

Four conclusions stand out. First, the number of employees engaged in regulatory functions is actually relatively small. Similarly, neither the proportion of the federal budget devoted to regulation nor private spending for regulatory purposes is large when compared with total federal spending or private spending for purposes other than regulation. The number of agencies and enactments is sometimes exaggerated because regulation is often not carefully defined. The growth of regulation, while sharing some features with government growth generally, is not to be confused with this phenomenon.

Second, if regulation is defined in terms of government powers, two periods of regulatory development are noteworthy: from 1887 to 1948, when extension of government control over participants, conditions of participation, and prices took place; and from 1948 to 1978, when extension of control over production and the quality of goods and services occurred.

Third, the late 1970s signified an end to the second period of regulatory expansion. Since 1978, pro-regulation forces have been on the defensive. The size, scope, budget, and continued existence of numerous regulatory agencies have been affected. Nontheless, these changes may not be permanent, as anti-regulation forces have suffered recent defeats and pro-regulation forces have made a partial comeback. The Rita Lavalle case, the public embarrassment of James Watt, and other incidents show the continued strength of pro-regulation forces.

Fourth, changes in business politics have had an important effect on these changes in regulatory policy. Iron triangles no longer dominate. They have been replaced by more elastic issue networks. These unstable networks have affected firms in two ways. They have allowed for the imposition of new constraints on the business firm, and have provided opportunities for a new wave of corporate political action. All of this has contributed to the creation of an adversary economy, in which a politicized business sector has become mobilized against regulatory agencies.

4 | Incentives and Constraints: The Case of an Aborted Industrial Policy

The government both provides incentives and imposes constraints on business activities. Some have referred to this as industrial policy. Incentives are intended to cause transactions to occur that otherwise would not occur if market forces were operating. Constraints are intended to prevent transactions from occurring that otherwise would occur if market forces were operating. Generally the government will offer incentives when market forces do not provide a benefit which is supposed to be in the public interest, but which is not in the interest of the firms participating in the market. Generally it will impose constraints when the social costs of private market activity are considered to be great and government action is needed to mitigate a market defect (see chapter 10).

Government actions that can be considered part of industrial policy include disbursements (direct subsidies); services (such as the provision of roads and waterways, and R&D); taxation (including tax credits); regulation (such as price controls); reorganization (the creation or termination of business organizations); exhortation (voluntary action, publicity, and jawboning); and market activities (purchases or loan guarantees).[1] Incentives are mostly disbursements, services, and market activities. Constraints generally fall in the category of regulation, but they can include exhortation and reorganization. Taxation can be an incentive or a constraint. Loan guarantees, price supports, and purchase agreements are examples of incentives. Battelle, for example, has found that during the years 1950-1976 the federal government provided some $117 billion in incentives to stimulate the conventional energy industries (oil, gas, coal, and nuclear).[2] On the other hand, among the barriers erected to mitigate social costs not accounted for in market transactions are air and water pollution control and occupational health and safety regulations.

Industrial policy is no simple matter, as incentives and constraints often are in conflict. Increased opportunities for business gain may be diluted by government-erected barriers to business development. The government often acts in a contradictory fashion, taking away with one hand what it delivers with the other. A regulation, moreover, may be both an incentive and a constraint, as it may simultaneously promote one business activity and discourage another. The requirement that best available pollution control equipment be installed, for example, is an incentive that promotes the pollution control industry and a constraint that restricts the activity of polluting industries.

Realizing that the government both discourages and promotes business activities is an antidote to simplistic notions of business-government relations that exaggerate business control or government dominance. The dual character of government impact, the paradoxical and contradictory way that the government directs the economy, is explored in this chapter. Reference is made to the synfuels program. "Synfuels Now, Repent Later" was the charge hurled against this program when it was proposed by the Carter administration.[3] Federal policy on synfuels—an agglomeration of schemes to produce oil and natural gas from shale oil, coal, tar sands, biomass, and other plentiful resources—provides an example for understanding the abortive character of industrial policy.[4]

SYNFUEL INCENTIVES

During the Carter administration, the federal government proposed to spend nearly $100 billion dollars in the 1980s to speed the development of synthetic fuels.[5] The initial proposal called for raising this money through taxes on oil company windfall profits. The program would be administered by a private corporation chartered and financed by the federal government. The corporation would be given the freedom to exercise its judgment on the most prudent investment of its capital. It would be the nation's wealthiest corporation, with assets more than twice those of Exxon.[6] Its goal would be to create the equivalent of 2.5 million barrels of oil daily by 1990, at a price of between $200 and $400 billion.

A social benefit that market forces otherwise would not provide is needed to justify the provision of such an incentive. The justification for creating the synfuels corporation was that decisions made by the private sector would not assure vital oil supplies. An additional governmental incentive was needed to bridge the gap between consumption and production of energy. Without government involvement, it was argued, the private sector would not produce sufficient oil and maintain adequate supplies of energy.[7] Incentives had to be applied to correct an alleged market defect, that is, to bring about an adequate supply when market forces did not seem capable of carrying out this task.

In the United States, only some fifty industrial corporations have total assets of as much as $5 billion.[8] Nonetheless, synthetic oil facilities capable of producing 50,000 barrels a day from shale might cost as much as $4.2 billion.[9] A coal gasification plant capable of producing 125,000 million cubic feet a day of substitute natural gas would require an investment of between $1.2 and $1.5 billion.[10] Moreover, sponsors of such projects faced the risk that the Oil Producing and Exporting Countries (OPEC) would suddenly cut prices because of world economic conditions and destroy the competitiveness of alternative fuels. Furthermore, there were technological risks that processes would not work economically after scale-up, both in terms of yield and efficiency and from operating and maintenance standpoints.

It was argued that the government should spend tax dollars to make synfuels more economically attractive to producers and consumers who otherwise would not be interested in buying or producing them in the same quantities if government support were not forthcoming. Without incentives, synfuels had limited prospects for development, because they were more expensive than competing fuels (oil, natural gas, and other conventional fuels). Without government involvement, the private sector would not be interested in investing, producing, distributing, or consuming synfuels in the quantities the government believed to be in the national interest.

Incentive Forms

The incentives for synfuels production came in a variety of forms. The five principal types were price control, direct subsidies, tax credits, loan guarantees, and deregulation.[11]

Price control. By means of rate regulation, purchase agreements, and other methods of controlling price, the government would keep the prices of synfuels below what they would be in a free market. This action would provide a subsidy to the consumers of the good, who would complete transactions they otherwise would forego. Government-set prices would induce sales and increase consumption at the expense of other forms of energy.

Direct subsidies. The government also could provide direct subsidies to the industry, such as revenues to finance the construction of synfuels demonstration plants. The government would promise to bear the cost and risk of the investment because the private sector was unwilling to do so.

Tax credits. Tax credits would increase the profits that a firm could earn from investing in a given synfuel. By reducing taxes, the government would make projects more attractive than they otherwise would be. A well-established company might even have good reasons for investing in non-profitable projects provided there were sufficient tax benefits to induce it to do so.

Loan guarantees. While tax credits tend to aid the well-established company in need of tax advantages, loan guarantees appeal to new enterprises in need of start-up capital. Well-established companies generally can obtain the money they need more readily than small firms, which may require loan guarantees to assure banks in the event they fail.

Deregulation. In the past, natural gas and petroleum prices were lowered through government decree, with the result that the government encouraged consumption and discouraged production of these fuels. Removing such rate regulation would induce synfuel use. Allowing energy prices to rise to their market level was supposed to compensate for the disadvantaged position of alternatives, such as synfuels, in comparison with conventional fuels.

The Argument against the Provision of Incentives

There must be a strong argument for incentives because of their paradoxical nature. When the government encourages activities like synfuels production, it discourages other investment opportunities. At least seven salient arguments were made against the provision of the incentives:[12]

1. It was not fair to force people to pay for these fuels through the tax system, when there was the choice of working through the market. Deregulation and allowing the prices of conventional energy to rise were sufficient to achieve policy aims. Doing so preserved a greater element of consumer choice. When prices rose, consumers would choose not to buy the higher-priced energy. By subsidizing synfuels, the government shifted the risk to taxpayers and forced them to pay for higher-priced fuel.

2. Market forces would naturally establish an alternative to present energy supplies without the artificial stimulation of incentives. When oil and natural gas reserves were sufficiently depleted, higher-cost sources would become more practical. To prematurely prejudice market forces in favor of synfuels as opposed to any other energy source could impose unnecessary costs on the consumer.

3. Private industry, not the government, was in the best position to determine the kind of technological change needed and to manage the commercialization process. For example, it was easier for the private sector to drop a project when it did not prove promising, because political and vested bureaucratic interests were less involved.

4. The federal government had the reputation for being "more talented at making bad investments than at terminating projects."[13] Even when cost overruns amounted to several hundred percent of the original price, the government often continued an uneconomic investment because of political pressures.

5. Money diverted to synfuels might be invested in less expensive alternatives such as conservation. There was nothing to prevent the federal program from forcing the creation of hundreds of "white elephants" which would have no use. A major breakthrough in a solar process such as photovoltaic cells would make the synfuels program irrelevant. Moreover, an international recession that depressed demand for all energy would make synfuels too expensive.

6. Synfuel facilities created a pool of benefits that might be distributed by politicians eager to serve their clients.[14] The creation of economically dependent constituencies imposed unnatural constraints on program change and development.

7. Finally, even if the government invested all its synfuels money in an effective manner, it might not achieve its goals. The magnitude of the task which it proposed was very large, and there might be a shortage of needed engineers, chemists, or equipment that would prevent synfuels development.[15] Sufficient demand pressures on the supply of individuals, such as process engineers and construction laborers, and on key materials and equipment would initiate rapid price increases which would increase total costs and jeopardize the commercial viability of projects.

The nuclear model and government involvement served as a negative example. As a professor of economics at Michigan State University, Robert Solo, commented:

This type of research and development operation—administered by minor and subservient bureaucrats without responsibility for the program outcome, dominated by advisory committees with representatives drawn from industry, which scatters grants among flocks of incoming proposals—has been used repeatedly. So far as I can tell, it has never produced significant technological advance and innovation.[16]

The rationale for providing incentives for synfuels development was challenged by many critics of government policy. Nonetheless, it was argued that the program was prompted not merely by a desire to reduce the nation's dependence on insecure sources of imported energy. The fate of Western civilization appeared to hang in the balance. Stabilizing international banking and trade and the dollar, and protecting America's allies and other values, in addition to keeping a lid on increases in the price of imported oil, were involved.[17] These were worthy goals that the market might not pursue rapidly enough by itself.

Some projects, it was insisted, are not undertaken by the private sector without government assistance. Large capital expenditures can involve considerable risk that private sector actors are not willing to bear. For example, firms often fail to invest during the earliest stages of technological development because the sums of money required may be very great and there is no guarantee that the results will be useful or profitable to the firm.[18] Moreover, certain technologies may look unprofitable to firms even though their social value is considerable. Thus, so-called market imperfections might justify government intervention. If the government attempts to make major technological breakthroughs which are in the public interest and would ordinarily be resisted by the private sector, then incentives may be justified.

Incentives are something that the government provides for the commercial development of a good or service that does not appear to be economically profitable for private producers and consumers to pursue without government aid. It is a political decision that is made, not a market judgment. The government must be able to justify subsidizing the good or service because of its ability to fulfill noble social goals for which markets would not provide.

SYNFUEL BARRIERS

Side by side with government proposals to offer benefits for synfuel development, there were government-imposed barriers. A sponsor of a synthetic fuel project faced the possibility that price controls, environmental constraints, permit delays, and court actions could alter the economics of a project.[19] An example was the energy industry's concern about future energy rate regulation. Companies were reluctant to invest because the future return might not justify the large risks. In their jargon, they were unwilling to take the "upside risks," because they perceived a probable government ceiling on their "downside potential."[20]

Another impediment was uncertain tax policy. The Energy Tax Act of 1978 provided an additional 10 percent energy investment tax credit on top of the normal 10 percent investment credit. The Crude Oil Windfall Profits Tax Act extended the additional credit to 1990 to companies that completed necessary engineering studies and filed applications for all environmental and construction permits by the end of 1982. However, because of the extensive time required to do engineering studies and the delays likely due to environmental permitting requirements, most potential projects could not meet this deadline and could not qualify for the additional tax credit.

Uncertainties existed about environmental policies. For example, would standards be promulgated only after plants became operational or would standards be known in advance.[21] This question was important because it involved the issue of whether the plants would need retrofitting after they were in use. It therefore affected estimates of project costs and expected profitability. Given the uncertainty, it was difficult for companies to determine if they should proceed with specific projects. Environmental regulations existed that had not been in force ten, twenty, and thirty years ago, and the configuration of environmental regulations that would be enforced in the future was uncertain.

Antitrust regulation was another uncertainty.[22] A synthetic fuel producer needs access to raw materials, the ability to transport the raw materials to a production facility, basic production capacity, and the ability to transport and market the fuels produced. Few companies are able to carry out all these functions. Most would prefer to share the risks by entering into joint ventures with other concerns. At a minimum, an integrated oil and gas company and an engineering firm would be involved. The oil and gas company would supply the site, a part of the market, and the capital equipment. The engineering company would provide the know-how and other necessary management services. The contemplated joint venture, however, would be closely scrutinized under Section 7 of the Clayton Act to see if there were "reasonable likelihood" that the venture would eliminate significant potential competition.

Barriers, then, are regulatory uncertainties that surround issues and prevent normal market planning. Instead of investment, there is hesitation because of the unknown impact of government policies on future income. A barrier is any type of policy uncertainty that prevents transactions from occurring that otherwise would occur were it not for the uncertainties. There is abundant anecdotal evidence about the relationship between these uncertainties and technological innovation.[23] Cogeneration, a process whereby industrial waste is used to generate electricity, is both technologically and economically feasible, but one of the barriers that has stood in the way of its general adoption has been uncertainty about state public utility commission rates and licensing regulations. Also, the use of composite fuels made of pulverized coal has been held back because of uncertainty about the interpretation of clean air laws.[24] Conversion of industrial boilers from oil to coal has been delayed for the same reason.[25] William A. Johnson argues that the main reason for the 1973 "energy crisis" was policy uncertainty.[26] The petroleum companies did not invest in new refinery capacity because of "uncertainty about federal energy policy," in particular, the possibility that Congress might enact "punitive" legislation and that the Department of Energy might issue "inconsistent and poorly conceived" regulation. Oil companies also have maintained that development of the Alaska pipeline was delayed because of uncertainties about the interpretation of the National Environmental Policy Act of 1970.

The anecdotal evidence provides many examples demonstrating that businesses are concerned about policy uncertainty. Uncertainty changes the way businesses operate and makes them hesitant about decisions they otherwise would make. A study supporting this view of the effects of policy uncertainty was done in Allegheny County (Western Pennsylvania). It found that many firms did not go beyond energy conservation housekeeping because of uncertainty about government policies.[27] Likewise, the work of K. Knight, G. Kozmetsky, and H. Baca shows that industry in general has viewed uncertainties about government regulation as a barrier to technological change.[28] Uncertainties about government policies prevent businesses from taking advantage of opportunities that would exist if it were not for these uncertainties.

Firms are unable to assess risk and opportunity, that is, to balance barriers and incentives and make the trade-offs necessary for investment in new technologies. However, more research is needed to determine whether uncertainties about government requirements impede all businesses with respect to all projects, or only some firms and industries with respect to some projects; and, particularly, whether it is simply a rationalization for decisions not to innovate or whether there is, in fact, a simple cause-and-effect relationship between policy uncertainties and reduced technological change.

OIL SHALE UNCERTAINTIES

The oil companies have argued that policies such as those involving prevention of significant deterioration in the 1970 Clean Air Act amendments have jeopardized oil shale development. Oil shale was one of the first synfuels considered for development after the so-called energy crisis of 1973. The passage of numerous new environmental and health and safety laws in the late 1960s and 1970s, however, provided a unique legal and institutional context for the development of this energy resource. To proceed with an oil shale project, a company had to acquire what amounted to the right to use the environment for four distinct purposes: (1) material inputs, including the right to use the land and water; (2) waste disposal, including the right to degrade the land, air, and water; (3) toxic exposure, including the right to expose people and nature to toxic substances and other dangerous conditions; and (4) area removal, including the right to remove from use areas that otherwise would be available for recreational purposes.[29] Obtaining the right to use the environment for these purposes was a difficult task, particularly because of the proliferation of new regulatory laws. The altered decision-making environment increased the complexity and unpredictability of government action. The increased uncertainty led to business hesitation about synfuels development. Let's examine the barriers in more detail.

Land availability. Nearly all the identified domestic oil shale reserves having commercial potential are located in the tri-state area of Colorado, Utah, and Wyoming. The federal government holds title to 7.8 million acres of the 11.01 million acres located in the Green River Basin, the most significant oil shale deposit.[30] During the nineteenth century, the government allowed claims to be filed and patents granted for the use of federal lands irrespective of specific land use considerations. The Mineral Leasing Act of 1920, however, established a system for leasing soft minerals such as coal, oil, and gas on public lands.[31] Because of legal conflicts arising from these laws, approximately 85 percent of all federal oil shale lands are subject to conflicting claims of ownership.[32] The most common form of conflict involves mining claims which can be traced back to the period prior to the enactment of the Mineral Leasing Act of 1920.

Spent shale disposal. The greatest environmental roadblock to oil shale development may be the disposal of spent shale. A 1 million barrel per day oil shale industry using high-grade shale would generate nearly 1.5 million tons of spent shale per day.[33] It takes a ton of shale to get thirty gallons of oil, and therefore the amount of solid waste would be enormous.[34] The 1976 Resource Conservation and Recovery Act (RCRA) was the first comprehensive federal solid waste legislation.[35] Though RCRA clearly gives EPA the power to adopt guidelines governing the disposal of spent shale, the agency has not elected to do so because it claims that it lacks sufficient information upon which to base recommended procedures.[36]

Air pollution control. Air quality problems and issues also are important. It was once believed that air in the tri-state oil shale region was relatively clean, but it was later determined that the background levels of different types of air pollutants exceeded federal clean air standards.[37] Policies are derived from the Clean Air Act, which was passed in 1970 and amended in 1977. The federal government established federal air quality standards, but the states had the right to establish more stringent local regulations than the federal government. Until recently, none of the processes being considered for a commercial-sized oil shale industry could meet both the federal air quality standards and those enforced in Colorado. However, Colorado changed its law in 1979 and was trying to do away with unnecessary regulatory obstacles to oil shale development.[38] Nevertheless, how the Clean Air Act would be interpreted and implemented in the future was uncertain.

Toxic subtances. The potential carcinogenicity of oil shale was first reported in relation to a Scottish oil shale plant, when sixty-five separate cases of skin cancer were identified during the period 1900 to 1921.[39] Early data from animal tests also showed that shale oil had carcinogenic properties.[40] Among the carcinogenic agents in oil shale and its derivatives, benzo-a-pyrene, or BAP, has received the most attention, largely because the analytical techniques for identifying this cancer-causing agent are well established.[41] As yet unidentified carcinogenic agents in oil shale, however, could be even more hazardous than BAP. It is unclear how the Toxic Substances Control Act would deal with these substances.

Occupational safety and health. The federal Coal Mine Health and Safety Act would affect oil shale operations, as room and pillar mining techniques would probably be used.[42] A 50,000-barrels-per-day oil shale operation would entail mining 55,000 to 70,000 tons of shale each day—equivalent to the largest underground mine in the United States and about four times larger than the nation's largest coal mine.[43] The surface oil shale industry of 1.5 million barrels per day would involve a mining effort approximately equivalent to the total annual coal tonnage mined presently in the United States.[44] An industry of this potential scope would be subject to provisions of the federal Coal Mine Health and Safety Act. Signed into law in 1969, this law established the first comprehensive code of mandatory health and safety regulations for the mining industry. It contains strong enforcement provisions and would have to be adapted to apply to the oil shale industry.

According to industry spokespersons, companies have been vulnerable to short-sighted political and bureaucratic delays.[45] One oil shale project originally projected to cost $379 million in 1972 ultimately was projected to cost $1.2 billion in 1977.[46] Another project that was estimated to cost between $204 million and $272 million in 1975 was projected to cost $800 million by 1978.[47] Because of the environmental, health, and safety regulations and an uncertain economic climate, it was difficult for industry to predict the ultimate costs of its investments. Environmental costs could account for anywhere from 10 to 55 percent of an oil shale investment.[48]

The oil shale evidence suggests that without certainty about government policies, private firm decision makers are unable to properly assess risk and opportunity and make the trade-offs necessary for investment in new technologies.[49] They have no method for weighing the constraints against the expected benefits. Policy uncertainties, therefore, may be a barrier to industrial development, preventing market forces from operating that otherwise would operate.

The Energy Mobilization Board as an Antidote to the Uncertainties

In 1979, the Carter administration proposed that an Energy Mobilization Board (EMB) be created to deal with the regulatory uncertainties associated with synfuels development. The board would have had three members appointed by the president and approved by Congress, and its purpose would have been to "cut through the red tape, the delays, and the endless road blocks" caused by regulatory requirements.[50] To accomplish this goal, Carter proposed that EMB be given "unique and unprecedented peace time power to preempt federal, state, and local laws to expedite the construction of new energy facilities that were in the national interest."[51] The new agency was supposed to have had the power to remove legal barriers standing in the way of high-priority energy projects, including any barriers that might hinder the development of synthetic fuels. It was modeled after one-stop permitting agencies, such as the state of Washington's Energy Facility and Site Evaluation Council, which had been established to deal with redundant permitting requirements. EMB members, under the president's plan, would have designated up to seventy-five projects for "fast track" regulatory consideration. They would have had the authority to draw up project decision schedules; set deadlines by which federal, state, and local agencies would have to accept or reject projects; and enforce schedules by stepping in and making a ruling whenever an agency failed to meet a deadline.

Disputes about EMB authority had to do with its right to override substantive laws when they caused delays in licensing and construction. The White House held that it did not want EMB to have such broad authority. It simply wanted it to have the power to waive "procedural delays" after a project had received all necessary approval and construction had begun. When the new legislation was being written, however, administration lobbyists made a different argument. They endorsed a sweeping waiver provision, drafted for the House by representative John Dingell (Democrat, Michigan), giving EMB power to override any law standing in the way of projects on the fast track.[52]

THE REACTIONS OF BUSINESS

Congress ultimately rejected the proposal to create an Energy Mobilization Board, but it did endorse a Synfuels Development Corporation. It promised to give the corporation approximately $88 billion in the long term, but appropriated only $20 billion in the short term.[53] The Synfuels Development Corporation would have the right to use government loan and price guarantees to speed synfuels development. These steps were taken to provide incentives, but similar steps were not taken to eliminate barriers. Conflicting and ambiguous requirements remained a problem.

The synfuels program enacted by Congress was intended to produce the equivalent of 500,000 barrels of oil a day by 1987, and 2 million barrels a day five years later. The second figure represented about 30 percent of 1980 imports. Business reaction to the paradoxical nature of government action—the provision of incentives without the elimination of barriers—involved the following elements: (1) some interest; (2) the formation of a trade association; (3) dire warnings; (4) fears of "red tape"; (5) the pursuit of projects without government assistance; (6) the seeking of additional assistance by large energy companies; (7) cooperation and the successful acquisition of benefits by some companies; and (8) continued uncertainty by many other companies.[54] As we will show, the program to produce 2 million barrels of oil a day by 1992 got off to a very bad start.

Interest

On the one hand, the lure of incentives touched off an "industrial gold rush." Large numbers of business executives converged on the Department of Energy with questions about how to get federal aid. Entrepreneurs moved in on the "synfuels bar" like a "band of alcoholics." A molasses farmer in Hawaii, the Seneca Indian nation, and a distillery in Maryland were among the hundreds of groups that submitted proposals to the Department of Energy. The *Wall Street Journal* described synfuels as "one of the biggest investment prospects in the 1980s." Major firms, such as Merrill Lynch, set up special synfuels groups and hired "energy experts" to concentrate on synfuels development.

Trade Association Formation

In the same vein, the construction and oil and gas companies in the synfuels industry formed a new trade association—the Council on Synthetic Fuels, with offices "a block up Pennsylvania avenue from the White House."[55] The council had forty-five regular members, companies with their own synthetic fuels projects either in place or on the drawing board, and fifteen associate members made up of engineering firms that designed or built synfuels plants. Membership in the trade association was expensive. It cost $15,000 a year for the big companies, and $5,000 a year for the associates.[56] The trade association produced two newsletters, one with 800 subscribers, which cost close to $400 a year, and another with 1,600 subscribers, which cost $200 a year. The association also became one of the half dozen or more concerns that were involved in the synthetic fuels conference business. The purposes of the association were to expand the industry and to explain to its members how they could take advantage of the burgeoning government program.

Dire Warnings

All this activity took place despite dire warnings from groups and individuals about the almost inevitable failure of the synfuels effort. For example, it was announced that a major Canadian tar sands project in Alberta carried a ten-year deficit of $35.3 million.[57] Critics also contended that so much energy would be required to produce synfuels that net energy production would be negative.[58] The Congressional Office of Technology Assessment warned that the goal of producing 500,000 barrels a day entailed significant technological, economic, environmental, and social risks. The target was "too visionary." The results were not worth the benefits and would create serious socioeconomic dislocation.

A former deputy secretary of the Department of Energy, Jack O'Leary, predicted that environmentalists would disrupt synfuels development "faster than they did the nuclear industry."[59] Opposition from environmentalists was immediate. They argued against coal gasification and liquefaction projects and for alternative solar energy and biomass projects.[60]

The financial community also expressed reservations. Involvement could turn corporations into entities whose profits were affected by government dictates.[61] From a stock evaluation point of view, these companies would command lower price earnings than corporations that were freer to set their own rates of return. Therefore, stock analysts predicted that corporations with synfuels connections would experience a relative decline in stock prices in future years.

Generally, there was agreement that the obstacles to creating a 2 million barrel a day industry by the end of the century were formidable. For example, a pilot plant had to operate for a minimum of two and a half years to provide the fundamental data for the construction of a larger unit.[62] After Exxon established pilot plants for coal liquefaction in June 1980, it would have to build four or five pioneer commercial plants to provide the equivalent of 50,000 to 60,000 barrels of oil a day.[63] Assuming, conservatively, that it would take six years to complete a plant, a new project would have to get under way every two or three months from 1981 to 1986, and this timetable did not take into account possible permitting delays associated with environmental impact statements. If built in the mid-1980s with 1985 dollars as a base, each plant would cost $3.7 billion. Eight plants would represent a capital investment of around $30 billion.[64] To justify this investment, the world price of oil in real terms would have to nearly double from its 1980 level.

Fluor Corporation, the designer of a synfuels plant under construction in South Africa, estimated that, at its peak, a construction campaign to create a 2 million barrel a day industry by the end of the century would require 153,000 new technical workers and engineers.[65] Where the new workers would be found was not clear.

Fears of Red Tape

There were also fears that the new synfuels corporation would create red tape. Conoco, for example, applied for a $4 million grant to do a feasibility study of a coal gasification plant, but the government refused to grant the money after a long administrative proceeding. The delay cost the company $100 million a year in interest. Construction costs were rising by $20,000 to $30,000 per hour, which added another $6 million to the costs of the project every two weeks.[66] Conoco decided to proceed and not appeal the government's decision, because delay had such profoundly negative financial implications.

Pursuing Projects without Government Assistance

Congress implied that it wanted the Synfuels Development Corporation to work mainly with companies that were not "experienced" energy producers. The motive was partly political, because Congress did not want to appear to be subsidizing the big oil companies. The Synfuels Development Corporation's charter said that its assistance could "not compete with or supplant" private investment available on reasonable terms.[67] Many observers interpreted this to mean that companies with huge cash flows, such as the large oil companies, could not seek assistance. These companies, who, some argued, had the know-how to produce synfuels, had to pursue projects on their own without government assistance.

Seeking Additional Assistance

The large oil companies, in any event, did not want the loan guarantees and price supports offered by synfuels legislation. They wanted fast tax write-offs, a law permitting them to depreciate synfuels development costs over five years instead of fifteen. Congress, however, granted them what they wanted only after the ascendance of Ronald Reagan and the revision of the general tax code. The large oil companies therefore had to pursue further policy changes through the political process before they felt comfortable enough to start development.

Cooperation

Some large oil companies, such as Gulf, managed to obtain government assistance. As a partner in an international venture, it was eligible to participate in the building of a synfuels plant near Morgantown, West Virginia. Most of the companies that received federal funds, however, were not large petroleum companies. The Great Plains coal gasification project, for example, was a joint venture by gas pipeline companies. The engineering firm W. R. Grace was involved in a feasibility study to produce methyl alcohol from coal. Union Carbide received funds to design a plant to produce minimum Btu gas. While these were not small companies, most of the firms that initially received assistance were not the traditional producers and distributors of energy.

Continued Uncertainty

Many companies never got beyond the stage of feeling out the situation, despite the "bonanza or gold rush type fever" that existed. These companies were not sure whether they should get involved and what the risks and the likely consequences were if they became involved.

The overall impact of government policy was divided between businesses that were risk-takers, which actively pursued the incentives offered, and those that were risk-avoiders, which did not become involved because of the uncertainties and red-tape. Very small entrepreneurs and large firms that were not in the oil business often tried to receive government assistance. Large oil companies sought a different form of assistance, which the government, at first, was not willing to offer. But many firms simply waited. Perhaps to their ultimate benefit, these fence straddlers did not get on the bandwagon.

ENTHUSIASM DISSIPATED

The initial enthusiasm displayed for the synfuels industry rapidly dissipated. Three major factors played a role: the new administration's opposition; an unfavorable court decision; and the plentiful supplies and stagnant demand for energy that existed in the 1980s.

Opposition from the New Administration

The Reagan administration played an important role in the early decline of the synfuels program: it tried to halt it before it could get going. David Stockman had been a major opponent of the synfuels program. Senior White House aides tried to prevent funded projects from being completed and worked to develop stringent criteria for federal assistance on future projects.[68] The Carter administration wanted to set aside $88 billion to finance synfuels projects, while the Reagan administration tried to draw the line at under $20 billion. The Conference Report of the Energy Security Act stated that "no time should be lost" before the development corporation became fully operational. Senate and House conferees expected that it would begin operations by March 31, 1980. However, as of July 15, 1981, it still had not started operations. The corporation had a chairman, but no board of directors, and its funding had been reduced by Congress from $20 billion to $17.2 billion for the period through June 1982.[69] Executive and legislative vacillation represented a significant barrier to investors.

The Great Plains Court Decision

The courts also put a damper on synfuels development. The Great Plains project was sponsored by a five-company consortium led by American Natural Resources, Inc., of Detroit.[70] It included Peoples Gas Co., Columbia Gas System Inc., Tenneco Inc., and Transcontinental Pipeline. The consortium had spent over $65 million during an eight-year period for a plant that, when completed, was projected to produce 125 million cubic feet of gas a day, the equivalent of 20,000 barrels of oil.[71] The synthetic gas would be mixed with natural gas, pumped through pipelines, and eventually consumed by about a third of the natural gas customers in the United States. Before investing the $1.2 billion to $1.5 billion to produce this synthetic natural gas, the Great Plains consortium wanted guarantees that it would be sold on a regulated basis, with the price averaged in with lower-cost natural gas.[72] It also wanted a surcharge placed on the ratepayers of the sponsoring companies during the period of construction. However, intervenors, representing the consortium's customers, sued. The customers included large industrial giants such as General Motors, and the appeals court found in their favor. It ruled that the Federal Energy Regulatory Commission had overstepped its power in authorizing the shipment of the synthetic gas through regulated pipelines. Moreover, the court disallowed the surcharge. This ruling brought the largest synthetic gas project on the drawing board to a halt.

Plentiful Supplies and Stagnant Demand

Perhaps the most important reason for the decline of the industry, however, was the existence of plentiful supplies and stagnant demand. One writer has compared the enthusiam for synfuels to a "recurring dream."[73] It happened in 1973-1974, after the Arab oil embargo, and in 1979-1980, after the Shah of Iran's fall from power and a slackening in Iranian oil production. Because of the instability of world politics, energy production was temporarily curtailed, supply declined, prices rose, and there was a resolve to establish a synfuels industry. Then, with high prices, demand was reduced, and surpluses replaced shortages. At this point, the resolve to create the new industry dissipated, as both industry and the federal government realized that it was cheaper to rely on conventional sources than to seek risky new supplies.

By the end of 1981, non-OPEC oil production had increased, world economic growth had stalled, and demand for energy had been significantly reduced. The realization set in that the price of energy would not increase at a pace faster than the rate of inflation. As a consequence, numerous alternative fuels projects were abandoned.[74] Occidental Petroleum and Tenneco reevaluated their Cathedral Bluff oil shale project in Colorado; Texas Eastern Corporation and Texas Gas Corporation modified their plans for a coal liquefaction plant in Kentucky; and Exxon made an abrupt departure from oil shale. After buying out Atlantic Richfield's 60 percent share in the huge Colony project in the Piceance Basin in western Colorado, Exxon had cash flow shortages and, for the first time in a decade, increasing hydrocarbon reserves. According to one commentator, "so huge was [Exxon's] 47,000 barrel a day project that its demise represents a major setback for the infant U.S. synfuels industry."[75]

Furthermore, predictions abounded that high-quality coal gas would not be needed in the future because of major new discoveries of natural gas.[76] Nineteen-eighty was the first year since 1965 that the United States added more natural gas reserves than it consumed. Moreover, it was predicted that fast-rising prices and improved drilling techniques were likely to ensure more discoveries in the immediate future.

Uncontrolled prices, conservation, and exploration had by 1983 depressed the price of oil by 30 percent in two years to $28 per barrel and had reduced U.S. imports by 50 percent from 5.3 million to 2.6 million barrels a day.[77] The U.S. Synfuels Development Corporation had committed only some $800,000 of the congressionally authorized $15 million. In 1983, nonetheless, it solicited investors to obligate all of this money by the year's end.[78]

The case of synfuels, with its ups and downs as an object of company interest and federal largesse, shows that the government's ability to influence the private sector in order to achieve policy objectives is limited. This case should serve as a warning to those who are calling for a "new industrial policy."[79] Government development efforts, such as the synfuels program, often go awry. Goals are not achieved. Promises are not fulfilled. In the case of synfuels, incentives were provided, but barriers were not removed. Very few companies were actually able to take advantage of the incentives offered. Many companies responded to what seemed to be an opportunity, but in a hesitant, uncertain, and inconsistent manner. Because of the paradoxical nature of government action, ultimately the whole program began to unravel and was put on hold by most companies, without prospect of much action unless the country again faced a critical energy shortage.

5 | Taking Advantage of Economic Regulation

Regulatory policymaking can be conveniently divided into three stages: (1) formation, when a new policy is proposed, formally considered, and approved; (2) implementation, when the policy is put into effect and has impact; and (3) evaluation, when it is assessed and altered. (See Table 5.1.) Understanding the distinction between these stages is important for understanding the organization of the remainder of this book.

The point made in these chapters is that the politics of regulation differs depending on the policymaking phase, and that the challenge to business likewise may change. This chapter focuses primarily on the first stage—formation—when economic agencies are created and regulatory policy achieves an initial form. The next chapter examines implementation, while the chapter following examines evaluation. This cycle of analysis is repeated for the new social agencies in chapters 8 through 11.

The next three chapters pertain to business management of the *old economic regulation*. One characteristic of this type of regulation is that it concerns rates, entry, and the conditions of service or business practice. Also, it is usually industry specific. The Federal Communications Commission, for example, deals with the communication industry. Similarly, the Civil Aeronautics Board deals with the airline industry. These agencies do not have common problems, such as pollution, that they manage across industries. Rather, their mandate is to affect the vital determinants of a single industry's success or failure.

Table 5.1
Policymaking Stages

Formation
Issue Creation and Expansion
—social, economic, and cultural conditions, and historical factors
—parties that create the issue
—issue entrepreneurs, coalitions, the media
—competing groups
—group strategies

Decision
—key decision makers that govern entrance of the issue onto the formal institutional agenda
—executive, legislative, judicial, and bureaucratic gatekeepers
—formal decision-making processes
—policy outputs, statutory mandates, authoritative decisions

Implementation
Delegation
—administrators
—motives, objectives, organization
—information, expertise, allies
—resources, standard operating procedures

Key Issues
—processes
—number of clearances, number of parties involved
—contextual factors
—policy specification

Evaluation
Effects
—costs, benefits
—distribution of impacts
—political change
—contextual change

Reform
—watchdogs, experts
—formal and informal methods of assessment
—the media, interest groups, congressional staffs, the courts
—advocates, opponents, strategies
—feedback and perhaps change

Adapted from Barry Mitnick, *The Political Economy of Regulation* (New York: Columbia University Press, 1980), pp. 81-83.

The distinction between policy stages will be illustrated by reference to examples from the history of the Federal Communications Commission. The first stage is *formation*. It results in a regulatory policy coalescing into coherent form and gaining official status. An agency is brought into being, and a regulatory statute enacted. Formation connotes gestation. It includes the period and the circumstances that produced the regulatory policy. During formation, the regulatory problem is defined and wins a place on the public agenda. Alternative solutions are developed and a specific strategy for dealing with the problem is formalized. Diverse actors are mobilized and authoritative decisions made.

In the case of the FCC, formation was initiated in the period between 1922 and 1933, when the agency achieved its present form and the Communications Act was proposed and passed. Broadcasters were distressed by "the Babel-like situation of the 1920's which in turn led to the Federal Radio Act."[1] As Cole and Oettinger write, prior to the Radio Act's passage "everybody was talking on the air at once so that nobody could be understood."[2] There was a limited number of spaces on the airwaves, but no restrictions on entry. During this period, the existing broadcasters aimed to create both an agency and a statute that would stabilize the relations among them.

In this first stage of policymaking, the statutory mandates that result often lack clarity. Although statutory enactment "climaxes a prolonged struggle for reform," the policy which is established rarely provides clear directions to the regulatory bureaucracy. Regulatory officials deal with "terms of treaties" that legislators "have negotiated and ratified." Public attention has been captured by the "battle for legislation," while "the hammering out of a carefully articulated set of regulatory goals" usually is ignored.[3]

The second stage of regulatory policymaking is *implementation* (see chapters 6 and 9). Authoritative decisions enacted when policy is formulated must be put into effect. The bureaucracy must make an effort to carry out the intent of decisions formally sanctioned by policymakers. The bureaucracy begins to have a direct impact on policy outcomes as it reaches out to client groups and businesses with whom it interacts. Whether officials are able to carry out policy intent and comply with the letter as well as the spirit of the law often depends on the reactions of those in the agency's environment.

In the case of the FCC, it is commonly believed that the implementation pattern from 1933 to the mid-1960s involved sharing of power among the regulatory bureaucracy, Congress, and the broadcast industry. An infamous iron triangle was supposed to have developed. The major issues revolved around the interpretation by the agency of a tricky phrase in the statute that Congress had passed: the "public interest, convenience, and necessity." In exchange for being granted the privileged status of receiving broadcasting rights, companies had to demonstrate conformance with this standard. A consensus prevailed among industry, Congress, and the FCC that the standard would mean responsibility for the dissemination of news about vital issues of the day, and the right of the public to have access to ideas and information from diverse and antagonistic sources.

If implementation begins with the agency taking "an aggressive, crusading manner" and adopting "a broad view of its responsibilities," it may end with the agency functioning as a "manager" for industry. According to Bernstein, the agency becomes concerned with the general health of the industry and tries to prevent changes that would adversely affect it. Bernstein argues that after aggressive, crusading beginnings, agencies are likely to become "guardians of the industries they are supposed to regulate."[4]

Evaluation is the third stage. It comes into being in response to assessments of the existing situation. The performance of the agency is examined by some group or individual—a "watchdog" in Congress, the press, the public, or the agency itself. Assessment leads to demands for change, and sustained evaluation over a period of time almost invariably results in some changes. Bernstein suggests that changes in regulatory behavior during a period of evaluation are not likely. There is little prospect for improved behavior after implementation: "In old age the working agreement that a commission reaches with the regulated industries becomes so fixed that the agency has no creative force left to mobilize against the regulated groups."[5] Nonetheless, Bernstein admits that the cycle of evaluation and reform can repeat itself. Recent history shows many examples of regulatory agencies that have been evaluated and reformed in their "old age." In the 1960s broadcast regulation came under increasing scrutiny from new actors in the policymaking process—the courts, citizen groups, and the White House. This scrutiny brought about changes in the FCC's basic character, mission, and operating procedures (see chapter 8). Basic changes in the character, mission, and operating procedures of other agencies, such as the Civil Aeronautics Board (CAB), also took place (see chapter 9).

During all three stages, businesses may use sanctions and incentives to change the preferences of government decision makers. They may lobby directly, or rely on indirect tactics, using pressure groups, brokers, and agents. They may initiate advertising campaigns, supply information, depend on the force of argument, or threaten to withhold votes. They may promise campaign contributions or jobs, or provide subtle rewards such as advice, prestige, and status. Opponents will try to prevent passage of bills businesses favor. They can interfere with the process of convincing and pressuring, and businesses may have to bargain, compromise, and change their original preferences.[6]

Economic regulation may involve "natural" monopolies. Regulation also can change a competitive situation into a monopolistic one and then protect the monopoly from potential competitors. It can bring about shared rules of behavior, increase prices, and stabilize and promote the profit of regulated firms. Government-established and -sanctioned monopolies are permitted because of inefficiencies and other situations that allegedly would result from a return to marketlike conditions. Old economic agencies thus may be captured by industries they are supposed to control.

Capture may be defined to mean that regulated businesses can take advantage of economic regulation. They can control the agency, neutralize it, or assure that it will not adequately perform its duties. Regulated firms can co-opt the agency into seeing things their way. Adversarial relations between business and government are supposed to be less likely under the old economic regulation. The process of regulation is supposed to lead to a community of interests between regulatory officials and regulated firms.

The formation stage, when an old economic regulatory agency is first created, its enabling statute passed, and its basic policy established, presents business firms with opportunities to achieve economic advantage and create regulatory policies in their favor. However, it also presents firms with threats, which, if not countered, can harm the firm. What follows is an analysis of the character of the corporate response to the initiation of new regulatory activity of the economic variety. It criticizes George J. Stigler's theory of corporate self-interest, provides a rationale for corporate political activity, and summarizes some basic notions about business's management of its affairs with government.

STIGLER'S THEORY

Stigler suggests that "regulation may be actively sought by an industry, or it may be thrust upon it."[7] His theory is that "as a rule," regulation is acquired by businesses or other economic interests and designed and operated primarily for their benefit. This is to be contrasted with another theory—that regulation is, "as a rule, instituted primarily for the protection and benefit of the public at large or some large subclass of the public."[8]

The classic example of firms seeking regulation involves the Interstate Commerce Commission. The 1870s and 1880s were a period of rate wars in the railroad industry, when attempts were made by the industry to institute collusive pooling agreements. Most of these agreements, however, did not last, as firms in the industry tried to gain relative advantage in particular markets. The railroad interests, according to one interpretation, sought regulation as a means of bringing about stability in the industry, which would protect their investments and assure profit. Similarly, in the 1920s and 1930s the large firms in the trucking industry suffered from substantial competition and consequent instability. They also sought federal regulation to reduce instability, regularize profits, and protect investments.

The basis of Stigler's theory is that business firms or other economic interests solicit the coercive powers of the state to stabilize or increase profits. He holds that there are four uses that business firms may make of the state.[9]

First and most obvious, firms may seek *direct subsidies* from the government—cash payments, contracts, awards, tax credits, and bonuses. Nonetheless, Stigler maintains that direct subsidies are not a very effective form of government aid to business, because there is no end to the business claimants for these government resources.[10] Unless the claimants can be limited in number, the subsidies soon disperse among a growing number of rivals.

Firms, therefore, may prefer *control over the entry of new rivals* to direct government subsidies. They may use regulation to restrict the rate of entry of new firms. The trucking industry provides an example. Until 1980 under ICC regulation, more freight had been hauled, but by fewer companies and fewer firms; and very few new firms had been granted the right to operate new lines in spite of the absence of significant economies of scale in the industry. On the basis of such examples, Stigler proposes the following general hypothesis: Every industry or occupation that has enough political power to utilize the state for its ends will seek to control entry.[11]

Another way firms take advantage of regulation, according to Stigler, is by seeking government aid to *control substitutes and complements* for the goods and services they produce.[12] A conspicuous example is the effort made by butter manufacturers to use state controls to suppress the development of margarine.

The final way that corporations may use regulatory policies for gain is to seek government-established *rates that guarantee profits*. Firms that gain government control of entry will seek rate regulation as well. They will want to be buffered from the pressures of competition and price, and they will also want the guarantee of a stable rate of return without any of these types of market constraints.

According to Stigler, then, firms not only seek direct cash subsidies; they seek government protection to relieve them of market pressures as well. They seek protection that, insofar as possible, eliminates the instability and unpredictability of operating in a free and competitive marketplace. Classical economics suggests that economic viability is bound up with conditions such as low-cost production and meeting market demand better than competition, but in the United States, because of regulation, many firms are in a position where they do not have to meet these tests of market viability. Firms have achieved government protection, favors, and special treatment and avoided being subject to pure market forces. They have received government aid which has reduced market instabilities.

Stigler lists three limitations on the use of government powers for these purposes. First, government protection does not work to the advantage of all firms. For example, small firms because of their political power may win advantages because of regulation, while large firms may lose certain advantages. Antitrust laws provide small firms with protection against elimination by larger, more cost-effective competitors. Moreover, Stigler maintains that procedural safeguards lead to delays that add to the costs of goods and services, which hurts both large and small business consumers. Finally, he argues that businesses must give up some freedom of control in exchange for the advantages of regulation.[13] Decline in managerial discretion is a disadvantage of regulation, a reason that firms should not seek regulation.

In many situations, however, the determination is made that these problems are slight in comparison with the advantages of regulation. Stigler's analysis suggests to the business manager the following axiom: "No industry offered the opportunity to be regulated should decline."[14] Few industries, according to Stigler, have done so. Railroads, airlines, telephone companies, broadcasting stations, electric and gas utilities, and other large industries have warmly embraced regulation when it was offered and have strenuously resisted efforts to remove it. Regulation has protected these industries against competition, shielded them from antitrust attack, and greatly reduced the risk of bankruptcy. While it may make very high rates of return difficult to achieve, it has virtually guaranteed a steady stream of adequate profits.

Stigler asks how business firms, which command the allegiance of only a minority of the population in a democratic society, maintain this form of government protection. How do they achieve the benefits of regulation? In essence, Stigler argues that the average voter does not have the time or information needed to make informed choices about regulatory issues that are of no direct material relevance.[15] Average voters are indifferent. Elected officials, who need support in the form of resources, votes, and organization, respond, not to the passive sentiments of average citizens, but to the strongly felt preferences of active minorities. In exchange for the government protection that businesses seek, they offer politicians the resources, votes, and organization they need to be elected and to stay in office. Elected officials also may receive compensation from favored firms in an indirect fashion; for example, firms may patronize the politicians' law firms or the banks in which they hold shares.

Large and wealthy economic interests, even if they command the allegiance of only a minority, are able to prevail over passive, disinterested individuals who have no focused interest in specific regulatory outcomes. Small investors and consumers have particularly difficult organizational problems in comparison with the interests having a larger stake in a given issue. They are dispersed and scattered, and the incentive for collaboration is less compelling. A permanent mechanism to assure advocacy for their position is often missing.

In summary, Stigler's theory makes the following points:

1. Corporations often seek government regulation for the purposes of profit and other sources of gain.
2. They achieve what they seek by exchanging votes, resources, and organization for government protection.
3. Regulatory agencies frequently end up serving the industries they are ostensibly supposed to control.

Stigler's arguments, however, overlook several factors.

Corporate political activity must be rationalized and legitimated in terms of broader social values. Most, if not all, special interest legislation has to be justified in terms of some alleged public benefit. The notion that regulation is created to achieve public interest purposes is contrary to Stigler's theory. Robert E. Cushman, for example, argues that agencies are created to solve major economic problems that come into existence either because of recurrent abuses in the regulated industry or because some goals in the national interest are not being accomplished by the private sector.[16] Similarly, Merle Fainsod and Lincoln Gordon maintain that regulation is initiated to control abuses and to solve problems.[17] Richard Posner, although he does not support the public interest argument, suggests that regulation is designed to compel the provision of certain services in quantities and at prices that a free market would not offer.[18] Examples include unprofitable airline service to small cities, public affairs programming by broadcasters, and commuter rail service. John Baldwin holds that regulation is an instrument used by the government to arbitrate disputes between parties with strongly opposing interests such as consumers and business, or truckers and the railroads.[19]

When it operates in the political arena, the corporation has to consider the broader public interest purposes that regulation is supposed to serve. The political arena expands the number of persons who must view a corporation's activities as legitimate. James Q. Wilson points out that, in politics, unlike the market, decisions must have justifications.[20] The ability of corporations to link their interests and activities to broad social norms and values is among the most important aspects of operating in the political environment and ensuring that objectives are achieved. Corporate strategists who seek to take advantage of regulation need to develop public interest arguments or risk failure.

Politicians that grant corporations favorable treatment are likely to be convinced only if there is a broad social interest in the regulatory solutions that the corporations propose. Politicians do not simply yield to corporate pressure. They are not simply exchanging resources and votes for political favors. Sam Peltzman, in an extension of Stigler's model, emphasizes that politicians seek to maximize their expected vote majority.[21] The probability of receiving support from a regulated industry is a function of the average net gain that the industry is likely to receive minus the money it must spend in campaigning, lobbying, and other activities on behalf of convincing the general public to support the politician. Barry Weingast insists that it is votes, not wealth, that politicians require.[22] Legislators, therefore, do not favor a single group to the exclusion of all others. Since they seek to maximize votes, they prefer to build broad coalitions.

Fainsod holds that the factors likely to affect a business group's success in influencing politicians include: resources, that is, financial capabilities to pay for lobbyists, provide campaign contributions, hire lawyers, and use the media; *and* opportunities for building coalitions within the context of broad social and political movements.[23] According to Fainsod, the influence that a particular industry exerts at any given time is largely a function of its ability to find effective political champions or allies and of its ability to fuse its demands into "a general program of wider appeal."[24]

Regulation requires some type of public interest rationale, and such rationales have an effect on political outcomes. William Comanor and Bridger Mitchell, for example, argue that regulation is a method or tool of planning.[25] Free market economies are subject not merely to business cycle booms and busts, but also to sudden and total dislocations of particular sectors that become obsolete because of shifts in technology and demand. The free market is risky. Market forces, particularly those associated with innovative activities, pose a threat to human beings who need time to adapt. Regulation is often designed to protect people and physical capital that have few alternative uses from the sudden shifts of market forces (see chapter 1).

Many scholars agree that the creation of the ICC was not simply a matter of corporate self-seeking. The private interests of the railroad industry were fused with broader public purposes. Albro Martin maintains that the railroads needed regulation that would enable them to cartelize, but this need was subordinated to the "public's mistrust of insulated aggregations of power."[26] Mitnick finds extensive contemporary support for the thesis that individual railroad executives supported regulation, because agreements among themselves to maintain uniform and stable rates, being based on good faith, were not binding by law and therefore tended to collapse.[27] However, he notes that such factors as an "ideological aversion to private monopoly, concentrated political power, and industrialism, and a belief in agrarianism and laissez-faire" also played a role in the ICC's creation.

Ostensibly, the ICC was created to see that the railroads would charge reasonable rates and end discriminatory pricing. The farmers and other shippers of the mid-nineteenth century complained that they suffered from

"extortionate rates," and that the railroads practiced extensive price discrimination against particular shippers, localities, and commodities.
Moreover, Mitnick finds "vivid contemporary descriptions of corruption,
fraud, and speculation in the industry."[28] Edward Purcell argues that the
commission was created because many economic groups in combination
favored regulation.[29] The broader view of the ICC's origin was that it came
into being as a compromise among contending economic interests, each of
which wanted some form of regulation.

The formative experience of many agencies involved similar compromises
among broad coalitions. Proconsumer sentiment, along with the hope
among businesses that the Federal Trade Commission would restrict the
predatory practices of their competitors, played a role in the FTC's creation.
Utility magnates were joined by Progressive politicians in calling for state
public utility commissions. Herbert Hoover said about the establishment of
government regulatory powers in broadcasting: "This is one of the few
instances . . . where . . . all of the people are unanimously for an extension
of regulatory powers."[30] The FCC was created in large part to allocate air
wave frequencies to control signal interference and improve service. The
CAB had the support of the airlines, but there was also widespread public
support for encouraging the growth of the young industry. In the case of
many of the old economic agencies, broad coalitions and public interest
arguments were involved. Proponents with a large stake in an issue were able
to convince those with a lesser stake because they could show them that
they had something to gain.

*A distinction must be made between the old economic regulation and the
new social regulation.* In the case of the newer regulation, businesses for the
most part have been opposed to policy developments. They have not
sought new regulatory constraints. OSHA was created over the objections
of business. EPA was formed even though it was opposed by the segments
of the business community that were to be regulated. Stigler's theory may
have been an advance over the traditional theory of economic regulation
which held that regulation simply was intended to provide a degree of
protection for consumers from the depredations of monopolists and from
shoddy and dangerous fly-by-night operators; however, his theory does not
fully take into account the new regulation. No one can argue that the new
agencies have been created to protect business interests. The Business
Roundtable did not view the creation of a consumer protection agency in
positive terms. It lobbied vigorously and effectively against the creation of
this agency. Stigler is wrong if he wishes to maintain that industry is likely
to favor regulation in every instance.

Moreover, the most common defect found among the old economic regulatory agencies is that they provide undue protection for business.
Providing such protection is against the public interest, because it leads to
higher prices and suppresses innovation. The most common defect found
among the new social regulatory agencies, however, is delay; goals are

rarely achieved in the time prescribed by statute.[31] Although some firms may benefit from delay because they have a desire to preserve the status quo, the latter problem is not the same as protection.

According to Wilson, there is a variety of conditions under which regulation becomes politically possible.[32] In some cases, business influence is likely to be strong; in other cases it is likely to be weak. The old economic regulation ordinarily allows for greater business influence. When benefits are concentrated and costs diffused, an industry is more likely to introduce and maintain an economic regulatory policy that is to its benefit. When benefits and costs are concentrated, competing economic interests are likely to initiate and sustain an economic regulatory policy that formalizes the rights and responsibilities of each side. However, in cases of the new social regulation, the distribution of costs and benefits may lead to reduced business influence. Concentrated costs and diffuse benefits may mean that businesses are unable to escape the burdens imposed by the public. The politics of the new regulation depend on the efforts of skilled entrepreneurs who can mobilize latent public sentiment by revealing a scandal or capitalizing on a crisis. They can put the opponents of a plan publicly on the defensive by associating the legislation with widely shared values.

THE CYBERNETIC THEORY

Marver Bernstein's theory, unlike Stigler's, is cyclical. It holds that regulatory agencies, established for public interest purposes, *subsequently* are captured by the industries they are supposed to control. Agencies are "pure" at their birth. They are not born "bad," but may become so, as the enthusiasm for regulation generated at the time of their creation dissipates. The agency flounders as it comes to depend more and more on industry for support, advice, and information. Bernstein's theory is overly pessimistic. He views reform in the case of the old economic agencies as atypical, and does not consider evaluation and feedback as common. Although he believes that reform and evaluation are possible, he sees the tie between the agency and business growing stronger as the agency gets older.

Posner contends that the capture theory is more of a hypothesis than a theory, as there is no reason why the regulated industry should be assumed to be the only party to have substantial influence on the agency.[33] Stigler himself ultimately adopts this position. Posner points out that the capture theory makes no attempt to explain why consumers cannot capture the agency as effectively as the firm does, or why a firm strong enough to capture an agency cannot prevent its creation in the first place.

In place of capture theories, the following *cybernetic theory* is proposed: Regulatory agencies should be seen as organizations operating in accord with "feedback" principles.[34] They are limited by bounded rationality, conflicting goals, and finite information. They make probes and adjust their behavior in accordance with changing circumstances. They go through cycles of *equilibrium* and *innovation*.[35] In the equilibrium stage, there is a well-established organizational structure for the regulatory agency. There are standard operating procedures, and instruments that the agency uses repetitively and predictably. In this stage, the agency experiences minimal conflict and criticism from external industry and consumer groups. The second stage, innovation, is more dynamic. The agency no longer satisfies external forces. Because the dissatisfaction grows, the agency is pushed into a search process for new policies with which to reestablish its acceptance. Through a process of trial and error, it develops different principles to govern its activities. The cybernetic theory corresponds to the case of the FCC and to the case of many other agencies, including the ICC, CAB, and the former Federal Power Commission (FPC), which are discussed in the following chapter. The notion of regulatory organizations being restricted to bounded rationality, responding to uncertainty, and being sensitive to feedback more adequately describes their behavior than theories of simple corporate self-interest or capture.

A RATIONALE FOR CORPORATE POLITICAL ACTIVITY

Pluralism describes the political system. It is also a rationale for corporate political activity. Business firms and other formal organizations are among the legitimate participants. If, by some decree, the legal status of the corporation were abolished immediately, it is quite clear that some type of organization would continue to exist and perform economic tasks in a way similar to the operations of business corporations. Various manufacturing and other business activities would continue. Automobiles would be built, railroads would ship goods to consumers, and factories for the processing of iron ore into steel would exist, for example. Large-scale economic units affect the political system in capitalist and communist societies. The persistence of large-scale organized activity depends not on corporate status, but on the critical functions that are performed.[36] Hierarchical organizations that provide jobs, vital goods and services, innovation, and productivity function in much the same way in societies where corporate status is not formally recognized as in societies where it is. Large-scale organizations constitute the basic economic units and play a role in politics in all complex industrial societies.

Barry Mitnick discusses three related notions of the public interest which may justify the participation of basic economic entities, such as corporations, in the political process: (1) a balancing notion, in which the public interest results from the "satisfaction of selected aspects of different particularistic interests"; (2) a compromising notion, in which the public interest arises when "particularistic interests are made to concede part of what they desire"; and (3) a trade-off concept, in which the public interest results from particularistic interests providing some good or service judged to be in the public interest in exchange for private benefits.[37]

Arguing for the legitimacy of corporate political activity does not condone abuses of the political process. The legitimacy of business participation does not imply that firms should engage in immoral or unstatesmanlike behavior.[38] Bribery, the trip to Acapulco, and other methods of influence-buying are not legitimate aspects of strategic behavior. Providing information, building coalitions, and gaining influence through accepted political channels are.

Moreover, a conception of the public interest that depends on group notions must take into account the fact that some interests cannot be mobilized as easily as businesses, nor can they exert the same economic power. These latent interests, often composed of scattered individuals, without resources, organization, or central purpose, must be represented by surrogates—policy entrepreneurs, bureaucrats, congressional staffs, or journalists—if the notion of fairness is to be achieved.

A CONCEPTION OF POLITICS

To distinguish legitimate political acts, it is necessary to develop a conception of politics. To the ancient political philosophers such as Aristotle and Plato, politics was certain ideals that the human community should strive to realize. They viewed politics in terms of virtues and ideals, not necessarily in terms of how humans actually behave. Modern political philosophy, beginning with Machiavelli, has been more realistic and has viewed matters more in terms of how they are and how humans behave, rather than how they should be. Politics in the modern sense is the study of means, not ends. Tactics play a greater role than strategy. How humans accomplish their goals and achieve power—how they get what they want— has received more interest than what they should be striving for or what they should be trying to accomplish.

There are certain ultimate considerations—liberty, justice, fairness, equality—which should occupy business leaders and inform their political choices. Business persons should ask themselves: What type of system should they be living in; what values should be represented by public choices; and what ultimate purposes are they and their companies serving? A concern for values should preclude the pursuit of short-term profit at the expense of the ultimate public good.

However, a sound conception of politics does not ignore the question of means. Consideration of ends without means is naive, and can do much harm, including leading to totalitarian extremes. Politics, according to political scientist Harold Lasswell, involves questions of power, of winning and maintaining possession of desired goods, as well as questions of ends. Typical political questions should include both the following concerns: What are the desired goods? and, What are the methods of achieving them? Politics focuses both on the question of ideals and on that of feasible means.

Methods of achieving desired goods include (1) the formal institutional route; (2) the group method; (3) the elite route; (4) through access to experts; and (5) by playing the system.[39] Traditionally, political scientists have viewed the allocation of desired goods in terms of institutions such as the executive branch, Congress, the courts, and state and local governments. These institutions have the formal power and the constitutional authority to make decisions. They are sources of legitimate sanctions and coercion. According to formal theory, the Constitution is a map of legal political activity. To understand how desired goods are allocated, businesses should focus on the operation of specific government institutions and their interactions.

Politics, on the surface, is dominated by these formal actors. Nonetheless, other features have to be considered. Group theorists emphasize the significance of such interests as business, labor, farmers, and consumers.[40] According to their theory, the interaction of these interests determines the allocation of desired goods. Legitimate activity occurs when individuals with common interests and shared attitudes join together formally and informally to press their demands on government. Government establishes the rules of the game and arranges compromises among competing groups. According to radical group theorists, government has no independent influence. The allocation of goods is determined by group strength, which is a function of group numbers, wealth, organizational strength, leadership, access to decision makers, and internal cohesion. The role of institutions— Congress, the White House, the courts, and state and local governments— is merely to arrange compromises among competing groups and to reflect the outcome of the group struggle.

Both institutionalism and group theory posit the existence of separate entities competing and cooperating to determine policy outcomes. These entities are either institutions—the executive branch, Congress, and the courts—which are governed by formal constitutional rules; or groups— such as farmers, laborers, and business people—which are governed by institutionally established rules. Elite theory and rationalism, in contrast, posit the existence of a dominant decision-making faction. According to these notions, members of ruling cliques share beliefs about the system and its preservation. According to elite theory, the activity of a small group of educated, wealthy, or privileged individuals interested in preserving the system and their place in it determines policy.[41] According to rationalism, allocation is controlled by a small group of non-partisan technicians and experts, who are trained in analytical methods and who attempt to achieve optimal choices that promote the general welfare.[42] Both theories hold that society is divided into the few who have power and the many who do not, although in order to maintain stability and reinvigorate the system there is a continuous movement of non-elite individuals into elite positions.

Experts are supposed to allocate desired goods on the basis of efficiency and rationality. Efficiency is the most output for a given level of input; the most social welfare for the least net expenditure. To select a comprehensive rational policy, experts are supposed to assess society's value preferences, establish goals, list alternatives for achieving these goals, determine the consequences of each alternative, and choose the option that maximizes net social benefit. Although there are barriers to knowledge-based decision making, the rational model of political action is important for analytic purposes. It helps to identify barriers to rationality, such as lack of goal consensus and lack of time and information to make an adequate list of options and predict consequences. It demonstrates how the allocation of desired goods strays from rational ideals (see chapter 2).

A final method of analyzing the allocation of desired goods is systems theory.[43] It views allocation in the following terms: (1) as inputs from an environment that makes demands and provides support; (2) as the transforming of demands and support into decisions and action; and (3) as feedback, where outputs influence the character of new input. A systems framework implies division of policymaking into distinct stages (formulation, implementation, and evaluation). It is cybernetic because of the feedback.[44]

Systems theory describes the overall framework of political activity without attributing outcomes to particular factors. Thus the determinants of policy in different arenas may be different. Pollution control policy can be the result of expert dominance, while defense policy can be the consequence of group or institutional conflict. Different decision-making stages, moreover, may be subject to different influences. The forces that frame policy are not fixed. The systems approach allows for the possibility that different areas and stages are dominated in different ways by different participants or types of activity. The image of "elastic nets" is appropriate. Lack of decision making as well as decision making occur, and deadlock is as common as action. Over-representation leads to a stalled society that cannot make vital decisions. The politics of confrontation and polarization may lead to policy paralysis with the government unable to create or implement coherent policy programs.

A FRAMEWORK FOR MANAGING GOVERNMENT RELATIONS

Legitimate political action is to be distinguished from illegitimate activity by the extent to which it conforms to notions of politics that consider both ends and means. Politics involves choices about legitimate ends and the discussion of ideals. It goes beyond the modern preoccupation with means. However, just as ends are considered, means also have a place. The activity of formal institutions, groups, elites, and experts in a policy process that includes formulation, implementation, and evaluation is important.

Aspects of a framework for businesses managing government relations include a coherent strategy, systematic evaluation, and mapping the policy process.

A coherent strategy. Firms should adopt a coherent strategy which takes ends into consideration rather than relying only on tactical maneuvers. They also need to systematically explore the problems of government relations by accounting for day-to-day negotiations with government at numerous levels by different officials. Company-government interaction is now so pervasive that it requires overall management from a strategic perspective, not just case-by-case decision making.

Systematic evaluation. Firms should list activities that involve the government and evaluate the interactions systematically. A list should be prepared including every section of the company that is dealing with the government, regardless of the branch of government or the issue. The list provides a basis for assessing interactions. Questions can be posed to determine which interactions are going well and which are going poorly and to assess their legitimacy or illegitimacy. As Dan Fenn observes, "Determining who is dealing with an activity for the company, making a judgment on how smoothly it is proceeding, and assigning some kind of priority would give top management [an] idea of how it is doing . . . and would serve to point out difficulties that might prove costly."[45]

Mapping the policy process. A map of the policy process should be prepared. The map should contain answers to questions such as the following: Who are the chief participants? What are their concerns, clout, and constituencies? It would identify decision makers, list power centers, evaluate influence, and explore the possibility of forming common causes.

Finally, businesses must understand the limitations of their activities. If the business community is to be effective in its dealings with government, it must see itself as an interest *and* as a set of values joining in a process with other interests *and* sets of values. No interest or value has special status. None has its way in every instance. All are participants that have to follow established rules of access and influence. With this recognition, a firm will be in a better poisition to decide when to initiate and when not to initiate economic regulatory action. Contrary to what Stigler argues, it may not be in the firm's interest in each and every case to pursue economic regulation. Allowing rigid models of corporate self-interest to guide the formation of corporate social policy will lead to unfavorable outcomes.

6	# Strategic Retreat and Frontal Attack

The life-cycle theory of economic regulatory agencies is that they are born pure (to serve public ends) and become corrupt (begin to serve private ends) during the implementation stage.[1] This theory is to be contrasted with the one summarized in the last chapter, which holds both that agencies are born to serve businesses and that they end up their servants.[2] Both theories maintain that corporations are able to take advantage of economic regulation after the regulatory law has been passed and implemented. However, these simple theories of business dominance do not do justice to the real situation of the old economic agencies.

In this chapter, the situation of these agencies is illustrated with reference to agencies such as the Federal Communications Commission and the Federal Trade Commission.[3] In the late 1960s, the threat of nonrenewal and unfavorable regulatory action began to hang like a "dangling sword" over the head of the established networks and broadcasters.[4] After the landmark 1969 U.S. Court of Appeals decision that persons or groups with no financial interest in broadcast licensing had standing, petitions to deny license renewals were filed against numerous stations. (Between 1969 and 1977, 360 petitions to deny renewal were filed against 828 stations.)[5] The power of the established broadcast interests was challenged. Even during implementation, businesses do not simply take advantage of regulation. They may have to retreat in the face of regulatory challenges. Cases from the history of various regulatory agencies, including the FCC, are used to illustrate tactics that businesses may use during these periods of regulatory innovation and business retreat.

REGULATORY CAPTURE

Because of vague statutory language and formulas such as "public interest, convenience, and necessity," agencies have a broad range of discretion during implementation. Special industrial interests may capture them to the harm or neglect of the general public. Regulated firms can engage in political activity, supply vital information to the regulatory agency, and otherwise convince significant numbers of officials to sympathize with their cause. The conditions that make business capture possible include the following:[6]

Political activity unopposed by the public at large. Since overall economic health can be significantly determined by an agency's decisions, firms have good reason to engage in political activity. While the firms' stake in the outcome is great, the stake of each citizen is quite small. The outcome has only a marginal effect on the price and quality of goods and services that each citizen consumes. It probably involves only a small portion of the average person's income. In the aggregate and in specific sectors, the effects of agency decisions are very great, but the effects on each individual are generally very small.

Case-by-case decision making. Decision making often is accomplished by case-by-case adjudication and negotiation. Policy is developed through the accumulation of precedents in individual cases. The general public and the media usually are not able to sustain an interest in these cases, and only the specialized press and industry trade associations cover them in any detail.

Industry information to the regulatory agency. The information agencies use in making decisions often comes from the firms they regulate, either as a consequence of agency procedures, which preclude effective participation by the broader public, or because of the indifference of the broader public and its inability to gather the resources and expertise needed to take part.

Sympathetic officials. Moreover, firms can rely on the fact that some government officials are likely to sympathize with their cause. Some officials serve for only a few years and then move back to industry. Others had important jobs before they took office. For example, over two-thirds of the FCC commissioners and high officials who served in the 1945-1970 period had positions in the communications industry either before or after their FCC tenure.[7] Because of the so-called revolving door, officials tend to feel a responsibility for a regulated industry's economic vitality and success.

Retreat in the Face of Regulatory Challenges

A pro-industry orientation of a regulatory agency may be upset when issues arise in which (1) a special interest group other than the protected industry has a major stake in the outcome (conflict between business groups); and/or (2) the broader public is aroused, perhaps by skillful political entrepreneurs.[8] Firms representing competing technologies (in the case of broadcast regulation, FM radio, UHF and cable television, and CB radio) saw potential profits from challenging the existing regulatory regime; and public interest lobbyists (often supported by "whistle-blowing" bureaucrats, "crusading" congressional staffers, or "muckraking" journalists) envisioned career advancement or the intrinsic reward of serving a good cause.

Moreover, many regulatory issues often are not clear enough to have a straightforward industrial interest opposed by an equally straightforward general interest. Many involve competing subgroups without a clear stake in the outcome, and coalitions form that cut across the simple industry/ public interest dichotomy. All sides must invoke larger values and appeal to broader constituencies to advance their cause.

BROADCAST REGULATION

The FCC's powers date back to the 1920s. The rationale for the agency's creation was not the public's concern with excessively high or discriminatory prices, or a related concern with inadequate competition or high profits. The agency came into being at the behest of the burgeoning broadcast industry. The industry's desire was to protect itself from the uncertainty of unfettered competition. The main issue was frequency allocation. Interference was a vexing problem that voluntary agreements among broadcasters had failed to solve.

The courts ruled that temporary restrictions laid down after World War I by the secretary of commerce on frequencies and the number of hours that stations could broadcast were unconstitutional. President Calvin Coolidge declared that the whole service of this most important public function "had drifted into chaos."[9] Congress, therefore, passed the Radio Act of 1927, which created the Federal Radio Commission and gave it broad licensing and regulatory powers. In the more comprehensive Communications Act of 1934, Congress incorporated the powers of the early commission with the newly created FCC. However, the FCC was never given the right to regulate profits or rates (a conventional feature of other economic regulatory agencies), as Congress intended that rate competition play a central role in broadcasting.

The FCC was made up of seven members appointed by the president. (It is now composed of five.) The act empowered the agency to license all broadcasting stations; prescribe the nature of the service in which each station could engage; make necessary regulations to prevent interference among stations; and, in general, promote "the wider and more efficient use" of broadcasting. The available channels were to be allocated among localities to provide "a fair, efficient, and equitable" distribution of broadcasting service. Licenses for operating were to be granted only on a temporary and conditional basis. The possession of a license was limited to a maximum three-year duration, and theoretically after three years it could be revoked.

To fulfill broadcasting's role as a public servant and to achieve diversity in program content, the FCC tried to establish stations in as many locations as possible. The available space on the public air waves was divided into a spectrum of four frequencies:

1. Lower frequencies were assigned to AM radio broadcasters.
2. Higher frequencies were assigned to FM broadcasting, which required more space on the spectrum than AM.
3. The still higher range of the broadcasting spectrum, known as VHF (Very High Frequency) was reserved for TV, for which a single channel required six times as much space as the entire AM band.
4. The highest frequency, or UHF, was initially set aside for future TV development.

As television development progressed in the 1940s, the FCC divided VHF into twelve stations. When geographically assigned so that two stations using the same channel could not interfere with each other (170 miles distance), this division provided most major cities with three VHF stations—one for each network (CBS, NBC, and what was to become ABC—which was then known as the "blue network"). In 1941, the FCC forced NBC to divest the blue network, and it became a separate entity.

Aside from these rules, the FCC had the power to determine who among competing interests was to be granted a license to operate. As there was only a limited number of allocable channels, this power was very important. Controversy always has existed about how licenses should be allocated. The mandate to grant licenses in conformance with the "public interest, convenience, and necessity" is very vague. This phrase has had to be defined. It has been interpreted as the right of the public to be informed through the "dissemination of news and ideas about the vital issues of the day"; that is, the public has the right to be informed without being captive to particular views, whether those of the government, broadcasters, or advertisers. The public, according to the FCC, has the right to ideas and information from "diverse and antagonistic sources." Stations have to demonstrate that they will provide information from diverse and competing sources about issues relevant to the needs of a community to obtain a license.

To enforce this concept of the public interest, the FCC promulgated rules, had the power to delay license renewals, and could threaten license revocation. Few licenses, however, were actually revoked. The agency's strength mainly was in the form of a threat. The powers of rulemaking and potential license nonrenewal compelled stations to voluntarily anticipate and conform to practices that the FCC considered important.[10] Through these powers the agency etablished the basic guidelines and ground rules for the broadcasting industry.

Recent Innovations

In recent years, as the FCC has made additional efforts to improve the character and quality of broadcasting, the broadcast industry has been on the defensive. The cybernetic theory appropriately describes such changes. A period of regulatory equilibrium, which lasted from approximately 1934 through the 1950s, came to an end in the 1960s, as new forces—the White House, the courts, citizen groups, and trade associations—emerged to challenge the iron triangle and the other industry-promoting features of broadcast regulation. Innovations took place that reversed the apparent longstanding friendly and intimate relations between the industry and the FCC.

The period of equilibrium prior to the 1960s was marked by policies favorable to existing industry. Existing industry consisted of two key elements: national networks—CBS, NBC, and ABC; and owners of local stations. If it were not for FCC rules, these elements might have merged as the networks owned some stations and would have owned more if they could, since much of their revenue and profit actually derived from station ownership. However, the FCC declared that networks could own a maximum of six stations. Thus, the FCC acted to preserve two separate and distinct elements in the industry—networks and affiliates—with some connection and overlap between these elements.

Traditionally, these elements tried to maintain control by creating a favorable regulatory environment for the development of AM radio, which they dominated in the 1930s, and for the development of VHF television, which they dominated since the inception of this medium in the late 1940s. A favorable regulatory environment to protect industry interest in AM radio and VHF TV involved erecting barriers to the entry of competing entities or substitute services and technologies.[11]

For example, using a highly controversial technical argument from questionable "expert" sources, the broadcast industry—supported by TV manufacturers and the owners of existing stations—was able in 1945 to hinder the development of FM radio despite the wishes of FM backers. The existing broadcast industry successfully promoted a proposal to change FM frequencies, thereby rendering the existing FM equipment outmoded. This change eliminated, at least initially, a potential competitor from the post-World War II communications market. Full commercial FM broadcasting initially was authorized in 1940 in the 43 to 50 frequency range. The 1945 decision, however, reestablished FM in the 84 to 102 range, thus making outmoded the existing operators and receivers, and holding back the development of a communications alternative.

The pre-1960 equilibrium worked to the advantage of the existing networks and station owners in other ways. The 1951 WBAL ruling protected existing owners from potential challenges to their licenses. In the WBAL case, the FCC reaffirmed the position that, in a comparative hearing for an existing station, the past performance of an existing broadcaster was the most reliable indicator of future performance. This implied that a good past record was enough to insure renewal, even if, for example, the competitor promised a better showing on matters such as integration of ownership and management, diversification, or local ownership. The burden of proof was on the competitor to prove inadequate or poor performance on the part of an existing broadcaster. Under the WBAL ruling, existing owners virtually were assured license renewal.

The equilibrium of the 1950s, with its favorable policies for existing networks and station owners, began to change in the 1960s. Feedback and reformulation began as responses to criticisms commonly hurled against the FCC and the broadcasters about the content and quality of their programs. Critics called for more diversity in television and for better quality shows. Television, it was argued, had failed to exploit its potential as a medium for educating, informing, and elevating tastes. It was dominated by a few powerful organizations and individuals who had enormous influence on the cultural standards and political opinions of millions. These organizations and individuals did not provide adequate choice to symphony lovers, and motorcycle enthusiasts, and other minorities who were not being served. The majority of entertainment shows appealed to large audiences and were not meeting the needs of smaller segments of the public.

This criticism affected the regulatory agency. Reform was spearheaded from within the FCC by Newton Minow, who was appointed commissioner by President Kennedy. Minow made a famous speech about the television "wasteland."[12] Dissatisfaction with poor shows, unwanted commercials, and irrelevant material played into the hands of other policy entrepreneurs, who, in turn, threatened network dominance.

Various challenges took place in the 1960s and 1970s that altered the status quo. Seven issues came to the fore: (1) UHF television; (2) the number and frequency of advertisements; (3) citizen group standing; (4) license revocation; (5) CB radio; (6) cable television; and (7) children's programming.[13]

First, the 1961 All Channel Receiver bill, by legitimizing UHF broadcasting, posed a threat to the competitive posture of existing broadcast interests. It required that all TVs manufactured be capable of receiving both VHF and UHF channels, which was a definite advantage for the fledgling UHF interests. They were given legal impetus to challenge the mainline network-dominated VHF stations.

Another challenge was in 1963, when the FCC proposed policies designed to control the number and frequency of advertisements broadcast by radio and TV stations. This proposal would have limited the economic viability and/or profitability of the existing stations. After congressional intervention, the FCC was given the right, on a case-by-case basis, to enforce in license renewal hearings a limit of sixteen minutes of commercial time for TV stations and eighteen minutes of commercial time for radio stations.

A third challenge was the 1967 United Church of Christ/WBLT decision, where the courts interfered to give citizen groups standing in license renewal decisions. In 1966, the U.S. Court of Appeals for the District of Columbia Circuit forced the FCC to give the United Church of Christ the right to challenge the license renewal of a Jackson, Mississippi, station on the grounds of discrimination against minorities. The court held that responsible community organizations had the right to contest license renewal applications. They had standing. This decision opened the way for public interest group judicial activism.

The fourth challenge to the existing industry came in 1969, when the commission took an unprecedented action. It actually revoked a broadcast license. This case involved competitors who argued that they would be more actively involved in the station's operation and would add to the diversity of control over mass communications in a region. In this case, WHDH TV in Boston, owned by the Boston Herald Traveler Corporation, lost its license. After losing it, the *Herald-Traveler* folded, destroying a local newspaper. There were legal limitations to the implications of this case, since the WHDH license had been contested from the beginning; however, many felt that the WHDH decision paved the way for other challenges to existing licenses. Previous to this decision, competitors believed that the only response from the FCC to their challenges was "blind reaffirmation" of the previous license holders.

A fifth challenge came from competition from CB radio, a technology which neither the broadcasters nor the FCC was able to control. FCC voted down a decision designed to limit the expansion of CB and prevent it from interfering with existing broadcasting. The FCC sided with CB users and CB manufacturers rather than with the existing broadcast industry. The situation that existed in 1951, when existing industry could suppress a potential competitor, FM, through regulatory action, no longer prevailed. In the mid-1970s, representatives of a competing technology, rather than those of the dominant industry, won their case.

The sixth challenge came from cable television.[14] The broadcast industry saw cable as a competitor and argued that it was destructive to the public's interest in free, over-the-air broadcasting. Cable companies and their allies, in contrast, maintained that cable provided a vast increase in consumer choice and freedom, as well as potentially great profits. The broadcast industry pressed the FCC for restrictions on cable, and challenged the new technology in the courts. In 1962, the FCC first asserted control over the microwave relay system used to import distant signals, and in 1965-1966 froze cable in the largest 100 markets and forbade importation of additional signals. The cable industry fought back. Despite the freeze, it grew in numbers, and its political strength grew as well. Many writers, attracted by the range of services that cable offered, produced books and articles that spread interest. By 1977, many of the regulations restricting its growth were lifted. In 1980, the rule limiting the number of distant signals no longer applied, and the exclusivity rule, requiring cable systems to afford stations protection against duplication of their syndicated programs, was removed. The FCC for all intents and purposes had deregulated cable TV.

A final challenge arose from citizen group complaints against children's television.[15] The citizen's group that initiated the complaints, Action for Children's Television (ACT), was the product of parents' indignation over the programs and incessant advertising that the networks offered. ACT called for daily public service programming for children, and an end to all advertising on children's shows. The broadcast industry fought back and claimed that it was only offering what children wanted to watch. According to the ratings, the programs parents favored were not popular. Moreover, in 1970, children's programming provided $75 million of the industry's revenues.[16] Although less than 5 percent of gross revenues, this amount accounted for a higher percentage of total profits.

Changes in Regulatory Behavior

Innovations in regulatory behavior made possible these challenges to broadcaster dominance. To begin with, the number of active participants increased. At least six of them became relevant, not just three, as in the old iron triangle theories.[17] Four were formal institutions—the White House, Congress, the courts, and the FCC—and two were private groups—citizen or public interest groups and trade associations that represented regulated industries.

A second change was in the relationship among the participants. The dominance of an iron triangle was predicated on relatively weak FCC commissioners, industry unity, and congressional support. However, commissioners Nicholas Johnson, Newton Minow, and Richard Wiley became activists and were in many ways anti-industry, or at least anti-status quo. Moreover, the industry trade association, the National Association of Broadcasters, represented a large and diverse group of broadcasters, and was less unified and therefore less successful than associations representing vocal and militant special interests—UHF broadcasters, CB radio operators, and cable TV interests. Finally, congressional support of industry and FCC actions decreased, as supervision by multiple committees increased, more investigations were held, and Congress took its powers of oversight more seriously.

While the traditional elements of iron triangle politics changed, new forces emerged to play an important role. Increased White House participation in the early 1970s, for example, was initiated because members of the Nixon administration were worried about the "ideological plugola" and "elitist gossip" that they saw as emanating from the media. A crackdown on broadcasting was attempted through the creation of a central White House office—the Office of Telecommunications Policy (headed by Clay White-head), which monitored the FCC.

The United Church of Christ/WBLT case allowed for increased public interest group and judicial activism. Viewpoints that would not have been represented in the past began to affect the course of regulation. Young graduates of prestigious law schools left eminent firms, and with grants from foundations set up groups such as the Citizens Communications Center, which handled cases representing black, civil rights, and anti-poverty concerns. The Stern Community Law Firm handled First Amendment cases and promoted counteradvertising (air time for rebuttals to advertisements dealing with public issues). The National Citizens Committee for Broadcasting, under the directorship of former FCC chairman Nicholas Johnson, aspired to be a large, broadly supported public interest group like Common Cause.[18] It lobbied Congress for better programming and was active in FCC proceedings and congressional hearings.

A new model of broadcast regulation emerged with the old influences on broadcast regulation—Congress, the FCC, and industry—in one triangle, and the new influences—the courts, citizen groups and trade associations, and the White House—in another.[19] The iron triangle, in effect, became a "Mogen David."

The broadening of forces playing a role in broadcast regulation politics affected the decision to deregulate cable TV.[20] In 1978, the FCC concluded for the first time that competition from cable television had improved television service to the public and would continue to do so in the future. In effect, it removed itself from regulation with this decision. Changes in White House and congressional attitudes were also important. During the Ford administration, the Domestic Council's regulatory reform group, whose chief economist was an anti-regulation figure, Paul MacAvoy, made deregulation arguments about cable and many other technologies. President Carter appointed new FCC commissioners whose votes were decisive. In 1976, the House Interstate and Foreign Commerce Subcommittee on Communications issued a report criticizing the FCC for continued regulation. The FCC was also criticized for its policies in this area by a House Investigation Subcommittee report.

The courts played a role. In *Midwest Video* v. *FCC* (1978), the Eighth Circuit Court decided that the FCC had no jurisdiction to impose access and channel capacity requirements. Meanwhile, the National Cable Television Association was growing in numbers, resources, and influence. Its revenues and membership were increasing, and its lobbying experience was mounting.[21]

The pattern of policymaking changed, as (1) new and old participants in policymaking sought conflicting goals; (2) none had sufficient resources to dominate the system; and (3) each had relatively equal strength.[22] The new pattern became one of mutual accommodation among competing interests.

STRATEGIC RETREAT

In periods of innovation, established businesses have trouble taking advantage of regulation. Rather than reaping particular economic gain, they are pushed into a defensive posture where they try to prevent disastrous consequences. Strategic retreat implies that under changing political circumstances a dominant regulated industry has to be prepared to give up something to new technologies and claimants for power. However, it must try to do so gradually and under carefully controlled circumstances. The established broadcast industry's response to the innovations of the 1960s and 1970s—such as VHF TV, commercial time controversies, license renewal revocation, and the CB challenge—involved strategic retreat; that is, giving up something to new technologies and claimants for power under controlled conditions.

The companies used a number of tactics. First, to avoid worse defeat on the UHF issue, the established broadcasting interests agreed to a compromise: they would support the All Channel Receiver bill. If they had to concede, they would only concede an intermixture of stations. Conceding on a lesser point to avoid a greater evil is a tactic that can be used in support of strategic retreat.

Another tactic is to have the government incorporate existing industry standards. If standards in some form are inevitable, then they should at least be standards that have been formulated and developed by industry and not by the government. This tactic of substituting industry standards for government standards was used by the broadcast industry to soften the blow of government-threatened commercial time regulation.

The same tactic was used in the case of children's programming. In 1972, ABC asked the National Association of Broadcasters (NAB) for a reduction in the number of commercial minutes permitted on weekend programs broadcast for children.[23] ABC wanted a reduction of from sixteen minutes to eleven minutes per hour. The NAB acted to change the industry code, limiting nonprogram material on weekend mornings to twelve minutes. In 1974, FCC chairman Wiley proposed that weekend time for children be brought into line with prime time—a nine and a half minute limit. The NAB again agreed. To avoid government regulation, industry cut commercial time in its code on weekend children's TV to ten minutes in 1974 and to nine and a half minutes in 1975. The three networks, however, lost nothing in gross revenues by taking these steps. In fact, gross revenues from advertising reached an all-time high in 1975 in spite of this reduction.[24]

A third tactic used to achieve strategic retreat is to insist on case-by-case rulemaking as opposed to general standards, if general standards are contemplated. Case-by-case decision making is preferable to general standards because it is likely to be more technical, and tends to be dominated by lawyers, who will argue about the details of precedent and about present interpretation. If further regulation is inevitable, case-by-case decision making, which industry resorted to in the commercial time controversy, is to be preferred over general rules.

A fourth tactic that will aid in strategic retreat is the use of bargaining and out-of-court settlements. The FCC is very reluctant to impose the "death penalty" of stripping a station owner of its license. Technical violations must be flagrant. The path of negotiation and agreement has advantages for both citizen groups and broadcasters. The citizen group often has limited objectives. It is usually expensive and time-consuming to pursue a petition to deny license renewal, and it is unlikely that the petitioner will get a hearing. Responding to a petition to deny is a great burden on the FCC, citizen groups, and broadcasters. It can be very expensive. In the early 1970s a station claimed to have spent $400,000, including court costs and extra staff time, in defending its renewal application.[25] Stations, therefore, are often willing to make many concessions to placate a petitioner. In order to avoid a formal hearing, the commission may permit stations to upgrade, particularly in regard to employment of minorities, before a formal petition is filed.

Another tactic firms can use is to strive for policy statements rather than rules. *Broadcasting* magazine commented in a 1974 editorial about the FCC's actions in regard to children's television: "Now that the FCC has concluded its long inquiry into children's television with a policy statement instead of a rule, a good many broadcasters are privately celebrating."[26] Rules are binding statements of law, while policy statements are not enforceable.

A sixth tactic that aids strategic retreat is to appeal to other decision-making bodies to reverse potentially adverse regulatory decisions. However, appealing to other decision-making bodies and widening the scope of the conflict may have its risks. Perhaps the appeal will be made to authorities that have no sympathy, are not as powerful as expected, and cannot reverse the prior decision. The established broadcast industry discovered, after the WHDH nonrenewal decision, that Congress, to whom it appealed, had no sympathy and could not deliver what industry wanted. The broadcast industry appealed to Congress to reinstate some version of the past performance rule by legislative fiat; but the media picked up on the broadcast industry's efforts, and magazines, including *Harpers* and the Sunday *New York Times*, ran scathing articles against industry collusion with Congress. The courts, responding to this controversy, established a new and more stringent test for allowing existing stations to retain their license—the test of superior performance. The existing broadcast owners, in order to reverse a political momentum that was going against them, then appealed to the White House; but the White House during the Nixon years was dissatisfied with the news media and sought changes in network news policy in exchange for arguing the broadcasters' position on license renewal.

Appealing to other decision-making bodies is a temptation during strategic retreat, but it is a temptation that has its risks, because the scope of a conflict cannot necessarily be controlled to industry's benefit.

A seventh tactic in support of strategic retreat is resignation. Sometimes an industry must admit that there are innovations, or claimants for power, that it cannot control. CB radio is an example of an uncontrollable innovation. There was little that either the established broadcasting industry or the FCC, for that matter, could do to police and control the introduction of this technology. CB radios were the personal computers of the 1970s. They spread like wildfire into the homes and cars of 20 million Americans in less than six years. With such a strange, cultlike phenomenon, the situation called for resignation—so long as resignation did not result in permanent damage to the industry.

An eighth tactic to control the damage is to develop economic interests in competing technologies. Due to increasing cross-ownership of cable television systems, broadcast owners are not as concentrated in one segment of the industry as they once were. By the mid-1970s, 25 percent of the cable industry was owned by existing broadcasters and the proportion was growing.[27] By the mid-1980s, the proportion owned by the existing broadcasters is expected to exceed 33 percent.[28] Cross-ownership weakened broadcaster resistance to cable TV, as the broadcasters themselves developed an interest in the technology's success.

A ninth tactic is to attack and try to weaken citizen group opponents. During the controversy about children's television, the president of CBS Broadcast Group was quoted as saying, "We must recognize the enemy and they are the consumer groups who went to Washington and told the FCC that they must put an end to all advertising on children's programming."[29] A weakened public interest sector has its effects. During the Carter administration, activist groups and public interest law firms fell on hard times. Staffs were reduced and foundation support decreased.

A final method of retreat is the use of symbolic gestures. When the controversy about children's television began, some broadcasters made changes in their policies on their own. Westinghouse Broadcasting Company, for example, announced the creation of a series of science-oriented programs for children which would have only limited commercials.[30]

Symbolic Gestures

Symbolic gestures may have a powerful impact. Another example comes from the cigarette industry.[31] In the early 1960s, it was confronted by an adverse regulatory climate. Release of the surgeon general's report in 1964 put the issue of smoking and health on the public agenda. Congress passed the Cigarette Labeling and Advertising Act of 1965, which required a health warning on packages and in advertisements, and the FCC interpreted the

Fairness Doctrine to mean that free broadcasting time and public assistance should be provided for anti-smoking forces. Between 1964 and 1970 per capita consumption of cigarettes by individuals fourteen years of age and older declined by an average of 1.6 percent per year.[32] After the anti-smoking advertisements of the post-1967 period, the decline was averaging 2.6 percent per year. Companies engaged in a fierce battle to maintain their shares of a shrinking market, spending over 50 percent more on advertising than they had in the previous seven years (1957-1964).

They had an incentive to discontinue commercials voluntarily, as it would free large sums of money they were spending on advertising. Indeed, the chairman of the Tobacco Institute, therefore, offered to end broadcast advertising. Industry supported the Public Health Cigarette Smoking Act of 1970, which completely prohibited television and radio commercials for cigarettes after January 2, 1971. Industry had three reasons for its action. First, the ban reduced industry advertising outlays, which after 1971 declined significantly. Second, it allowed promotion of "safer" low-tar and -nicotine cigarettes by requiring that information about tar and nicotine be placed in all cigarette advertisements. Third, and most important, it eliminated anti-smoking advertisements. The Fairness Doctrine required that both sides of an issue be aired, but, in the absence of pro-smoking advertisements, public interest groups could not claim "equal time." Cigarette consumption increased at an average annual rate of 2.5 percent in the five years immediately following the new law, and low-tar and -nicotine cigarettes were the fastest growing segment of the market.[33]

From a public interest perspective, the threat of increased smoking was not abated by the change in legal standing. Industry achieved its goal without capturing the regulators. However, its support for regulatory innovation tilted an unfavorable regulatory situation in its favor. The tobacco industry successfully retreated in the face of regulatory challenge through a symbolic gesture.

FRONTAL ATTACK

In contrast to strategic retreat, the history of the Federal Trade Commission during the 1970s provides an example of frontal attack to beat back a regulatory challenge.[34] As the decade began, the FTC was under intensive fire. Attacked in 1969 by a very critical Nader report and subject to a thorough investigation by the American Bar Association, the agency undertook some basic changes in its policies.

In 1970, Caspar Weinberger was appointed FTC chairman by President Nixon. Weinberger endorsed administration proposals to increase FTC enforcement authority and urged that this authority be broadened to award damages to consumers. He also favored an automobile quality control act in which the government would establish standards for the durability and performance of new vehicles. Miles Kirkpatrick, his successor in 1971, had directed the American Bar Association study of the FTC and was even more committed to revitalizing the agency than his predecessor.

A major reorganization was accomplished, with existing functional bureaus being abolished or shifted to new bureaus. The Deceptive Practices and Consumer Protection bureaus, which reflected the agency's new priorities, gained in prominence. A council of legal experts proposed changes in administrative procedures, which had been criticized for causing delays, and the commission took a number of other substantive actions that indicated a new "toughness." For example, it required that businesses show supporting evidence for their advertising claims.

Some of these changes were symbolic. After all, the FTC had been very active in the 1950s initiating a major suit against the drug manufacturers during the Eisenhower administration. But some of these changes were more substantial. The agency put less emphasis on its older voluntary compliance programs, fur and textile labeling activities, and programs to protect small businesses. Rather, it emphasized consumer protection and antitrust actions. It initiated suits against major businesses, including the petroleum companies and cereal manufacturers, charging eight primary refiners with monopolization and conspiracy and charging the cereal manufacturers with shared monopoly among the largest firms. After the Magnuson-Moss Act became law in 1975, the commission favored rulemaking rather than litigation, but about a quarter of its new rules were very controversial.[35] Four stand out, because they aroused the ire and indignation of significant groups in the business and professional community. Opposition to proposed children's advertising rules came from the National Association of Broadcasters, the Grocery Manufacturers of America, the Association of National Advertisers, and other representatives of the cereal, sugar, toy, broadcasting, and advertising industries. Opposition to rules requiring funeral homes to provide itemized price information came from the National Funeral Directors Association. Opposition to mandatory inspection and disclosure in used car sales came from the National Automobile Dealers Association. Moreover, organized physicians and optometrists opposed many FTC activities, including FTC restrictions on state abolition of advertising.

The opposition and indignation of many different business and professional groups led to a frontal attack against the FTC's policies. The Chamber of Commerce led a group of thirty to forty business associations and companies in lobbying against the FTC. The business groups that were part of this coalition included the National Association of Manufacturers, the National Federation of Independent Business, the Grocery Manufacturers of America, the Toy Manufacturers Association, many advertising groups, and insurance associations. They favored a legislative veto provision that would give both chambers of Congress ninety days to veto any commission rule. The intent was to curtail the agency's discretionary powers. The veto, declared unconstitutional as a tool of congressional policy in 1983, was not the only consequence of the frontal attack. The FTC also cut back several other proposals, because of the massive opposition to its policies that came from the business community.[36]

From 1979 to 1981, Congress publicly attacked the FTC, branding its activist programs abuse by a "runaway bureaucracy." September 1979 hearings charged that the FTC had roamed "far beyond its congressional mandate." According to Mark Moran and Barry Weingast, changes in congressional composition had an important impact on the agency: "In 1977, the Senate oversight committee experienced nearly complete turnover, bringing to power legislators with markedly different preferences than their predecessors."[37] Only two of thirteen subcommittee members returned in 1977. Most of the major figures associated with the consumer protection movement were no longer in power. The congressmen who replaced the FTC's supporters acted to reverse prior policies.

The FTC was a scapegoat for congressional criticism of excessive government regulation. According to James Singer, the commission became "a sitting duck for members of Congress who wanted to demonstrate their determination to curb big government."[38] A frontal attack by the united business community was successful. However, after the 1982 House elections, the coalition that supported the FTC (the Consumer Federation, National Consumers League, AFL-CIO, United Auto Workers, and other civic groups and labor unions) regained some strength.[39] Democratic victories in the House and the defeat of some FTC opponents restored support for keeping the agency's remaining powers intact. The frontal attack did not turn the agency around entirely, but merely deflected it from its prior commitment to tough law enforcement.

REINVIGORATING STATE UTILITY COMMISSIONS

The 1970s also witnessed the revitalization of other regulatory agencies including many of the state utility commissions. Rising electricity rates brought increased consumer activism. The period of upward pressure on rates started in the early 1970s and gained momentum after the 1973 oil embargo. It came after a long period of stable or declining rates. Contributing to the upward pressure, in addition to higher oil prices, were interest rates, inflation, environmental quality and nuclear safety requirements, and limited technological advance. After 1970, rates increased 90 percent in five years.[40]

The political environments of the state utility commissions became very turbulent. Numerous and diverse actors took part in efforts to assess and reformulate policies, including commissioners and their staffs; governors and legislatures; consumers and producers; environmentalists; local governments; the Department of Energy; and other federal and state agencies.[41]

An important lesson to be learned from these changes involves the variety of the state responses. Key actors were often different in the various states. In a study of the utility commissions of three southern states, David Welborn and Anthony Brown found that Tennessee had very little organized consumer activity, while Georgia had a great deal.[42] Gubernatorial involvement was greatest in Kentucky. Georgia and Kentucky had official watchdogs in the attorney general's office, while Tennessee did not.

Lifeline rates, favored by consumer advocates, were adopted in California and defeated in New York.[43] These rates priced the first several hundred kilowatt hours of electricity below cost to protect disadvantaged citizens. The failure to enact lifeline rates in New York is attributed to the inability of the pro-lifeline groups in New York to organize sufficient support for their cause. The New York commission, under Joseph Swidler and Alfred Kahn, was professionally run, unlike the California commission, which had been politicized under governors Ronald Reagan and Jerry Brown, and was an inviting target for left-wing consumer interests. The specific politics at state levels had important effects on outcomes.

ENDURING FEATURES OF REGULATION

Iron-triangle or other theories of simple business dominance are not adequate in explaining regulatory behavior during implementation. Even in the phase when most scholars agree that industry should be able to take advantage of regulation, the evidence indicates that the industrial posture may be defensive, warding off agency thrusts at industry prerogatives, rather than reaping economic gain from regulation. A number of features of agency behavior contradict the simple theory of industry dominance.

1. An agency has a crucial position as the principal, although not always the most powerful, agent in the regulatory process. An agency can always threaten not to renew a license or to change the ground rules to the detriment of business.

2. An agency generally strives for modest changes—some acceptable level of innovation short of radical departures. It tries to partially satisfy different interests (in the case of the FCC, these interests were FM, AM, VHF, UHF, CBer's, and cable operators) without unduly infringing on the rights of any and without regard for any specific notion of a transcendent public interest.

3. Officials generally would prefer to take small steps and reverse themselves rather than risk the large mistakes that are possible with sweeping innovations. Therefore, they try to be flexible in their policy choices and sensitive to feedback. They try to direct attention to immediate problems in a series of sequential stages. They focus on bottlenecks and generally limit consideration to proposals which are only marginally different from existing policies.

4. Regulatory outcomes are likely to change over time, but not as simple life-cycle theories propose, that is, from public serving at birth to private serving during implementation. Rather, outcomes may move among various levels of regulatory performance without a necessary or predictable pattern.[44]

Agencies may be adversarial, arbitrating, mediating, or legitimizing.[45] Adversarial agencies aggressively promote the interests of businesses' opponents. Arbitrating ones attempt to independently balance conflicting concerns in terms of some notion of a transcendent public interest. These agencies are technocratic and idealistic, but are often naive with respect to actual political realities. Mediating agencies, in contrast, try to secure acceptable political compromises that can withstand political tests. Only legitimizing agencies, in contrast to the rest, are captured by the businesses they are supposed to regulate, and simply serve business interests. An incrementalist approach to regulation, which allows for periods of disequilibrium and change and movement from one type of regulatory performance to another has more descriptive power than conventional industry-dominance theories. This approach has implications for business in that it signifies constant vigilance to the many small regulatory struggles that continue for long periods of time.

7

Deregulation: Opportunities and Problems

Deregulation presents opportunities and problems for business. Some companies want to prevent it, some promote it, and some are unable to prevent the demise of agencies they wished to preserve. After deregulation, all companies must live with the uncertain consequences of government efforts to remove requirements. The economic environment in which they operate becomes very turbulent.[1] For example, after airline deregulation an established company in the airlines industry, Braniff, failed. Pan Am has been operating on the brink of bankruptcy. Newer entrants, such as People Express and New York Air, have not been making a profit. Some airlines, however, such as Delta, US Air, and Southwest, have been prospering, even though the recession and higher fuel prices meant that times were difficult for the entire industry.

The older "regulation mentality," so prevalent among firms before deregulation, is an impediment to effective management in the period after deregulation.[2] The older mentality has been characterized as a limited focus on markets, limited attention to growth, and lack of concern about costs, while the main focus is on the regulatory agency. This older mentality gives way to a competitive mentality in the post-deregulation period. At companies that survive the emphasis is on the customer, planned expansion, and cost competitiveness.

Adjustment to the altered situation, with its emphasis on innovation and risk, is difficult. To meet changing marketing needs and competitiveness requirements, a flexible organization is necessary, and companies must have a strategic orientation. Skills in strategic management, hitherto unnecessary, become critical.

Arguments against economic regulation have been made time and again by economists of the left and of the right who maintain that it contributes to inflation, protects industry from competition, and stifles innovation. The natural gas shortages of the late 1970s, for example, were attributed to poorly conceived rate regulations that did not allow supply to balance demand. But a negative evaluation, however widely held by economists, does not mean that there will be policy change. Evaluation is political in nature. Actual change needs a broad movement for reform.

Stigler's theory suggests that evaluation will not bring about change because regulated industries are likely to resist deregulation, and regulatory agencies are likely to survive threats to their existence because of industry support.[3] However, the evidence presented in this chapter indicates a more complex pattern.[4] In the four examples of deregulation that are discussed, none corresponds entirely to Stigler's classic paradigm.

The deregulation movement took off in the late 1970s. Regulatory reform bills were passed that affected the trucking, natural gas, airline, banking, and railroad industries. For example, the Airline Deregulation Act of 1978, the Natural Gas Policy Act of 1978, the Staggers Rail Act of 1980, and the Motor Carrier Reform Act of 1980 were the products of this period. Other agencies made changes on their own. The Securities and Exchange Commission (SEC) eliminated control over brokerage fees, and the FCC and FTC changed the rules affecting the Bell System. The giant telephone company ended its opposition to "foreign" equipment attachments and accepted loss of intrastate assets in exchange for the right to enter nonregulated markets.

Until World War II, the old-line economic agencies had expanded their authority and jurisdiction, continually developing more detailed rules and restrictions. In the 1950s, however, technological changes began to create new competitive opportunities, particularly in communications and transport. Under the existing regulatory regime, lengthy hearings and extensive evidence were necessary for price changes, mergers, entry, and the abandonment of unprofitable service. The regulatory milieu, which was legalistic and burdened by administrative lethargy, inhibited technological change.[5]

Economists demonstrated repeatedly and insistently that economic regulations were costly. Each of the major objections to airline deregulation raised by the CAB, the airlines, and others was refuted at congressional hearings. The impetus for Senate support of trucking deregulation was based on "literally thousands of PH.D dissertations, books, and scholarly articles" that, with few notable exceptions, were highly critical of existing regulation.[6] The trucking industry apparently had difficulty producing credible experts to testify at congressional hearings. According to Paul Quirk and Martha Derthick, the primary reason that senators and representatives supported deregulation was the powerful and "almost uniquely persuasive case for it on purely intellectual grounds."[7] Economists argued that competition without regulation was possible, that prices would be lower, that productivity would increase, and that the costs of switching to market mechanisms were negligible.

Deregulatory bills, introduced over the years, failed to pass until the late 1970s, at which time the academic criticism had reached its peak. This criticism always received a welcome reception within the executive branch, where the Council of Economic Advisers was sympathetic to the economists' viewpoint. Although every president from Kennedy to Reagan had supported basic changes in economic regulation, in almost every case the changes were not forthcoming. What made a difference in the late 1970s was that the affected industries were in some important cases split about the merits and demerits of regulation. Different companies within an industry took different positions. Contrary to Stigler's theory, industry unity could not be assumed. The economists' arguments had made inroads among those who were supposed to be the staunchest supporters of regulation. Defecting companies, such as United in the case of the airlines, played a decisive role in changing the politics of regulation. A major factor in the success of the deregulation movement was this "deterioration or narrowing" of industry resistance.[8]

Some firms saw that strategic advantage—increased markets, growth, and inroads on the competition—could be gained from deregulation. The anti-government, anti-regulation mood of the late 1970s also contributed to the success of the deregulation movement; but this success was relatively short-lived. After 1982, there was little left that needed to be reformed. The next frontier might have been electric utility deregulation.[9] However, the natural monopoly characteristics claimed by some for this industry probably precluded further deregulation. The case for reregulation in transportation, power, and communications, moreover, was being made frequently, as political interests and businesses felt the effects of reform and did not always like what they were experiencing. Administration support for deregulation also weakened. 'The Republicans and their business allies should be smashing the old molds," a writer in *Fortune* stated, "and they're not."[10] Congress, because of a concern with overwork and other reasons, pulled away from its commitment to periodically review and reauthorize all federal programs—the so-called sunset proposals.

The heyday of the deregulation movement was 1978-1980. Four cases of deregulation from this period will be examined, with commentary about the role businesses played in bringing about deregulation and the effects deregulation has had on these businesses.

ICC-TRUCKING: THE CLASSIC PATTERN

The classic pattern is industry support for regulation and success in preventing deregulation. The trucking industry, by and large, is opposed to ending Interstate Commerce Commission regulation, and until recently was able to prevent complete regulatory elimination. However, a far-reaching liberalization of trucking regulation occurred between 1978 and 1980, despite trucker opposition, and this liberalization continues, albeit in muted form, in the Reagan administration.[11] First, we will describe the pre-1978 pattern, and then the post-1978 reforms in trucking regulation.

In the pre-1978 period, industry gained from regulation a system of rate-making and entry that virtually guaranteed its financial health, even though there were inefficient operations and marginal operators within the industry. Financial health was guaranteed by price rules which generally led to routine renewal of rate proposals high enough to cover the fully allocated costs of the average carrier. Truckers survived, but there were limits to their profitability and growth.

ICC regulation prevented price competition, virtually guaranteed profits, and controlled entry. It provided stability, but did not present the opportunity of great rewards. Risk-taking, in the form of efforts to make inroads on another firm's markets or to substantially lower costs through some major innovation, were virtually ruled out. To operate, a common carrier needed an ICC certificate of operating authority, which spelled out the precise service it could offer. Operating authorities were typically a trucker's most valuable asset in that they guaranteed a portion of what may be referred to as a government-protected monopoly. They were bought and sold for substantial sums of money and were not unlike frequency rights, which in a similar manner guaranteed TV station owners a portion of such a monopoly.

Prior to 1978, the trucking companies did not have to deal with the market and did not have to seriously consider the problem of competitive position. In exchange for virtually assured financial health, but not the potential for great growth or extraordinary profits to individual firms, the regulated industry had to provide the public with some benefit. It had to serve the "public interest, convenience, and necessity," which was defined as providing equal treatment to small and big shippers alike by charging them the same rate for the same service, regardless of how much more it actually cost to handle the goods of the smaller shippers. The industry justified its right to protection through this form of cross-subsidization.

The disadvantage was that the industry had to cope with bureaucratic costs. Coping with bureaucratic costs was a minor disadvantage when compared with the instabilities of the market. There was another plus from regulation. In addition to a virtual guarantee of financial health, the truckers gained a rate structure that protected not only the efficient operators but also incalculable numbers of marginal and poorly managed firms. The same policies that protected the marginal operators also handsomely overrewarded the good managers.

If trucking firms received protection that gave them stable, if not extraordinary, profits from regulation, the public lost. It had to pay the higher costs of regulated trucking. Depending on the nature of their shipments, shippers paid between 9 and 15 percent less to unregulated intrastate carriers than they would have had to pay to regulated interstate truckers for the same kind of service.[12] It was estimated in the late 1970s that the regulation of trucking cost society between $1.4 billion and $6 billion annually.[13]

How did the truckers maintain this protection from the rigors of marketplace competition, which is at odds with the economist's criterion of a successful policy—the most efficient use of society's resources? They did so through a political coalition that in every contest between regulators and deregulators in the twenty-five years prior to 1978 led to regulatory maintenance. Proposals to reform the regulation of trucking were made during every administration—Republican and Democratic—in the postwar period. Initiatives were made to reform trucking regulation in the mid-1950s, the early 1960s, the mid-1960s, the early 1970s, and the mid-1970s. In every instance, the reform proposal had minimal effect. Little basic change took place. Evaluation in these cases did not lead to reform. The economic interests of the truckers prevailed until 1978, when everything changed.

Until that time, the politics of trucking deregulation was not favorable to change. Truckers, labor unions, and railroads supported continued regulation. In opposition were academics, mostly professional economists, who portrayed the inefficiencies of the system in learned articles.[14] In this contest, the academics were weak. Expert judgment was ignored. The truckers, who owned the operating rights, were opposed to deregulation because it threatened a system that guaranteed their financial success. The Teamsters Union, on the other hand, feared deregulation because free entry could open the industry to a flood of non-union trucking firms. The railroads opposed deregulation because lower rates might enable motor carriers to capture traffic from the rails. (Freight carried by the railroads would be switched to lower-priced trucks.) This coalition of trucking operators, unions, and railroads faced opposition from academic economists who had no compelling reason, other than professional advancement, to pressure the government for change.

In addition, and perhaps as significant, the shippers—who used the services provided by the truckers—did not endorse deregulation, even though they stood to be its greatest beneficiaries. An end to regulation might create opportunities for new firms to enter trucking markets. It might foster innovation, lead to competition, and lower prices, but individual shippers were not sure what was likely to happen. The instability that would result from new ratemaking procedures dictated their policy. They preferred the present system, however inefficient, to unpredictability. The competitive implications of proposed changes were not clear. Shippers were not sure whether deregulation meant that they would have higher or lower rates. As they did not know, they were cautious about change. The small shippers, in particular, were opponents of deregulation; while the large shippers had more to gain and were more likely to favor it.

The politics of deregulation, however, changed dramatically in the late 1970s. Consumer groups, the media, and a combination of liberals and free market conservatives were induced to work for reform. The existence of successive administrations in Washington which promised to fight unnecessary regulation provided ample opportunity for the deregulators. Congress held numerous hearings on the subject. Of great significance is the fact that the principal opponents of regulation were organized into an ad hoc coalition that was dominated by several large corporations, of which Sears was the largest.[15] Other participants in this coalition included Common Cause, the American Conservative Union, the Nader-related Transportation Consumer Action Project, the American Farm Bureau Federation, the National Federation of Independent Businesses, and the National Association of Manufacturers.

The case against trucking regulation was made with rhetorical vividness and simplicity. The reformers took advantage of opportunities for "attention-getting ridicule and moralism."[16] Senator Adlai Stevenson III of Illinois, for example, during debate in the Senate, made fun of the arbitrary distinctions between regulated and unregulated commodities. The media took note, and their coverage of trucking deregulation, if not extensive, was sufficient to maintain the interest of a broader public.

Under this assault, the fragmented industry front began to disintegrate. Owner operators (the "independent" unregulated truckers) and private carriers (firms that operate trucks to carry their own goods or products) saw the possibility of expanding their scope of operations if changes in the existing system were made.

Before Congress acted, the ICC showed that it favored reform, and, under Carter administration appointees Darius Gaskins, Jr., Marcus Alexis, and Thomas A. Trantum, substantial deregulation took place.[17] The agency moved from what had been a protectionist attitude to the belief that "competition was a good thing."[18] It made it easier for firms to get into the trucking business and for truckers to lower their rates. The burden of proof was on the opponent of a new entrant or a price reduction. No longer could established companies routinely protest against every new applicant for operating authority and against every carrier that requested a price reduction.

The commission received more applicants for operating authority and made more approvals. New applicants began to take some of the traffic from the existing companies. They were especially interested in capturing the round-trip business, which was particularly profitable. Shippers, in addition to rate cuts, received other benefits, such as additional hauling capacity "whenever and wherever" it was necessary.[19] They had the choice of more companies offering more and different services, as the ICC granted liberal and less restrictive rights to operate.

The effects on the trucking industry were substantial. Management had changed its emphasis. Greater stress on marketing, cost control, and operating efficiency had replaced attention devoted to regulation and public relations. Long-term planning and innovative rate and service concepts became important. Relaxed rate control meant widespread rate cutting and discounting. Relaxed entry control meant expansion of existing carriers into new territories, entry of new carriers, and a general increase in competition, but not at all points or for all commodities.

In 1981, many trucking companies were in poor financial shape because of the combined effects of deregulation, high labor and fuel costs, loss of business to new entrants and independents, and the recession.[20] Many carriers made additional managerial and organizational changes, particularly in their marketing and planning functions. These functions were the most difficult to carry out because of the turbulence unleashed by regulatory changes.

Shippers enjoyed rate discounting and improved service, although the improvements varied by routes, points, and products. Deficiencies in service for small communities did not materialize. However, service did decline for some products and some destinations. Moreover, shippers had to acquire negotiating skills in dealing with carriers in connection with rates and service. They had to show initiative in developing new ideas and had to accord greater importance to the management of transportation and logistics, as opposed to functions such as production and marketing.

In the competition that developed, established trucking firms (the common carriers) were at a distinct disadvantage. Unlike contract carriers and independents, they did not necessarily have sufficient business to use their trucks economically. They carried very high overhead costs: salespersons, who solicited business; warehouses, where freight could be stored in between trips; and terminals, where the freight could be moved from one truck to another before delivery to a final destination. The common carriers also tended to use union labor, which was expensive, while the independents did not.

The American Trucking Associations, representing the common carriers, fought back against the unfavorable regulatory situation. It accused the ICC of going farther than Congress had intended. It made its criticisms known during oversight hearings. It brought lawsuits regarding the ICC's interpretation of the 1980 law. These attacks on the law bore fruit. In 1981, the federal court of appeals remanded two ICC policies involving entry control.[21] One involved the awarding of broad new operating authority. The other concerned the removal of restrictions from existing operating authorities.

The established industry was successful in another area—presidential appointment of a new commission chairman. President Reagan at the beginning of his term chose Reese Taylor, who planned to curb the number of firms entering the business and to trim the scope of operating rights. It was charged that Reagan's appointment of Taylor was a political payoff to the Teamsters, who supported his election after receiving a promise that the administration would not hastily deregulate trucking. The Teamsters experienced major losses under deregulation. Many members were laid off, as the industry began to switch to cheaper, non-union, labor.

However, the Reagan appointments were not strictly one-sided. The president also appointed Malcolm Sterrett and Frederic Andre to the commission. Both were supporters of deregulation. During his administration, ICC policies became less predictable than they had been. The agency was less inclined to move toward complete regulatory freedom, and yet at the same time it showed signs of limiting regulation and promoting competition. Stigler's theory says that regulated firms oppose deregulation and have the power to prevent it, but the evidence from this case shows a more complex pattern, with neither regulators nor deregulators gaining the upper hand.

FPC–NATURAL GAS

The second case, natural gas deregulation, clearly runs contrary to Stigler's theory. In this instance, the producer segment of the industry has consistently opposed regulation.[22] For years it tried to remove regulation, but to no avail until recently, when concessions were made and deregulation initiated. Why was the natural gas case different from the trucking case? What was wrong with the producers? According to Stigler's theory it made no sense for them to oppose regulation. It made no sense for them not to have taken advantage of regulation and to support its preservation.

However, natural gas regulation in its basic design was different from trucking regulation and, for that matter, from airline and railroad regulation. The object of natural gas regulation has been consumer protection, that is, absorbing possible windfall profits earned by producers and preventing their transfer to consumers.[23] The producers can earn windfalls through the sale of existing older stocks, which progressively cost less to produce, at uniform prices. Instead, regulation sets the prices the producers charge for both old and new stock on a cost-of-service basis. To eliminate windfalls, ratemakers set tiered prices depending on the costs of production in individual categories.[24]

Natural gas regulation, therefore, has not benefitted producers, at least in terms of price protection. The government generally has set artificially low prices for natural gas to stimulate the development of a market for a fuel thought to be in the national interest. Natural gas replaced coal for home heating with a cleaner, easier-to-handle source of energy. The government, therefore, aided the growth of the industry by providing incentives to expand the number of customers who could afford this fuel.

The benefits and costs of regulation to the three elements in the industry (producers, transmitters, and distributors) are different. Until the landmark *Phillips Petroleum Co.* v. *Wisconsin* case of 1954, regulation applied only to the transmitters and distributors.[25] Distributors, for the most part, had monopolies, as economies of scale made it difficult to establish more than one company per area. As a result the local gas distributors were regulated by state utility commissions. The Natural Gas Act of 1938 gave the FPC the right to regulate transmitters, the pipeline companies that transported the gas interstate and sold it to the distributors. Twenty-two large interstate companies transported over 70 percent of the gas shipped interstate.[26] The transmission segment of the industry had elements of monopoly and monopsony and therefore regulation was considered appropriate in this instance also.

On the other hand, the largest producers were the major oil companies. Although they produced gas as a by-product of their search for oil, and the twenty largest producers accounted for 70 percent of industry sales to major pipelines in 1971, thousands of small, independent producers led in the search for new gas.[27] They used new drilling methods to search exclusively for gas, rather than for gas as an oil by-product. In 1974, 86 percent of new gas wells and 70 percent of new reserves were discovered by independents.[28] Of the three parts of the industry, the producing segment by virtue of the existence of the independents was the most competitive. Because of this fact, there was great surprise when the Supreme Court found in the *Phillips* case that the FPC had the right to regulate the price of the new gas discovered by producers.

Producer price regulation, it is alleged, caused, or at least aggravated, a series of natural gas shortages in the late 1970s.[29] A number of points can be made about the shortages.[30] To begin with, they were serious, as in some parts of the country consumption was cut back as much as 50 percent and overall, curtailments in the winter of 1976/77 were 20 percent.[31] In addition, the curtailments varied depending on the pipeline that served a particular area. For example, the pipeline serving North and South Carolina had a 40 percent deficiency in the winter of 1975/76, while the pipeline serving Massachusetts experienced no cutback.[32] Furthermore, the short-ages appeared to be those of supply. Until 1967, the trend had been increasing reserves. During the early 1960s, proven reserves were sufficient to supply gas for about 20 years at the existing production rates.[33] By 1967, however, this figure had fallen to 15.9 years.[34] From 1968 to 1975, the ratio of total reserves to production continued to fall, reaching 9.3 years in 1975.[35]

A final point to note about the shortages was that they appeared to be related to the problems in allocation caused by regulation. The newly discovered gas went into intrastate rather than interstate markets. In 1975, the "new" gas price in the regulated interstate market was about $0.52 per million cubic feet (Mcf), while the "new" gas price in the unregulated intrastate market was around $1.32 per Mcf, and in some markets was as high as $2.00 per Mcf.[36] Between 1969 and 1975, new gas prices rose 158 percent in regulated interstate markets, while they rose almost 650 percent in unregulated intrastate markets.[37] Therefore, between 1969 and 1973 producers committed over 90 percent of net reserve additions to the higher-priced intrastate market.[38] This shift from interstate to intrastate markets represented a major reason for the shortages in the interstate markets and the resulting curtailments.

The shortages had adverse effects on regional balance. Some industries, heavily dependent on natural gas, had a tendency to move south to avoid the threat of further curtailment. The politics of natural gas pricing always had been influenced by regional factors, but the threatened displacement of additional northern industry exacerbated the situation. Traditionally, the gas-consuming states of the North favored low wellhead prices, while the gas-producing states of the Southwest opposed control of wellhead prices. The Supreme Court in the *Phillips* case had in effect decided in favor of the gas consumers of the North. As a result of the *Phillips* decision, however, almost all new natural gas discovered went into the more lucrative unregu-lated intrastate market and almost none went into the unlucrative regulated interstate market. No producer in its right mind was willing to produce for the latter market, as long as it knew that by assigning gas to the unregulated market it would receive double or triple the price.[39]

Natural gas producers therefore consistently opposed price controls. They had the cooperation of southwestern congressmen, and were opposed by consuming-state representatives who favored the existing system. If the FPC had been "captured," it was by these northern consuming interests.[40]

Until recently, these interests successfully defeated a series of deregula-tion proposals. However, in 1978 Congress passed a new Natural Gas Policy Act that promised to gradually deregulate the price of new natural gas. Under the act, the natural gas industry's campaign to deregulate prices met with some success, but success of only a marginal and limited kind. The bill-drafting process actually was a series of compromises between those who wanted to promote increased production—by letting gas prices go up—and those who wanted to hold gas prices down and protect consumers.[41] The outcome was a measure that provided for slow, grudging, and partial deregulation of natural gas in the interstate market, while at the same time it imposed price ceilings on the previously unregulated intrastate market, which at the time accounted for roughly 45 percent of production. Two factors may explain the natural gas producers' ability to achieve partial deregulation, shortages, and discrepancy in prices.

The shortages. The most obvious aid to the producers' position was the curtailments to service, which changed congressional attitudes about deregulation.

Discrepancy in prices. The maldistribution of resources caused by different pricing schemes in the inter- and intrastate markets was another major reason for deregulation, because it exacerbated regional tensions.

Deregulation of new gas prices altered supply and demand for this resource. By 1982, a critical shortage gave way to a surplus.[42] The major producers, the oil companies, always had been somewhat ambivalent about production, because their major investment was in petroleum facilities, and gas competes with petroleum in the marketplace. As a consequence, the independents always had been the real driving force behind the push to find new supplies. After deregulation, independent producers were joined in their efforts to find new supplies by pipeline and distribution companies who wanted to take advantage of the new higher prices. Pipeline companies established exploration and production divisions, and distribution companies started their own drilling ventures.

The Natural Gas Policy Act of 1978 allowed the prices of new gas to rise, but the swiftness of the actual price increases was not anticipated. Pipeline companies, fearful because of the shortages, also signed long-term contracts for expensive new and deep-well gas and for costly foreign gas. Another result of the sudden price increases was that members of Congress introduced bills to stem the tide. However, few congressmen were willing to do away with deregulation entirely. Instead, they called upon producers and pipeline companies in 1983 to renegotiate their contracts to eliminate automatic price escalation provisions.

Despite consumer outrage over higher gas bills, the Reagan administration wanted to push ahead with the further decontrol of prices. It argued that ultimately prices would be lower if full deregulation took place and cited petroleum deregulation.

Some analysts believed that full deregulation would benefit producers of old gas because under the current system they had the lowest price ceilings. It would, in effect, restore their windfall. However, it would hurt producers of new and expensive gas, and suppliers and equipment producers for these firms. In the uncertain regulatory climate, the pipeline companies gradually began to recognize that: (1) shortages were over; (2) gas could not compete in a price war with residual oil; (3) flexibility had to replace security as the central principle of pipeline purchases; and (4) pipelines had to limit themselves to purchases whose terms reduced the company's average supply cost.[43]

Curtailments and the strategic use of the situation by the natural gas industry contributed to partial deregulation of prices. Congress finally accepted the argument that only higher prices for natural gas would spur increased production, but the ultimate fate of gas deregulation was still undecided. The case of natural gas corresponds to none of the suppositions in Stigler's theory. The natural gas producers opposed regulation and ultimately fought to partially defeat it. Since deregulation, they have had to live with increasing uncertainty about demand, not supply.

CAB-AIRLINES: A MIXED CASE

In terms of correspondence with Stigler's theory, airlines deregulation by the Civil Aeronautics Board is a mixed case. In accord with Stigler's theory, the regulated industry, with some significant exceptions, favored regulation and fought to have it retained. However, unlike Stigler's theory, which emphasizes the power of affected interests, the airlines failed in their efforts to prevent deregulation. Deregulation occurred in spite of significant opposition from the industry.

The CAB, created in 1938, was more like the FCC and the ICC than the FPC. The regulated industry sought regulation. It was not thrust upon industry, as it was thrust upon the natural gas producers. The 1938 Civil Aeronautics Act, in fact, read: "Competition among air carriers is being carried to an extreme which tends to jeopardize the financial status of the air carriers and to jeopardize and render unsafe a transportation service appropriate to the needs of commerce."[44] (According to W. Glen Harlan, there is a "cyclical character to the airline industry, as the situation under deregulation may be reverting to the condition of 1938."[45] The industry may again have little choice but to seek re-regulation.) The fledgling airline industry in the 1930s had suffered a period of low profits and failing investments. After price-fixing and pay-off scandals in the 1920s, the industry's biggest companies—United, American, TWA, and Eastern—lost a guaranteed contract with the U.S. Post Office to carry the mails. By 1935, anxious industry leaders organized a trade association, the Air Transport Association, to halt what was referred to as cutthroat competition. They called for regulation to end scandal in the industry and to improve safety for the public.

Get rid of "fly-by-night operators," the existing companies maintained, and the public would feel more secure about flying. The CAB, created at the behest of these companies, was supposed to protect the airlines from potentially debilitating intra-industry competition and to oversee the public's interest in the development of the industry.

The functions of the CAB were not unlike those of the FCC or the ICC. It had the power to award routes—the licensing or franchising function—analogous to the FCC's right to grant frequencies and the ICC's right to grant shipping rights. It also had the right to determine prices, not unlike the ICC, which also had the power to determine shipping rates. Like the ICC and FCC, the CAB did not have a mandate to regulate safety. This responsibility was in the hands of the Federal Aviation Administration (FAA). The CAB also had a vague charge—to protect the "public interest, convenience, and necessity"—which was supposed to govern performance of its functions; and like the other agencies, the CAB was accused of being captured by industry, of giving into industry pressures on important decisions.

In short, the CAB was a typical economic regulatory agency. Rate setting, for example, was supposed to have been managed in industry's favor. The CAB periodically reviewed average industry costs, then it added a standard 12 percent, which it called "reasonable profit."[46] The CAB, in addition, did its best not to authorize new major domestic carriers. Between 1950 and 1974, it received seventy-nine applications from companies wishing to enter the domestic scheduled airline industry and granted none.[47] It virtually froze entry to protect the five big airlines—United, TWA, American, Eastern, and Delta—which accounted for 70 percent of domestic business.[48] After 1938, overall entry into the industry was limited to supplemental carriers, which provided charter service, and to local service and commuter carriers, which carried travelers in small airlines over short distances.

Among the charges brought against the CAB were that (1) route applications were subject to serious delays; (2) the board's standards in awarding new routes were obscure; (3) between 1969 and 1974, there was a route moratorium under which the agency refused to hear applications by existing airlines for new routes; and (4) the large number of meetings between board members and industry members was improper.[49] Critics of the agency also pointed out that a "revolving door," through which top airline executives who served in the CAB often returned to industry and vice versa, was promoting the development of policies favorable to industry.

In the early 1970s, the airlines faced a deteriorating political situation and the industry was willing to retreat. It tried to compromise with the critics who accused industry of capturing the CAB. The forces that opposed industry, however, were too strong and were able to defeat the industry initiative to stem the tide of complete deregulation. While almost every academic economist in the country accepted the conclusions of Richard Caves, whose 1962 book, *Air Transport and Its Regulators*, argued against continued regulation, in this instance the academics were not alone.[50] They were joined by numerous followers. Evaluation became reform, because it gained the momentary backing of a broad political movement.

The Ad Hoc Committee on Airline Regulatory Reform, which favored deregulation, included an unlikely assortment of organizations representing conservative Republicans, liberal Democrats, Naderites, retailers, students, and business interests, including defecting airlines—United, Pan Am, Frontier, and Hughes Air West.[51] The Ford and Carter White Houses, the Council of Economic Advisers (CEA), the Council on Wage and Price Stability (COWPS), the Antitrust Division of the Justice Department (ATD), the Department of Transportation (DOT), and some voices in the CAB also favored deregulation.

In wishing to retreat in the early 1970s, the airline industry was not that much different from the broadcasting industry, which had to make a strategic retreat in the face of regulatory challenges in the 1960s and early 1970s. However, the airline industry, unlike the broadcast industry, did not stem the tide. In the airline case, total deregulation—not modification or reform—was the result. The Airline Transportation Association, the industry lobby, sought a compromise—some shift in the burden of proof in awarding entry, but continued rate regulation and CAB protection. However, this compromise did not prevail. The 1978 Airline Deregulation Act dictated complete deregulation. The law ended route control in 1982 and rate control in 1983, and the CAB was supposed to be abolished by 1985.[52] Of all the cases discussed here, airline deregulation demonstrates the most complete change in existing regulatory practices.

The airline industry was unable to make small concessions to avoid greater losses, as the broadcasters and others had done for various reasons. To begin with, the industry was divided. Therefore, it did not resist deregulation as vigorously. Some airlines, including one of the big carriers, United, supported deregulation. The airlines thus did not take a united stand against deregulation. Also, in giving their support, the airline unions were not as strong as the Teamsters. Moreover, consumers of airline services were predominantly the public, not another class of businesspeople. The public, unlike shippers in the case of trucking deregulation, was less concerned about instability, and was aroused by a skillful policy entrepreneur to support deregulation.

The Policy Entrepreneur

The politics of airline deregulation was different from the politics of trucking and gas deregulation, and an important aspect of this difference was the decisive role played by a policy entrepreneur, who used congressional hearings and the media to arouse broad public support for policy change. A policy entrepreneur may be defined as an innovator, a person who takes an academic idea, a "candidate for reform," and gets it "off the shelf" by having the government adopt and implement it. An entrepreneur, in a sense, is a transferer of a technology who moves evaluation from theory to practice. Ralph Nader was a policy entrepreneur who changed government regulatory policy in the late 1960s and early 1970s in accord with arguments that first had been articulated by academics such as Stigler and Bernstein.

Stephen Breyer was also such an entrepreneur. Breyer describes his entrepreneurial behavior quite vividly in a chapter in his book, *Regulation and Its Reform*.[53] A Harvard Law School professor and an expert in administrative law, Breyer was invited in the 1970s by Senator Edward Kennedy of Massachusetts to be on the staff of the Administrative Practices Subcommittee and to hold hearings on the subject of airline deregulation. Breyer had approached Kennedy with the idea of doing the studies and then holding the hearings. Kennedy would benefit from the image of a liberal senator supporting what heretofore had been regarded as a conservative idea. To promote the image of an effective legislator who was not bound strictly by ideology, Breyer argued that Kennedy should become an advocate of economic deregulation. In this way, he would win respect from economists who believed that the general welfare could be promoted by creating free market conditions in previously regulated markets.

Kennedy gave Breyer the ability to organize hearings, because he was dissatisfied with the role that the Administrative Practices Subcommittee, which he headed, was playing. It was too diffuse and disjointed in its efforts. It was drifting from issue to issue without focus or coherence, and had not accomplished much substantive change in the way government was run. Kennedy thought that by tackling the deregulation issue, he could bring favorable attention to himself and to his subcommittee. He would be recognized as a catalyst for change.

Breyer carefully planned the hearings to achieve Kennedy's purpose. In his opinion, the success of the hearings was dependent on certain actions.[54] It was necessary to (1) gather information and consult professional economists; (2) do comprehensive research to learn how to refute the arguments of industry; (3) produce a concrete transition plan and alternative to regulation; and (4) assemble a coalition and confront the political factors that ultimately determine if reform can be enacted.

Breyer planned the hearings as if they were a mode of theatre—a dramatic presentation that had to be carefully staged to achieve maximum results. The purpose of the hearings was to prove the theory that had been advanced by the economists—that more competition and less regulation was needed. The hearings, therefore, were structured so that each day "told a story" and related a different aspect of the same problem.[55]

The hearing day itself was organized to provoke debate and create drama. The critical element was to make a decisive point that the media would carry to millions of Americans. Points were to be made through provocative questioning. The hope was to get, in Breyer's word, a "zinger," to catch the witness in an untenable contradiction of logic and fact that anybody, even if they knew nothing about the subject, would recognize.

Breyer defines a *zinger* as interrogation that makes an important point for one side in a debate; is unanswerable by the other side; and shows that the other side cannot answer only because it is "wrong" and its opponent is "right."[56] For example, on the second day of the hearings Breyer wanted to establish a simple but devastating point about CAB regulation. In the unregulated intrastate market, rates were 75 to 100 percent lower than they were in the regulated interstate market. To fly from Los Angeles to San Francisco in the unregulated intrastate market cost, at the time, only $18.75, while to fly from Boston to Washington, D.C., an equivalent distance, on a regulated interstate carrier cost $41.67. In questioning the Airline Transportation Association (ATA) representative, Senator Kennedy got the admission that the expert could not account for the difference in fares. The expert's reply was "weak and evasive": "I don't have a complete answer to where the differences are, Senator, and there are other differences I have not been able to get any data on."[57] The industry association's own study showed that only a small percentage of the difference on most routes could be attributed to anything other than regulation.

Breyer got another zinger when Senator Kennedy questioned the CAB Commissioner O'Melia. The exchange between Senator Kennedy and O'Melia, which was on the six o'clock news that evening, went as follows:

KENNEDY: Are you familiar with the 1965 staff study on unregulated intrastate airlines? This study concluded that while using low fares the intrastate carriers attracted the traffic of competitors, reduced their fares, brought down average fares. . . . Are you familiar with that?

O'MELIA: I am familiar with it, but when I don't know an answer I would like to address it to . . .

KENNEDY: Given that kind of result, what takes place in the Board when you receive a study like that?

O'MELIA: As far as I am concerned, if it were brought up to date now, and I am sure these hearings will bring it up to date, and as far as I am personally concerned, as one Board member . . .

KENNEDY: What does that really mean? Will you be a little more specific?

O'MELIA: Yes, I will. If the ratemaking system which the Board has evolved over the years has some defects in it based on the cost studies that you are finding here today . . .

KENNEDY: You would encourage development of a similar service or give direction to a carrier who wants to duplicate that service from Boston to Washington. You could do that, could you not, if the Board wanted to do it?

o'melia: Yes.

kennedy: Then you can do something about it.

o'melia: Oh yes.[58]

O'Melia's concession under cross-examination by Kennedy illustrated Breyer's point to a wider public in dramatic fashion. It got the hearings favorable media attention and imprinted in the minds of the public, in almost mythic terms, the message that airline regulation was a "rip-off," because flying could be made less expensive if the government deregulated the carriers. According to Breyer, the key issue in communicating with the public was vivid symbols that could be presented to the public via the media.[59] Political visibility was achieved when broadcast journalists did stories that conveyed to the public that reform was not simply desirable. It was necessary.

The Results of Deregulation

The results of airline deregulation, however much was promised, have been mixed. In 1980, a CAB study reported generally positive outcomes. Adjusting for fuel price increases, fares were down somewhat. Productivity gains were recorded.[60] Inflation-adjusted unit costs fell 32 percent because of higher load factors, installation of more seats on aircraft, and greater utilization of equipment.[61] Passenger miles increased and service to small communities did not perceptibly decline. The rush of commuter airlines into small markets actually increased the number of flights by 2 percent.[62] However, the airline industry in the early 1980s also experienced a serious downturn. Jet fuel prices doubled between 1979 and 1980.[63] The steep recessions of 1980 and 1981-1982 reduced the number of discretionary fliers, such as vacationers.[64] The strike by air traffic controllers limited flights to and from the nation's busiest airports. Despite lower fuel bills, lower interest rates, and a slowing of labor cost increases, 1982 was the third straight year of record losses for the eleven largest airlines.[65]

Dramatic changes took place in the airline industry after deregulation. The major airlines were in a war with aggressive smaller competitors to hold market share. Weak carriers were slashing prices to stay viable. Travelers were becoming accustomed to cheaper fares and were coming to expect a permanent discount structure in pricing.

Moreover, industry was cash-short and jet manufacturers were experiencing serious difficulties in selling airplanes. According to industry calculations, for each $200 million in profit the airliners make as a group, they buy $1 billion worth of airlines. With profits severely limited, carriers were not buying new aircraft.[66]

Arguments were made favoring a return to regulation. Industry representatives brought up the safety threat that might exist in a highly competitive environment where fly-by-night operators were using old aircraft. Cost minimization, industry officials maintained, could lead to maintenance shortcomings.

Not all companies in the industry, however, were complaining. Deregulation and the economic conditions of the early 1980s tended to favor the medium size airline that was flying medium size jets. These carriers used the freedom provided by deregulation to use these jets on longer, more profitable routes. They were flying Boeing 737s and DC-9s on routes ranging from 200 to 1,500 miles. Having a smaller plane on the longer routes actually became an advantage as a greater percentage of seats could be filled. Piedmont, Ozark, and US Air took on new routes and avoided the empty seat phenomenon that plagued the big carriers, which were loaded down with the large wide-body jets. These smaller carriers also had lower overhead costs than the giants, which had large investments in maintenance facilities and airport gate equipment. The larger companies, in addition, had not shown the managerial capability to take advantage of the new situation. They were used to operating in a regulated environment and were slow to adjust to the change.

Policy entrepreneurs and dramatic hearings, which have the ability to arouse the public through a simplistic message, did not play the same role in the ICC and FCC cases, where industry was able to stem the tide of deregulation to a greater extent. The role that policy entrepreneurs, hearings, and the media can play in the politics of regulation refutes contentions that under all circumstances industry is able to dominate the regulatory process and maintain it for its benefit. Under conditions when policy entrepreneurs are active and dramatic congressional hearings take place, it is possible for evaluation to become reform, for actual change to take place.

ICC-RAILROADS

The case of railroad deregulation by the Interstate Commerce Commission is also anti-Stigler. As in the FPC-natural gas case, the regulated railroads sought deregulation and were successful in achieving their goal. They were successful even though there was major opposition from consuming sectors, coal users, and coal producers, who complained that coal was not being used more extensively to replace foreign oil because of exorbitant railroad prices. If deregulation were put into effect, they argued, these prices would go even higher. It was easy enough to get the coal out of the ground, but moving it to markets was difficult because freight rates had gone up dramatically since 1969.[67] If deregulation took effect, prices would rise even more rapidly, and would discourage further coal use.[68]

Coal users and producers fought the rail deregulation bill. They made it a regional battle, dividing South against North. The state of Texas and its utilities, local officials, and representatives took up the cause of maintaining regulation. They were committed to building coal-fired power plants and were dependent on the railroads for delivering coal at a price consumers could live with. Texas users mobilized producers, other aggrieved utilities, the Consumer Energy Council (an important pressure group), and Senator Russell B. Long of Louisiana against the Carter administration's rail deregulation bill.

The railroad industry, although needing higher rates to improve rail lines and cars that had been damaged from carrying heavy coal, was distrustful of deregulation. It had lived comfortably for years with regulation. Sheltered from competition, many lines preferred that the existing situation continue. However, a majority in the Association of American Railroads decided, with some qualms, to support deregulation in order to achieve higher rates in the face of falling profits. Railroad deregulation was aimed at raising capital for the ailing rail industry by giving railroads more leeway in adjusting their rates upward. The industry had a need for billions of dollars to finance maintenance which had been deferred, and which was now threatening safety and causing the railroads to operate at reduced speeds on bad stretches of track.

The industry viewpoint in favor of deregulation prevailed in Congress.[69] Shippers believed that gradual escalation of rates under statute was preferable to more precipitous action by the ICC. On October 14, 1980, President Carter signed railroad deregulation legislation, which allowed rate hikes that would boost railroad profits. Beside giving railroads considerable freedom to raise prices free of ICC interference, the deregulation act let railroads abandon routings and branch lines more freely. Part of the nation's 191,000-mile rail network was taken out of action. One-third of Conrail's lines, which were operating at a deficit, were ripe for abandonment.[70]

Shippers, in response to the prospect of higher rates, were trying to get the railroads to sign long-term contracts. Companies that were captive to the railroads—bulk shippers such as coal producers, iron-ore miners, and raw chemical and clay manufacturers—had no alternative now that the prices were being deregulated.

Like the FPC-natural gas case, the ICC-railroad case did not correspond with Stigler's model. What is remarkable about the case is the considerable political pressure the railroad industry had to overcome to achieve its goals. It had to defeat a major coalition of consumer interests, which connected its arguments to the energy crisis and American dependence on foreign oil, powerful political rhetoric at the least.

STRATEGIC IMPLICATIONS

These cases dealing with the ICC, the FPC, and the CAB are additional proof refuting simple-minded allegiance to a theory of capture. Each instance of regulation had its own micro-setting where different political configurations prevailed. The ICC-truckers case conformed more to the classic paradigm, primarily because the truckers had influential allies and were successful in their efforts to maintain regulation, albeit in a very modified form. The FPC-natural gas case refuted both contentions of the simple capture theory. The natural gas producers neither favored regulation nor fought to maintain it. Rather, the opposite was true: they opposed regulation and fought to do away with it. The ICC-railroad case was another example of the power of industry to do away with regulation. Against almost overwhelming odds, industry achieved the deregulation it was seeking. In the CAB case, although most of the airline industry—in accord with the capture theory—fought deregulation, it was not able to maintain the existing regulatory system. The ICC-railroads and FPC-natural gas cases were examples of industry power, while the CAB-airlines and ICC-trucking cases were examples of industry succumbing to powerful public interest pressures. In these latter cases, industry division, expert unanimity, and unfavorable publicity played a role in industry defeat. As indicated, the mobilization of political pressure, accomplished by a skillful policy entrepreneur using congressional hearings and the media for his purposes, was crucial in the airlines deregulation case.

The variety of settings and outcomes raises strategic dilemmas for the manager. To begin with, how do managers determine the benefits and costs of continued regulation? Each firm may reach a different conclusion. Efficient, growth-oriented, and innovative firms may have more reason to favor deregulation. The advantages of continued regulation, on the other hand, are likely to be greater for large, less efficient companies that need protection. Smaller, growing concerns may believe that they can give existing firms a beating under conditions of deregulation, while existing firms, fearful of such a prospect, may want continued regulation. Industry unity, therefore, cannot be assumed, and individual company defections— if there are opportunistic firms in an industry—are to be expected. Industry ability to stem the tide of deregulation may be more limited than ordinarily thought, precisely because the unit of analysis is the firm and not the industry as a whole, and each firm has interests that may differ from those of the industry of which it is a part.

Many industries now face the challenge of surviving under conditions of deregulation. Among the lessons they should learn are the following: (1) an industrywide contraction of profits occurs with substantial cost cutting, including the need for staff reductions; (2) in attractive markets competition increases; (3) weak firms become weaker faster than strong firms become stronger. In the airline industry, performance differences among trunk carriers (based on return on sales or assets) more than tripled as competition grew for the attractive routes and there were major layoffs of personnel. Some of the winners to emerge from this upheaval were some national companies with a full line of services; low-cost producers; and local or regional carriers.[71]

National companies with a full line of services (for example, Delta Airlines). Such firms prepared prior to deregulation for gradual, planned expansion. They gathered accurate information on cost to establish price levels on new routes that would return a profit. Delta, for example, decided to expand cautiously, and not to move into every market. It only added a few routes in the Northwest and Southwest. In contrast, Braniff added many new airplanes and applied for 400 new routes all over the country and the world. In expanding aggressively, Braniff encountered huge start-up costs and low load factors. It had to generate cash flow by desperately cutting fares. In contrast, Delta decided to keep its "economy" fares higher and concentrate on holding regular customers with cheaper rates for regular coach and first-class travel.

Low-cost producers (for example, Southwest and Peoples). Often new entrants, these companies focused on a small segment of the market and offered limited service and "no frills." They "cream-skimmed" from the top firms, entering where the profits were highest or passenger travel was greatest. They could lower costs more rapidly than older firms because they lacked staff and management overhead costs that the older firms had acquired and could not abandon immediately. Formerly regulated firms were not as cost sensitive. Unions and the culture of being a formerly regulated company often led them to place less emphasis on controlling costs than on employee and public relations. While the older firms had structural rigidities and were not able to respond quickly to market changes, the new entrants used low price as a strategic weapon. They drove down prices across the board to gain immediate market share at the expense of the older airlines.

Local or regional carriers (for example, US Air). These companies realized that they should focus on a narrow, but profitable, niche, and they made strong showings after deregulation, perhaps because of their focus on secondary markets where competition was less intense. In addition to having the advantages of smaller jets and lower overhead, they experimented and took calculated risks to discover their place in new markets. They did not become national airlines simply for the sake of being national airlines, but tried to find secondary markets where the competition was less intense.

Managers must be aware that competition will intensify after regulation is eliminated. They have to respond to the opportunities and problems with a new mentality that is at odds with their older regulatory orientation. Increased competition requires "greater emphasis on marketing, closer contact with customers, and improved cost control."[72] Managers must be prepared to incorporate greater attention to competitive analysis in their planning processes. Significant adjustments have to be accomplished in a short period of time after deregulation.

8 | Limits to Business Power

One of the most important political questions is, who gets what, when, and how? Charles Lindblom argues that governments cater to business.[1] Business exerts "disproportionate power."[2] Government shows toward it a "degree of solicitous concern that is not matched by an equivalent concern for any other group."[3] According to Lindblom, the business community, along with government, constitutes one of the "two great leadership groups in Western society."[4] The power of business rests on its ability to carry out important public functions—to organize the work force, motivate it,. and pay it. Businesses create jobs and taxes without which governments could not survive. To provide jobs and taxes, governments must induce business enterprises to carry out tasks that governments seek. Lindblom goes so far as to hold that businesses cannot be commanded or coerced.[5] Governments must induce them to carry out vital functions by means of incentives, prerogatives, indulgences, autonomy, or whatever they need.

Lindblom's theory is fairly typical of what many political scientists and economists believe about business-government relations. But does government actually "indulge" business? The evidence from the old economic regulation indicates that the pattern of business-government interaction is more complex. In few cases does the theory of simple indulgence hold true. Regulated industries retreat, they only partially achieve their goals, and they sometimes lose to forces claiming to represent the public interest. Sometimes they wield power, but sometimes their power is limited by skillful policy entrepreneurs, who challenge the "privilege" of business by rallying consumers and citizen groups and using the findings of academic critics.

There are limits in our society to the power of any group. The Founding Fathers intended that the power of single interests be limited.[6] Their ideal was pluralistic competition: not the dominance of a single interest or faction, but the sharing of power among groups and institutions. In this chapter, the limits to business power imposed by the new social regulation are discussed. The legal dictates of this regulation are of a different quality than the economic enactments directed at businesses in the past. These legal dictates are examined, various factors that account for a decline in the power of business are presented, and reasons to believe that this decline is neither as significant as critics allege nor as final as they maintain are given.

THE NEW SOCIAL AGENCIES

The new social regulation represents a change from prior limitations on corporate power. The word *regulation* once applied almost exclusively to government control of prices and licensing in such fields as transportation, electric and gas utilities, and oil and gas production. However, the late 1960s and early 1970s marked the growth of regulation that involved employment opportunity, health, safety, and environmental protection. The new agencies and their dates of creation included: the Equal Employment Opportunity Commission (EEOC), 1964; the Environmental Protection Agency (EPA), 1970; the National Highway Traffic Safety Commission (NHTSA), 1970; the Occupational Safety and Health Administration (OSHA), 1970; and the Consumer Product Safety Commission (CPSC), 1972 (see chapter 3).

The focus of the new agencies was not on a single industry. Jurisdiction extended to the bulk of the private sector and at times to activities in the public sector as well. The government even regulated its own practices in the areas covered by the new regulation.[7] The broadened scope of the new agencies made it difficult for a single industry to dominate a given agency in the manner of the traditional model.[8] What *specific* industry would be able to capture the EEOC or OSHA, or would have the incentive to do so?

The concern of the new federal agencies was not with the health of a particular company or industry, but with the segment of the business that fell under the agency's jurisdiction.[9] The ICC, for example, deals with the basic mission of the trucking industry (to provide transportation services to the public) as part of its supervision of rates and entry into the trucking industry. The EPA, on the other hand, is interested almost exclusively in the effects of a company's operations on the environment. This single focus on many different industries prevents the newer agencies from becoming too closely identified with the overall progress and well-being of the companies or industries they regulate.

It is argued that the rise of new social regulation signifies a decline in business power.[10] Businesses, large and small, cannot operate without considering numerous government restrictions and regulations, both new and old. Costs and profits are affected as much by these requirements as by management decisions and changing customer preferences. The types of management decisions which increasingly are subject to governmental influence and control include what type of business to enter; what products to produce; under what conditions the products can be produced; where they are to be made; how they can be sold; and how much they will cost.[11]

A good example is the steel industry.[12] Labor costs are influenced by state and federal health and safety agencies. The cost and availability of raw materials are affected by the Bureau of Mines, the Department of Energy, and state utility commissions. Processes also have been heavily controlled. Steel companies must reduce air and water pollution in a time period set by the government and by using the best available technology. The size of the market available to domestic producers of steel is affected by foreign trade policies; and price levels may be influenced—albeit implicitly—by jawboning. Product characteristics also have been affected by consumer product agencies and by the purchasing criteria of the federal government. Moreover, the government also regulates the general business environment in which the steel industry operates. In short, it controls the industry's inputs, processes, and outputs as well as the overall business environment. A similar analysis could be made of the automobile, chemical, paper, and other large, basic manufacturing industries.

In fact, virtually every major department of such companies is likely to have "counterparts" in federal agencies that influence internal decision making:

- Corporate research scientists receive guidance from agencies that affect technological innovation.

- Manufacturing engineers are guided by standards set by safety and occupational health agencies.

- Sales personnel must follow the procedures of consumer product safety agencies.

- Officials who decide about site location have to be concerned about the ability of the company to conform to environmental statutes.

- Personnel staff must comply with equal opportunity edicts.

- Other employees, including statisticians and accountants, deal with paperwork requirements.[13]

It is difficult for a single person in the business world to comprehend the broad scope of government involvement; but there are few aspects of business activities that totally escape government review or influence from either the new social regulation or the old economic regulation.

The existence of both types of regulation may represent a decline in management autonomy, with possible adverse consequences, including: (1) an increase in red tape; (2) a need for increased economies of scale; (3) the diversion of capital from investments in new plants and equipment to investments in regulatory compliance, which increases prices; and (4) a possible decline in productivity in the affected industries.

One study done by the Brookings Institution estimated that productivity growth declined by nearly 20 percent in the 1970s, partially owing to increased environmental control costs and health and safety regulations.[14] The productivity growth rate in the late 1970s slowed to about 1 percent per year, a rate which would allow minimal improvement in the average standard of living and even less ability to address other pressing social problems.[15] However, other reasons for a decline in productivity aside from the new regulation have been noted. These reasons include oil price rises, a shift in jobs from manufacturing to services, declining support for research and development, and the entry of the "baby boom" generation into the work force.[16]

THE RISE OF PUBLIC INTEREST GROUPS

If there was to be an interest or faction capable of dominating the newer agencies, it was not likely to be the regulated industries, but rather a group or interest preoccupied with the specific tasks the new agencies performed— environmental cleanup, elimination of job discrimination, establishment of safer working conditions, or reduction of product hazards. Public interest groups, therefore, and not private concerns, were in a better position to capture the new social agencies. Thus, it has been argued that instead of business dominance, the 1970s witnessed the growing power of public interest groups in creating and controlling new agencies.

How can we understand the emergence of public interest groups and their ability to challenge business influence and power? Scholars have defined public interest groups as those who pursue goals designed to benefit society as a whole, goals that are of no immediate benefit to the leaders or the organizations they represent.[17] E. E. Schattschneider, in a classic example, compares public interest leaders to non-death row convicts who advocate abolition of the death penalty even though they are not likely to benefit from this change in policy.[18] The scholarly definition is in accord with the image public interest leaders try to project. Ralph Nader, for instance, during his controversy with General Motors, declared: "General Motors executives continue to be blinded by their own corporate mirror image that it's 'the buck' that moves the man. They simply cannot understand that prevention of cruelty to humans can be sufficient motivation for one endeavoring to obtain the manufacture of safer cars."[19] The claim made by scholars and public interest leaders alike is that purposive incentives—the ideological satisfaction associated with efforts to achieve collective goods—motivate public interest leaders.

Jeffrey M. Berry, a Tufts University political scientist, surveyed lobbyists of eighty-three national public interest groups in Washington, D.C., during the fall, winter, and spring of 1972-1973.[20] He divided public interest leaders into two groups—founders or entrepreneurs, and professional staff. Forty-seven percent of the groups he surveyed were started in the 1968-1972 period and in many of them founders were still present.[21] The founders, often charismatic leaders, established the initial goals and purposes of the organization and defined the boundaries for organizational changes. Staff then decided, with little supervision or control from external forces, what issues to take up and what causes to emphasize.

The critical factor in organizational formation was not some disturbing event, such as a change in government policy, the business cycle, or technology, but strong leadership on the part of charismatic leaders and founders. These organizational entrepreneurs were individuals like Nader —usually young scientists, law students, or lawyers, who with "great determination" created public interest organizations. Roughly two-thirds of the groups were begun by charismatic founders.[22] Founders attracted followers, some of whom became the organization's staff. In exchange for affiliation, the staff received material, solidarity, and, especially, purposive incentives—the ideological satisfaction of being a part of a cause.

The staff was young (two-thirds were under forty) and inexperienced (65 percent were recently graduated lawyers, and another 30 percent had master's degrees or were working toward Ph.D.'s).[23] Sixty-four percent were Democrats as opposed to 42 percent being Democrats among the general population, and many placed themselves in the left of liberal, but right of radical, category.[24] The jobs that the staff performed were eagerly sought by the "best and brightest" of a generation that had demonstrated against the Vietnam War and campaigned for Eugene McCarthy or George McGovern.

In 30 percent of the organizations, the staff literally embodied the organization because there were so few members.[25] Most groups, with a few prominent exceptions (Common Cause, for instance), had small memberships. Seventy-five percent had less than 100,000 members, and 57 percent had less than 25,000 members.[26] Moreover, in the groups with members, members exerted little influence on policy. Influence flowed from staff to members and not vice versa. Formal democratic procedures were not present, and boards of directors were weak or ineffectual. Staff was constrained only by the possibility of a significant portion of the membership refusing to renew its association.

A large portion of organizational resources came from foundations.[27] Berry estimates that one-third of the groups that began in 1967-1972 obtained at least half of their total income from foundations; close to 45 percent of the groups received some foundation money, ranging from 10 percent of their total budgets to over 90 percent; and over 11 percent received more than 90 percent of their funds from foundations.[28] In the "boom years" before the stock market plummeted, the Ford, Carnegie, Field, Stern, Rockefeller, Bernstein, Cummins, and Midas foundations and others were eagerly seeking agents of "constructive social change." Usually, they would give public interest leaders seed money to initiate a new organization or project. The expectation was that in a few years' time the public interest leaders could make the organizations self-supporting. Public interest leaders, however, often found it difficult to shift from foundation to membership support, nor were all of them capable of doing so. Some, after initial grants ran out, had to survive on a hand-to-mouth basis with small "emergency" grants that carried them for a few months at a time.

To obtain members, the public interest leaders usually had to send out mailings to an "attentive public," that is, to a well-educated, prosperous middle and upper middle class that read magazines such as the *Nation* and the *New Republic* and was more liberal than the rest of the population. Direct mailings to this attentive public, however, were a risky venture. Groups traded mailing lists and all competed for the same slack funds of a small portion of the population. Moreover, this attentive public was fickle. It was known for the unpredictable and uncontrollable way it switched attention from issue to issue. Very often, therefore, the mailings did not cover expenses. To increase the likelihood that they would be successful, public interest leaders often had to offer selective benefits, such as publications, or exclusive services, such as outdoor facilities, for joining and contributing.

In spite of the difficulties of maintaining support and attracting members, the public interest groups were far from poor. In Berry's estimation, they were quite well off.[29] Fifty-nine percent had incomes of over $100,000 a year, 19 percent had budgets of more than $1,000,000, and only 13 percent had budgets of less than $50,000 annually.[30] Maintaining the appearance of poverty, however, was an important symbolic aspect of maintaining public support.

Nonetheless, public interest leaders worked long hours for relatively low pay (76 percent earned less than $20,000 a year) because they considered their work to be a "higher calling" where motives and intentions were beyond question.[31] They received the satisfaction of good conscience in return for their exertions. Their hard-to-get, low-paying, demanding jobs were satisfying to the conscience because of the absence of alienation—the lack of distance between self and institution. The goals of the individual and the goals of the organization were nearly identical. Organizations usually were small and short on standard operating procedure. Berry describes them as being more like a cadre of friends, of comrades and equals, than formal institutions with strict rules and impersonal relations. The public interest leaders had few formal duties and no regular hours—just crises that had to be coped with rapidly and with little time for reflection.[32]

To be part of this scene it was worth foregoing material pleasure and comfort, which may be the key to the public interest groups' success. Much of a staff person's time was spent at press conferences and hearings, or talking to congressional staff members and reporters. A good portion of the rest of his or her time was spent preparing for these occasions—receiving tips from citizens, bureaucrats, or corporate "whistle blowers," or carefully scrutinizing government documents in search of scandal and corruption. The excitement, the glamour, and the touch of power involved in this activity made up for the low pay and lack of job security. As long as talented and ambitious individuals preferred the satisfaction of serving their conscience to pecuniary gain, public interest groups flourished.

BUSINESS DECLINE

There were at least five factors that permitted the ascendance of the public interest associations and accounted for a decline in business power. The first was the increasing sophistication of the natural and social sciences, which left many unanswered questions regarding the long-range effects of various technological practices. The long-run consequences for society of choices that business and government were making were often unknown. For instance, whether Right Guard was delivered as a spray propelled by fluorocarbons was not merely Gillette's marketing decision when scientific research showed that there might be significant risk of skin cancer associated with the decision.[33]

Second, increasing affluence and growing social awareness increased society's demand for public goods and services that the government gave to all and from which no individual could be excluded.[34] Environmental quality was an example. In 1965, the Opinion Research Corporation found that 28 percent of those polled considered air pollution to be a serious problem, but by 1977, despite the fact that almost two-thirds of those polled felt that fair to great progress already had been made in dealing with the issue, nearly 51 percent nevertheless considered the problem to be "very or somewhat serious."[35] Public support for pollution control policies remained fairly high in spite of economic difficulties.

Third, society became more "communal."[36] An aspect of this development was increased "externalities," defined by Daniel Bell as "costs (or occasionally benefits) generated by one party (be it a corporation, municipality, or private individual), but borne by other parties or by the society as a whole."[37] Nitrogen oxide emissions from automobiles into the air or disposal of wastes into the water are examples. The important fact about externalities is that, except by resort to the courts, the only way they can be "internalized" and borne by the responsible parties is through the actions of government, which makes rules and enforces them through fines and penalties.

Fourth—another aspect of being a communal society—was rising entitlements.[38] People in modern societies came to believe that they were entitled to protection from hazard. A revolution of rising entitlements has occurred in the United States in the areas of civil rights and social rights.

Fifth, a paradox, noted initially by the French sociologist Bertrand de Jouvenal became important.[39] De Jouvenal noticed that people find that when their incomes double, they do not live twice as well as before. The commodities they acquire, when provided to everybody, are less desirable.[40] An obvious example is traffic congestion. As more people drive, the negative effects of increased traffic reduce the satisfaction of driving. Individuals find that the auto increases personal mobility and freedom, but that the massive use of this mode of transportation leads to great frustration. Such paradoxes are multiplied in many ways in a modern society. Earlier generations could enjoy remote national parks in relative isolation, but when thousands descend upon these limited spaces on summer weekends, the aesthetic pleasure and sense of isolation are reduced.

Shifts in the Structure of National Political Institutions

Facilitating the growth of the new social regulation were basic changes in the structure of national political institutions.[41] Congress changed in very fundamental ways.[42] First, individual congresspeople had very large staffs that allowed them to challenge the information-gathering and policy-generating capabilities of executive branch officials.[43] Additional congressional staff meant extra work and ideas. More demands and commitments were presented to legislators for action.

Second, the power of committee chairmen was reduced. Conservative southern senators and congressmen such as Wilbur Mills, James Eastland, and Howard Smith could not use their positions as chairmen to obstruct new proposals. Congress was fragmented; its leadership was weakened; and the power within it was dispersed, while the resources of individual members were enlarged. Individual members of Congress gained at the expense of committee chairmen, party leaders, and interest groups. As Wilson comments, Al Ullman could not dominate the Ways and Means Committee as Wilbur Mills had done; Robert Byrd did not have the power Lyndon Johnson had as Senate majority leader; and although Tip O'Neill was stronger than Carl Albert, he was not the same type of leader as Sam Rayburn.[44]

Third, media coverage of the Senate presented opportunities to skillful and ambitious senators. They were able to preside over dramatic televised hearings into auto safety, the drug industry, or malnutrition and obtain favorable national attention. They had the resources—the staff and the budgetary authority—to promote issues that reached national constituencies with which they became identified. Such institutional factors facilitated innovation by Congress and promoted the creation of additional regulation.

Legislative Innovation

Legislative innovation in the 1970s was influenced by some of the following factors: (1) the prevailing public philosophy, (2) various crises, (3) symbolic politics, and (4) various other pressures on congresspeople. As Alan Stone remarks, inaction generally is easier for legislators than action, as less than 10 percent of the bills introduced are ever passed.[45] However, legislative success may increase because of the prevailing public philosophy, the set of themes about the role of government and its limits prevalent in society at a particular time. In the late 1960s and early 1970s, a philosophy developed that encouraged regulatory expansion. The curbing of business power through strict government controls was a common theme, which public interest associations played a major role in developing, articulating, and publicizing. They stressed the undesirable side effects of technological change and viewed with suspicion the allocation of goods and services via the market. Books such as Rachel Carson's *Silent Spring* and Ralph Nader's *Unsafe at Any Speed* were read widely. Television documentaries were made about matters of concern to consumer activists and environmentalists, as environmental demonstrations and calamities became part of the everyday news.

The prevailing public philosophy sets the stage for legislative action, but it requires specific crises, scandals, and emergencies to overcome the tendency of legislators to ignore situations. The crises, scandals, and emergencies must appear as major threats involving the imposition or threatened imposition of very great costs, which legislators have trouble ignoring. Sometimes crises develop gradually and sometimes they erupt suddenly, but in either case they play an important role in overcoming legislative lethargy. For example, Senator Estes Kefauver's 1962 amendments to the Pure Food and Drug Act received only lukewarm support from President Kennedy and his advisers and outright opposition from the drug manufacturers until the thalidomide case was made known to the public. Thirty-five thousand deformed babies were discovered, mostly in West Germany, among women who had taken a presumably harmless sleeping pill in the early stages of pregnancy. The publicity surrounding the babies heightened demand for strong drug protection laws. The drug companies realized that they could not oppose all regulation given the public concern. However, they did not give in on certain provisions involving patent and price controls, which Kefauver and his supporters thought crucial. The new law was passed in weakened form to take into account the drug companies' opposition to these provisions.

Without the scandal the likelihood that any bill would have been passed was minimal. As Eugene Bardach and Robert Kagan comment:

The growth of regulation is not merely the product of the steady and relentless forces of logic and political and economic interests. Regulatory victories, as well as initiatives, are products of intermittent events or "occasions" that fire the political imagination and overwhelm the normal defenses of antiregulatory interests. Most prominent are physical catastrophes; scandals that expose presumptive laxity, corruption, or incompetency in the regulatory agency; dramatic scientific discoveries; . . . and changes in administration.[46]

Symbolic politics influences the behavior of legislators. "Gestures and speeches" make up the "drama of state."[47] Legislators involved in the symbols of politics often do not examine the true costs, benefits, or alternatives of proposed policies.

In a media-oriented political system, concerns are chosen for attention by senators and the young attorneys on their staff because of their symbolic value. An example is automobile air pollution. The 1970 Clean Air Act imposed stringent emissions standards that had to be achieved in a very short time period without regard to cost or technological feasibility. The statute was drafted without evidence about the health benefits. The purpose of the statute's drafters was to appear "pure" on the environmental issue and to demonstrate their opposition to the automobile industry, at the time a very popular thing to do. Symbolic posturing was needed by Senator Edmund Muskie of Maine, who was preparing to be a presidential contender. To maintain his image, he had to outdo what President Nixon proposed on environmental issues. Therefore, he drafted a very "tough" law. The auto industry did not vigorously oppose passage of the new law, an apparently surprising fact. However, the industry reasoned that it would prefer a law that promulgated impossible standards to one that had standards that could be realistically achieved. As Howard Margolis comments, 'There is a certain comfort in being asked for the impossible; you know you will not actually have to do it."[48]

In addition to their concern with symbols, legislators are subject to other pressures and incentives. Provided by their constituencies, interest groups, the White House, fellow legislators, business associations, and party leaders, these opportunities and constraints affect their choices. Their goals include getting reelected, achieving prominence within Congress, and establishing the "right" policy. Resources that can be provided, such as money or the ability to sway large numbers of voters, are very important to them. The "correct" policy from a cost and benefit standpoint is just one consideration among many. Rarely is it the most important consideration.

THREE EXAMPLES OF REGULATORY FORMATION

Three examples of regulatory formation are the creation of the Occupational Safety and Health Administration and the Environmental Protection Agency in 1970, and that of the Office of Surface Mining Reclamation and Enforcement in 1977. The first initiative came from an executive department; the second received a healthy push from a Nader report; and the third was able to pass Congress because of industrial competition.

In the case of OSHA, Labor Department officials were trying to create new programs that they could administer, and congressmen responded to their initiative because of their need to be associated with new programs.[49] But nothing happened quickly. President Johnson introduced an occupational safety and health bill in 1968 and hearings were held by Senate and House committees, but no bill was passed. Representatives of labor argued in favor of the legislation and representatives of business argued against it. There was a stalemate until 1969, when the Nixon administration introduced a bill of its own.

The Nixon administration was concerned about winning labor support from the Democratic party at a time when the party was increasingly associated with "hippies" and "anti-war protesters."[50] A mine disaster in West Virginia gave further impetus to passage of the legislation. As it became increasingly clear that some legislation would be enacted, businesses began to support the administration's position. They feared that Congress would enact a more stringent statute acting on its own.

The Occupational Safety and Health Act of 1970 passed with lopsided majorities in both the Senate and the House. Its passage was aided by the activist spirit of the times. Ralph Nader and his associates were not directly involved in passage of the bill; however, their support for other safety legislation softened the resistance.

In the case of the EPA, public interest advocates, such as the Naderites, played a more direct role. The "transferers" of the notion that vague legislation contributed to inadequate regulatory performance were members of a Ralph Nader organization, the Center for the Study of Responsive Law.[51] This group had two task forces: one on air and one on water pollution policy. The former, led by John Esposito, published *Vanishing Air* in 1970; the latter, led by David Zwick and Marcy Benstock, published *Water Wasteland* in 1971. In the period when Congress was considering amending pollution control statutes, these task forces published books that were very critical of Congress's previous work. The Naderites wrote detailed case studies of bureaucratic efforts to implement earlier air and water pollution control laws in which they demonstrated that poorly conceived, politically compromised legislation led to regulatory incompetence. They recommended the adoption of strict new statutes that eliminated the possibility of delay and forced the bureaucracy to achieve goals by specific dates.

Although the substance and specific recommendations of the Nader reports were important, the timing and staging of their appearance were also significant. Their appearance after the 1970 "Earthday" celebration, in the midst of a general public debate about environmental degradation, had an impact on a central figure in Congress's deliberations: Senator Edmund Muskie, who was chairman of the Subcommittee on Air and Water Pollution of the Senate Committee on Public Works. The appearance of *Vanishing Air* in May 1970 after the Earthday demonstration of April, demonstrates how a timely accusation can evoke a commitment to a particular posture from an elected official. The report accused Muskie of not taking a tough stand against private industry, and the media gave this criticism of a potential presidential candidate extensive coverage. The stories emphasized the task force's charge that Muskie had "sold out" to political expediency and industry interests. Muskie was indignant. At a press conference the day after the report appeared, he maintained that his subcommittee had not acted "for the dark, secret conspiratorial reasons" suggested by the Nader report. He criticized those who adopted a tactic of "excessive confrontation" and promised to strengthen the air pollution law before the end of the year.

In assessing the influence of public interest leaders like Nader, James Q. Wilson has argued that a "symbiotic political relationship" existed between some of these activists and subcommittee chairmen who were interested in gaining national prominence. He gave the example of auto safety legislation, where Senator Abraham Ribicoff of Connecticut and his Senate Subcommittee on Executive Reorganization of the Senate Committee on Government Operation worked together with Nader against the auto manufacturers. While this theory of a symbiotic relationship between a congressional committee and a public interest advocate may apply to the passage of various consumer laws, it does not fit the case of the 1970 Clean Air Act amendments. In this instance, Senator Muskie's subcommittee on air and water pollution and the Nader task force were antagonists, not collaborators. In the case of the 1970 and 1972 pollution control laws, the influence of public interest leaders rested on their ability to embarrass a key senator.

The passage of the Surface Mining Control and Reclamation Act of 1977 (SMCRA) involved a far different political climate and set of political interests. The pro-regulation mood of the early 1970s had by this time subsided. It therefore required substantial business divisiveness to assure passage of this bill. As surprising as it may seem, businesses may join forces with anti-business groups and urge passage of specific new regulatory enactments. They do so because the proposed regulation will affect different firms differently. Some will face higher costs than others, and therefore competitive advantage can be gained by the firms in the low-cost position.

Government regulation often has significant competitive effects; what hurts one business may help another. Significant variations, therefore, may be found among firms in terms of their political preferences and behaviors with regard to particular regulatory proposals. In the case of SMCRA, the coal industry was divided. Western coal interests thought that they could gain significant advantage by supporting the legislation. Their size and experience with state laws led them to believe that they could comply with the law with little trouble. They had a favorable topography, long-term supply contracts, and longer-term time horizons. It was easier for them to absorb and pass on the incremental compliance costs than for smaller, eastern firms to do so.

The smaller eastern firms were put in a very disadvantageous position because of the legislation. They were selling coal to meet spot demand and they worked on small margins. The additional costs of reclamation could mean the difference between profit and loss, between staying in business and getting out of it. James McGlothin, director of the National Independent Coal Operators Association, testified that "the bureaucracy of acquiring a permit will totally eliminate small and medium-sized operators from continuing in the surface mining business. Most of these operators do not have registered or certified engineers, hydrologists or the equipment and technicians to do core drilling, or most of the experience required to obtain a surface permit under the Act and to continue compliance therewith."[52] One would expect that, to the extent that regulation impinges on profits, it would be opposed by all firms equally. However, the immediate regulatory impact, increased costs, may be offset by other long-term advantages, such as eliminating a competitor or gaining market share at its expense. This division among mining firms largely explains passage of SMCRA in 1977 after much of the enthusiasm for increased regulation had subsided.

Strange Bedfellows

The new regulation was often sustained by strange coalitions. In 1977, when EPA and the White House agreed on a proposal to require sulfur-removing equipment called flue gas scrubbers on all new coal-fired utility plants, the idea was advanced by an "odd couple" coalition of eastern and midwestern coal mining unions and environmentalists. The purpose of the

United Mine Workers was to prevent a shift to cleaner-burning western coal, which is generally surface mined in areas where the national miners' union is less powerful. The miners feared jobs losses if utilities shifted to cleaner-burning western coal to comply with environmental standards. The environmentalists, on the other hand, feared a decline in environmental quality if strict environmental quality standards were not supported. Both groups supported scrubbers in the belief that scrubbers would save the miners' jobs and protect the environment.

For a change, labor unions and environmentalists united, but the cost to the general public of installing the scrubbers, according to EPA's own estimates, was around $1 billion more per year than relying on western coal, as advocated by the utilities.[53] The utilities' concern with low costs may have conformed more closely with the desires of the general public than the miners' concern with jobs or the environmentalists' concern with air quality.

BUSINESS RESURGENCE

Neoconservatives argue that problems such as unnecessarily high pollution abatement costs, unrealistic emissions standards, and needless delays are caused by the disproportionate power of public interest groups.[54] They attempt to show how these groups achieve power by forging key alliances with significant political actors such as bureaucrats, judges, politicians, labor unions, and corporate executives. They argue that the resulting disproportionate power has contributed to significant policy problems, such as higher pollution control costs than necessary to achieve stated objectives and unrealistic pollution control standards and timetables.

The new regulations, however, cannot be adequately understood in terms of disproportionate public interest group representation alone. Rather, there are at least two reasons to believe that the limits on business power imposed by the new social regulations are neither as significant as critics allege nor as final as they maintain, and that a business resurgence has indeed occurred.

First, some issues involving alleged disproportionate public interest group power must be understood in terms of competing values that transcend interest group lines.[55] An example is arguments neoconservatives make that current EPA regulations result in less pollution abatement at higher costs to society than are necessary. They cite the following case where EPA could reduce pollution by the same amount but at a lower cost to society: EPA treats the steel industry and the paper industry similarly despite evidence that marginal cleanup costs are higher in the steel industry than in the paper industry. This case is supposed to demonstrate that EPA is not utilizing a regulatory scheme which emphasizes marginal costs of abatement. As a result, society is supposed to be paying more for a given amount of pollution abatement than is required.

Neoconservatives have maintained that the major reason for the higher costs is the "bureaucrat/decision maker." Lilley and Miller, for example, argue that regulatory agencies tend to lure personnel who "believe in regulation." It is not surprising, they feel,

that EPA has a reputation for having a staff composed largely of "environmentalists." . . . These officials behave as though driven by a desire to "punish" a transgressor. Understandably, kicking around some company because it has done something wrong can be fun. Treating all polluters as sinners is also much easier than making quantitative judgments about optimal levels of cleanliness of the air and water, but it leads to inefficient regulations.[56]

Lilley and Miller blame the overrepresentation of environmentalists in the EPA for high abatement costs; however, the same problem also can be understood as a trade-off between the competing values of equity and efficiency.

An equitable regulatory policy has been defined as one which treats those subject to it fairly, "that is, treats like cases alike on the basis of rules known in advance and applicable to all," while an efficient regulatory policy has been defined as one that achieves its purposes at minimal cost.[57] According to these definitions, enforcing regulations more heavily against the paper industry than the steel industry violates the canons of equity by favoring one group over another. When viewed from the perspective of equity and efficiency, EPA policies tend to be more equitable than they are efficient. They treat like cases alike without necessarily minimizing total economic cost.

High abatement costs can be attributed to a bureaucracy filled with environmentalists; but it also can be seen to result from the conflict between equity and efficiency. Arguments about the disproportionate power of environmentalists may be exaggerated. Rather than revealing that the bureaucracy has been infiltrated by public interest advocates, such arguments may mask fundamental value conflicts that society has trouble resolving.[58]

When evaluating regulatory agencies, different individuals will apply different standards, and the agency will have defenders and detractors, depending on the standards that have been applied. Some of the evaluators, such as economists, will stress efficiency—the greatest good for the greatest number. Others, perhaps public management specialists, will stress program performance—achieving goals at the lowest total cost to society. Still others, who may be referred to as politicians, will stress responsiveness—accommodating clients and vital interests in the agency's environment. Bureaucrats, on the other hand, may be interested in an agency's survival, consumer groups with the extent to which it serves consumer goals, and so on. The goals used in evaluating an agency will be diverse and contradictory.

Decline in business power also may be less permanent than neoconservative critics imply. At the end of the 1970s, businesses became better organized and capable of defeating public interest group initiatives for additional social regulation (see chapter 3). The year 1976 was a watershed. In that year, the Business Roundtable, along with older business organizations— the Chamber of Commerce and the National Association of Manufacturers —was able to defeat a bill for a consumer protection agency. The defeat stemmed the tide of regulatory advance that had been occurring steadily throughout the late 1960s and early 1970s, when more new regulatory agencies were created than in any other period in American history. The Business Roundtable, which, unlike other business organizations, relied only on the chief executive officers of companies for its lobbying efforts, is just one example of the reassertion of business power.[59]

The 1970s began with a period of public interest group advance and business decline and with government becoming more involved in the affairs of the firm than it had been in the past. The late 1970s were a period of business advance and public interest decline, with business leaders becoming more involved in government decisions than they had been in the past. The net effect may have been a merging of public and private realms, but neither business nor public interest dominance.

The Coal Policy Project

A concrete example of an effort in the late 1970s to constructively merge public and private interests was the Coal Policy Project.[60] Started by Jerry Decker, Dow Chemical Company corporate energy manager, and Larry Moss, a former Sierra Club president, the Coal Policy Project aimed to bring together business people and environmentalists to find alternatives to adversary relations. The group tried to develop a nonadversarial forum for resolving disagreements in a manner acceptable to both parties. It aimed to negotiate a set of mutually acceptable recommendations for many of the environmental issues that plagued coal production and consumption. Among the participants were seven environmental groups and fifty-nine private companies.[61] The project was sponsored by four foundations, and funds and technical advice were provided by four government agencies.[62]

Proceedings of the Coal Policy Project were governed by the "rule of reason."[63] It was deemed inappropriate to resolve issues through the use of tactics that may achieve a successful outcome in litigation, such as delay or obstruction, or through *ad hominem* methods, such as personal attack. Participants were told that they could achieve success only by dealing with the facts of the case.

An extensive list of rules was adopted for the forum. They included:

- Not withholding data because they are negative or unhelpful to one's case
- Not using delay to avoid an undesired result
- Not using "tricks" to mislead
- Not questioning an opponent's motives or personal characteristics and habits
- Leaving room for an opponent's orderly retreat and "exit with honor"
- Avoiding dogmatism and extremism
- Conducting research and investigation as appropriate to the problem under consideration
- Isolating subjective elements in technical analyses

Five task forces were formed to cover the broad range of coal-related energy and environmental issues. Each task force was co-chaired by an industry and an environmental representative, each of whom conducted meetings on a rotating basis. Each task force had an equal number of representatives from both sides. Each developed its own agenda with the intention of establishing negotiated outcomes to various issues based on some of the following principles:

- Development and use of new emissions control technology
- Compliance with government standards
- Fair and economic competition
- Efficient and expeditious reclamation of abandoned lands
- Improved decision making for siting
- Reduced procedural delays and increased citizen participation
- Proper price information for consumers

Despite a great deal of initial mistrust and suspicion, business persons and environmentalists working on the Coal Policy Project developed a common framework for solving many problems, a far cry from the situation in the early 1970s.

Since the new social agencies have come into existence, businesses have been working within the system to reverse the tide of regulation.[64] They have communicated with the staff of congressional subcommittees and have been successful in striking out clauses and adding riders to bills pending before Congress. They have played an "insider's game" of working within the system and trying to find compromises on matters of vital concern.[65]

If business involvement in politics is to go beyond successful tactical maneuvers, however, something more may be necessary, as Walter Guzzardi suggests:

Now, while the political climate is more favorable, business' task is far harder—to determine the guiding philosophy, indeed the ultimate justification, for big business in a new era. Just what kind of accommodation with big government does big business seek? Like government, business too has been a desecrater of the altar of free enterprise. What new construct does business have to propose? Does it want competition or protection.?[66]

In the 1980s the country may be ready for a different business philosophy. The conservative mood means that there is an opportunity for business to "have a new agenda enacted."[67] However, " business must first determine what it believes in, and where it stands, especially on issues of competition and protection."[68] Whether business is ready for a new era remains to be seen. The temporary ascendance of business in politics may be followed by a decline, similar to the decline experienced by public interest groups in the late 1970s.

9 Opportunism and Stonewalling

Under all regulation, but especially under the new regulation, the government commands businesses and tries to control their behavior. It establishes standards and uses sanctions such as fines and imprisonment to obtain compliance with stipulated directives. The 1970 Clean Air Act and the 1969 Federal Mine Safety Act, for example, authorized fines and criminal penalties for violators of $25,000 per day, and for repeat offenders of $50,000 per day.[1] Violation of the 1976 Toxic Substances Control Act had fines of $25,000 per day.[2] Similarly, automobile manufacturers could be fined $10,000 per vehicle in violation of emissions standards.[3] There are many examples where, under the new regulation, the government commands businesses and threatens punishment to achieve its objectives.

Even with such penalties, companies may not comply for a variety of reasons, including the following:

1. Lapses or ambiguities in communication
2. Insufficient resources
3. An objection to the policy
4. Lack of sympathy with the actions the policy requires
5. Doubts about the authority upon which the policy is based[4]

The probability of compliance increases with the ease of compliance and the perceived urgency of compliance, but decreases with uncertainties about government policies.

Moreover, it has been suggested that compliance decisions may be evaluated in a manner similar to investment decisions.[5] Companies may choose among compliance alternatives. They have a variety of responses, from seizing the initiative to closing shop (see Table 9.1). A firm may enthusiastically comply. It may treat the requirement as an opportunity for gaining competitive advantage. It may stonewall, that is, use the legal system to avoid compliance by looking for loopholes in the rules, influencing authorities, trying to redefine the terms of compliance, and/or litigating. In this chapter, after standard setting and enforcement are discussed, the range of corporate responses to the imposition of commands by the government is developed and some reasons for varying responses to government requirements are given.

THE CHALLENGE TO MANAGERS

At one time, social responsibility and not compliance was the issue.[6] Emphasis was placed on the conscience, individual choice, and the ethical demands of business leadership. After changes in regulation in the late 1960s and early 1970s, however, the ethical dimension was often replaced by legal requirements. Legal requirements raised new issues for manage- ment. Pollution control, occupational safety, and minority hiring require-

Table 9.1
Compliance Decisions

Firm Action
Take advantage of requirement

Challenge requirement

Close up shop

Range of Compliance
Full
Partial
None

Firm Strategy
Seize opportunity
(e.g., introduce new product)
Stonewall (e.g., use courts and
judicial process to delay implementation)

Adapted from Roland J. Cole and Paul Sommers, "Business and Government Regulation: A Theory of Compliance Decisions," *Journal of Contemporary Business* 10, no. 1 (1981): 145.

ments were opportunities for the application of business skills in managing resources and projects. Managers could apply their skills to eliminate pollution, provide safe jobs, and employ the disadvantaged. Social problems might be opportunities for growth and profit. For example, in the lat 1960s, Westinghouse, like other companies, rushed into the social problem solving business by employing analysts who were hired to solve the problems of other companies.

However, the new constraints imposed by the regulatory laws of the 1960s and early 1970s were a threat as well as an opportunity. They signified that corporations were the objects of popular discontent. Auto safety was only one of a number of widely publicized issues. Public confidence in business was declining. The Yankelovich polling organization, for instance, was finding fewer favorable responses to the statement, "Business achieves a good balance between profits and public service."[7] A number of polls supported this trend, though it should be remembered that business was not alone among institutions suffering a loss of public confidence during this period.[8] Demands previously expressed in the press or on the streets became actual government programs. With the imposition of the new regulation, the emphasis changed from the 1950s debate about corporate responsibility to the concrete problem of altering practices in conformance with new legal requirements.

Compliance issues were faced in at least four functional areas in the corporation.[9] First, *personnel* managers had to make decisions bearing on the composition and treatment of the work force. First occasioned by discriminatory practices against blacks, these requirements later extended to Chicanos, native Americans, and women. Minority issues affected entry level hiring and facilitating advancement of minorities to managerial and professional ranks. In virtually all large corporations huge deficiencies existed in the proportion of high-level jobs occupied by minorities and women.

The Civil Rights Act of 1969 created the Equal Employment Opportunity Commission. In 1972, EEOC, which was receiving complaints at the rate of 52,000 a year, was given the right to initiate its own suits in addition to the authority to respond through conciliation to employee complaints. The penalties associated with the legal actions taken by the EEOC could be substantial. In a very large settlement, AT&T was ordered to make lump sum payments of some $15 million to cover 36,000 workers.[10] The Office of Federal Contract Compliance, through the Department of Labor, also conducted compliance reviews. If compliance was not forthcoming, it had the power to cancel government contracts with violating firms.

The second functional area where compliance demands had an impact was *product safety*, which became an issue in the 1960s after quiescence in the period after World War II. Such issues as the thalidomide disaster and the

Corvair controversy were instrumental in reawakening public interest. The technological content and potency of many products increased the risk and hazard of product malfunction. Thousands of disabling injuries and deaths each year were attributed to a wide variety of poorly functioning consumer products, from plastic soda bottles and monosodium glutamate to powerful drugs and unsafe toys.

Compliance demands had serious implications for the firm as the degree of liability attributed to the manufacturer for use of its products increased. The manufacturer had been liable for injury regardless of negligence on its part.[11] Now it also was held accountable by the Consumer Product Safety Commission.[11] The CPSC frequently required performance and design standards covering product composition and added safety features. Product recalls, public warnings, and customer refunds were more common.

The third area where compliance with new regulatory requirements was necessary was in *selling and marketing practices*. Many of the complaints registered by the consumer movement related not to the product itself but to the fashion in which it was sold; to consumer experiences in purchasing.[12] Prior to purchase, the consumer is influenced by advertising and packaging. At the time of purchase, he or she confronts the selling practices of the vendor. Corporate behavior at each stage became subject to public criticism and to renewed government requirements.

The fourth area where firms had to comply with new regulations was *environmental quality* and *workplace health and safety*. These regulations also affected the design and operation of production processes. Noncompliance caused delay and could lead to abandonment of projects. Noticeable and cumulatively significant were delays that resulted from thousands of meetings each year between company and government officials to negotiate schedules for achieving compliance with rapidly changing and expanding federal, state, and local environmental and health and safety regulations.[13] The burden of these regulations, such as the 1970 Clean Air Act, the 1972 Federal Water Pollution Control Act, and the 1977 amendments to these acts, was experienced in financial and operational terms. McGraw-Hill surveys showed a steady increase in the expenditure of manufacturing firms for pollution control equipment, but as indicated earlier these expenditures peaked in the mid-1970s (see chapter 3).

Considerable effort was made by EPA to demonstrate that economic dislocations caused by compliance with its requirements were relatively minor. However, macroeconomic studies suggested that pollution control expenditures did contribute to layoffs and inflation.[14] In the late 1970s, approximately 20,000 employees lost their jobs because of plant closings, and the additional inflation attributable to pollution control was between .3 and .5 percent.[15] In addition, some industries, such as electric utilities, faced severe capital shortages because of large pollution control expenditure requirements that limited their capacity to update outmoded equipment. Another case in point was the steel industry, where capital spending for pollution control contributed to a rise in the ratio of debt to total capitalization. In addition, many plants, such as a Bethlehem Steel plant in Johnstown, Pennsylvania, had to be shut down at least in part because of large pollution control expenditures.[16] Cost estimates for compliance with environmental regulations only partially reflected the technical difficulties and operational uncertainties. In some cases regulations could not be met because the technology was not currently available. The steel industry, for instance, maintained that it had not developed a satisfactory means of abating air pollution in its coke-making practices.[17]

Cumulative Effects of the New Regulation

The cumulative effects of the new regulation on firms could be substantial. General Motors estimated that it spent more than $2.2 billion in 1974-1975 to meet government requirements.[18] Dow Chemical claimed that compliance with federal rules cost it $268 million in 1977, up 82 percent from 1975.[19] Caterpillar Tractor claimed costs of $67.6 million in 1976, with most of these costs allocated to meet the demands of two agencies, EPA and OSHA.[20] R. J. Reynolds reported spending $28.9 million in 1977 to meet regulatory requirements.[21]

PPG, the nation's leading producer of flat glass and one of its top producers of paint and chemicals, represents the plight of a fairly typical manufacturer. It felt the effects of a wide variety of new regulations. It had to deal regularly with dozens of federal, state, and local officials as the new requirements concerned both top managers and line managers of the company. Problems and frustrations in dealing with the new regulations included an EPA requirement that assumed air pollution emissions were three times as great as PPG believed, and an OSHA requirement to control lead that involved costly engineering controls, rather than personal protective equipment.[22] PPG managers also expressed frustration about the duplicative nature of the requirements and their ambiguous character. They wanted more flexible rules that reflected the considerable variations in health and safety conditions that existed in the industry. According to the manager of the firm's environmental affairs division, regulations were too "stringent" and "numerous," and were not "applied uniformly."[23]

PPG had to install anti-pollution equipment at substantial cost. However, it also benefitted from market opportunities provided by the new requirements. For example, the trend toward lighter-weight cars provided a market for glass and plastics that were needed to replace metals. Also, with greater awareness of the need for energy conservation, sales of insulation products increased.

As the impact of the new requirements was large, PPG felt compelled to establish a Washington-based office to monitor legislation and regulatory developments in such areas as EPA's new source performance standard for glass manufacturing; specifications for railroad cars carrying an assortment of chemicals; developments in the Toxic Substances Control Act and the Resource Conservation and Recovery Act; and OSHA's generic policy on cancer-causing chemicals.

Firms like PPG experienced six types of costs because of the new social regulation.[24]

1. *Direct Compliance Costs*
   License/permit/registration fees
   Changes in work routines
   Changes in physical facilities

2. *Administrative Costs*
   Inspections/reporting/record keeping

3. *Start-up Costs*

4. *Opportunity Costs*

5. *Cumulative Impacts*
   Prices
   Quality
   Growth
   Profits
   Competitive position
   Innovation
   Employment

6. *Psychological Costs*
   Relationship with government
   Relationship with employees
   Managerial autonomy
   Satisfaction of doing business

What Roland McKean calls avoidance and enforcement costs were involved.[25] Whatever the regulation might require, some firms were likely to violate the rules or were likely to seek to get around them and avoid the penalties by hiring attorneys and looking for loopholes. They might try to influence the authorities in other ways, by trying to conceal offenses or lobbying to change the law. These activities were *avoidance costs*, which included the need to acquire information about regulations and the methods available to avoid their impact.[26] *Enforcement costs* were the efforts the regulatory agency had to make to counter this avoidance.[27] These costs included monitoring industry's behavior to detect violations, deciding what to do about the violations once they had occurred, and going to court and punishing the violators when necessary.

Avoidance costs which the firm experienced included:

* finding out about loopholes
* deciding what to do
* paying legal and clerical staff and consultants
* bargaining
* lobbying
* litigation
* advertising and public relations

On the other hand, the enforcement costs for the regulatory agency included:

* inspection
* devising forms for required reports
* checking required reports
* using officials to detect violations
* deciding who to prosecute
* conducting hearings, appeals, and litigation
* collecting fines or meting out punishment

Small businesses often suffered more than large companies. They were particularly concerned about the added paperwork requirements. The Federal Paperwork Commission estimated that paperwork costs to private industry ranged from $25 billion to $32 billion in 1977, and that a substantial portion of the costs was unnecessary.[28]

Industry estimated that it spent $10 billion per year in the late 1970s to meet government safety, environmental, and other regulatory requirements.[29] The diversion of private investment from productive uses, according to Edward Denison, resulted in a loss of approximately one-quarter of the potential annual increase in productivity during those years.[30]

Responding to the New Regulation

Responding to the new regulation was among the most important challenges that managers faced. Different firms made different responses which included a wide variety of behaviors. One writer describes behaviors as "denying, fighting, acquiescing, passively accepting, and creative problem solving."[31] A company might bargain with regulators, arguing that its responsibility in a particular case was minor, especially in comparison with other firms in the industry. It might fight the imposition of additional standards through advertising or public relations campaigns or drawn-out court battles. It might lobby against the standards and assert that they were unreasonable, lacking in scientific sense, costly to implement, and technologically impossible. A company might also cooperate with regulators and try to meet "the letter of the law."[32] The company might be so scrupulous in meeting the letter of the law, however, that it missed the law's true spirit.[33] A company also could try to reconcile the standards with its needs through business analysis. Projected gains might be balanced against possible losses: perhaps the company could benefit from the requirement.

In developing a corporate social policy, a firm might display all of these responses in one form or another. From the outside it would appear as if it behaved inconsistently, moving from response to response without reason or purpose. The imposition of a new standard and the requirement to comply with its provisions were challenges that firms responded to in different ways.

POLICY DRIFT: THE CORVAIR AND PINTO CASES

Sometimes a corporation was not able to develop a coherent response. Corporate behavior during the Corvair and Pinto cases illustrates the results of such drift. After the Corvair had been on the market for a few months, it was clear to auto experts and industry officials alike that the car's handling characteristics were unusual: the car would go out of control without warning. People who were injured in auto accidents involving Corvairs began to sue. At least thirty lawsuits were filed in the three years after the car's introduction.[34] The crucial question was why General Motors waited so long before making changes that would have thwarted the Nader attack that subsequently embarrassed the company and destroyed the market for this car. What were the reasons for this drift?

Nader's explanation of the company's slow reaction was an economic one. The redesign and production of a new suspension system would cut into earnings and would make the Corvair less competitive with its rival, the Ford Falcon. Another explanation for drift was the discounting of relevant information by GM executives. They discounted public sensitivity to the issue, believing that the car's safety record was not unusual in light of the experience of other small subcompact and compact cars of the time. The Volkswagen Beetle, for example, had a far worse safety record.[35] Moreover, driver negligence was often cited in court cases as a contributing factor in the accidents. According to Paul Halpern, "In the Corvair case GM miscalculated primarily because, given the relative stability of its political-legal environment, it did not anticipate the environmental change which took place five years after the car was introduced and almost ten years after it was initially designed."[36]

But Ford executives made the same miscalculations in the Pinto case, in spite of the obvious changes in the political-legal environment and the publicity surrounding GM's earlier problems. Company executives knew from early test crashes that the fuel tank of the Pinto ruptured and was likely to ignite if the car was rear-ended at relatively moderate speeds.[37] However, they did nothing about it. One reason was the demands of the production schedule.[38] The Pinto—initiated in 1969 and on the market in 1972—had one of the shortest production schedules in modern automotive history.[39] It made no sense in terms of either time or money to make a last minute fix, especially after tooling had taken place. Project managers at the division level refused to act.

Meanwhile, the Pinto became one of the best-selling subcompacts, with nearly 2 million in sales between 1971 and 1976.[40] Although demands for a recall were heard as early as 1974, nothing happened until 1977, when journalist Mark Dowie of the magazine *Mother Jones* publicized Ford's test data.[41] One year later the National Highway Traffic Safety Administration (NHTSA) recalled all the Pintos that had been manufactured between 1971 and 1976. Pinto sales immediately slumped, causing great concern at Ford because the company had been relying on the car to meet federal fuel economy standards.

Both the Corvair and the Pinto hurt their respective companies. They also damaged the credibility of American companies in their competition with the Japanese for the small car market. In both cases, auto executives knew what the problem was and knew that the problem could be fixed, but it took four to six years before they responded with retooling, and then they responded only after substantial regulatory pressure. Numerous product liability suits had been filed by maimed or injured persons who collected damages in court settlements, and the companies were embarrassed by policy entrepreneurs who publicized the safety problems and undermined the market for the cars.

Ford executives learned nothing from GM's experience despite the increased regulatory assertiveness of the government in the 1970s. By the time the Pinto was introduced government enforcement powers in the product liability area had increased. NHTSA, for example, had recall authority. As Halpern remarks, product liability litigation was "no longer the only game in town."[42] The cost of notification letters alone was $285,000.[43] Labor time for a retrofit was more expensive than it was on the assembly line. Parts cost more. Revenues declined because of decreased sales. The financial implications hurt in innumerable ways. Policy drift had a negative effect on the company's reputation and on its ability to compete in the marketplace.

It is hard to understand why Ford executives let matters get to this point, especially after the Corvair incident. Halpern speculates that drift in policy was related to insensitivity of production units to larger organizational concerns.[44] At the production level, the primary goal was meeting immediate deadlines at cost. This goal defined the task environment. The time lag between production and the consequences was significant. Moreover, people in the divisions did not face the ultimate consequences. If the company was embarrassed by a suit, the comptroller at corporate head-quarters had to write the checks to the plaintiff. If forced to comply with a recall, the company lost markets, but only after those who had been involved in the design and production of the car had been rewarded for successfully meeting yearly production and profit schedules. Division level employees had no incentive to take into consideration the long-term consequences of their actions. Without a corporate social policy that permeated the organization, penetrated to the division level, and influenced the work habits and basic motivations of employees, the corporation was motivated by priorities that stressed immediate profits at the expense of long-term integrity.

STANDARD SETTING

As the Corvair and Pinto cases demonstrate, managers have to take the new regulation seriously. Agencies are engaged in standard setting to cover a wide variety of practices, and firms, and even government agencies, must submit to frequent inspection. Corporate managers need to be aware of the strategic and competitive implications of the standards the government has promulgated, and have to develop methods to cope with inspection and enforcement costs.

During the late 1960s and early 1970s, the National Highway Traffic Safety Administration developed numerous standards, involving technical subject matter and difficult scientific and engineering questions. Standards were set for head restraints, brakes, tires, bumpers, and fuel economy.[45] Moreover, the way these standards were developed was not the way a rational policy planner would conduct the task, with cost-benefit analysis to determine which safety improvements made the most sense. The goal was not to maximize benefits for the least cost. If cost-benefit analysis had been done, that brake maintenance rather than installation of a new brake system was more cost-effective would have been realized.[46] Mandating special devices to stop speeding rather than requiring head restraints made more sense.

The process of standard promulgation rested heavily on statutory requirement and precedent. It involved negotiation, revision, modification, and delay. The Administrative Procedures Act required "public notice and comment"; NHTSA had to provide a reason for a rule; and the courts could dismiss the rule if they found it to be "arbitrary, capricious, or abuse of discretion."[47] To develop a rationale for a standard, NHTSA gathered preliminary information from members of its staff, outside experts, members of industry, and the general public. Sometimes it did so through an

"Advance Notice of Proposed Rulemaking." It had to keep a record of the information it gathered. The agency then had to formulate a preliminary standard and issue a "Notice of Proposed Rulemaking." It held informal hearings or public meetings where affected industries, consumer groups, and others submitted comments. It modified the proposed standard, and asked for more comment. Further modification and comment might then be necessary. Eventually, the agency issued a final standard, after much give and take and negotiation with the affected parties.

Any of the parties might appeal the decision to the courts. The courts then examined the standard to see if NHTSA had committed procedural or factual errors. They tried to determine if the standard was "reasonable." The courts, however, often had trouble making this determination. Judges often found it difficult to determine if a particular statistical or scientific study supporting the standard made any sense.[48] In addition, agencies often relied on precedent, with standards being based on pre-existing industry standards; but reliance on industry standards could create serious problems. These standards were generally voluntary. Voluntary standards could be rejected by firms if they did not make sense. Firms could selectively comply with them. However, with mandatory standards they did not have this choice. Reliance on inappropriate industry standards, for example, cost OSHA greatly.

Developing new standards was a demanding task, because the agency needed reliable and accurate information from external sources. NHTSA, for example, lacked the in-house capability to generate this information, and none of the external sources of information was considered entirely trustworthy.[49] Most of the information had to come from the regulated companies. Experts who had access to the relevant facts worked for industry. Even independent consultants had to depend on industry for information. The agency believed that it obtained reliable information only when opposing firms acted as a check on each other's information. Another check was consumer groups, but they might be biased or lack the requisite technical expertise.

In actually formulating standards, difficult and sensitive issues were involved:

1. All risk could not be eliminated. The agency therefore had to make decisions about a tolerable level of risk.
2. It had to choose between detailed and specific rules and general and unspecific rules. Detailed and specific rules eliminated bureaucratic discretion and industry uncertainty, but they might prove to be inflexible and inapplicable to specific industry problems.
3. The agency had to decide whether to phrase standards in terms of ultimate goals or in terms of particular technological requirements. Performance standards had

the advantage of giving industry an opportunity to choose the means to accomplish the goals; however, they presented the possibility that the agency might establish unrealistic ends for symbolic purposes.

4. If the agency chose a design as opposed to a performance standard, it had to decide whether the design would be state-of-the-art or technology-forcing. If the standard demanded that companies make a breakthrough and was technology-forcing, then it gave them possible reasons for not being able to meet requirements.[50]

The process of formulating the standards was as much political as it was technical. The process involved different parties in negotiation. Each had different interests and influence. While auto manufacturers emphasized the costs of NHTSA's standards, consumer groups emphasized the benefits. NHTSA, which wanted to appear neutral, had the power to set the standard. However, no matter what it did, companies could challenge the standard in the courts. They also could influence the political environment, for example, by publicizing that the standard would raise prices and contribute to unemployment. Consumer groups also had the power to appeal to the courts and could press their demands with Congress and publicize their position in the media. Industry unity could not be assumed. In the case of NHTSA tire standards, Uniroyal provided the agency with a method for rating treadwear traction and blowout resistance without which there could have been no standard.[51] Standards developed were not the best that were possible from a cost-benefit perspective, but were the best from the perspective of agreement among conflicting parties.

Once adopted, standards were likely to have diverse competitive effects on an industry. For one thing, the added cost of compliance erected barriers to entry for new firms in the industry. Only some firms would have the expertise and financial capability to comply. The cost curve of compliance would be substantially lower for these firms. These firms were in a position to benefit from regulation.

However, immediate and long-term competitive effects often were unknowable because of industry and regulatory uncertainty. Firms had the right to appeal. They could and did argue that standards reflected only an "inspired engineering guess," because in many cases this argument was true.[52] They claimed that standards were based on "soft information," because in many cases this fact also was true.[53] Appealing firms almost always had a case because they could argue that the record was incomplete. Standards were not set according to policy-planning ideals, but according to a complex political and legal process.

Standards that were finally promulgated were often vague. The fact that they left unsaid more than they said and that they lacked substantive detail provided avenues for further dispute. For example, the National Highway

Traffic and Motor Vehicle Safety Act of 1966 made automobiles with a defect "related to safety" subject to recall.[54] However, NHTSA did not give a precise meaning to the phrase by providing objective criteria which would determine the existence of a safety-related defect. In 1973, in the *Federal Register*, it declined to issue a standard, preferring instead to rely on case-by-case determinations. General Motors challenged this approach. The agency later changed its stance. Its standard, based on the premise of a "large number" of failures, was then refuted by the courts, which determined that gross abuse by the vehicle owner could negate determination of a defect. Standard setting and resetting in various administrative and judicial forums provided businesses with many opportunities for intervention, but issues were rarely settled with any conclusiveness.

Once adopted, a policy was likely to change. To eliminate or change unreasonable standards industry had to press its case. In the case of OSHA, removal of defective standards that the agency borrowed from industry took much time and effort. The publicity campaign against these standards, which was based on anecdotal information about "ridiculous rules," made splendid media copy. Nonetheless, it was difficult for businesses to contend with an agency that had the entirely unobjectionable task of eliminating workplace disease and injury. Elaborate due process procedures made it particularly difficult to eliminate what industry considered to be unreasonable rules.

ENFORCEMENT

In the meantime, enforcement was a constant challenge for managers. Social regulation often was based on the premise that firms need the threat of punishment to compel them to comply. Enforcement must be strict. Leniency and discretion were not proper. Congress, therefore, enacted strict statutes that allowed little room for discretion. Ambiguous phrases such as *reasonable* and *feasible* were eliminated.[55] Statutes mandated ambitious levels of protection and set fixed deadlines for achievement. The 1970 Clean Air Act, in its attachment to goal achievement, excluded concern about the costs of compliance. Many new regulatory statutes shifted the burden of proof by requiring regulated firms to keep detailed records and to seek agency approval before undertaking an activity. Penalties were severe and the range of legally available remedial actions was wide.

The 1977 Clean Air Act Amendments extended criminal liability to "any responsible corporate officer."[56] Agencies in some cases could impose sanctions directly without having to go to court. Inspectors had little discretion to tailor the regulatory program to the situation of individual companies. They were explicitly forbidden to overlook minor violations, take into account extraneous circumstances, use oral advice or warnings, or take other action that might adapt enforcement to the reality of specific circumstances.[57]

Imposing uniform requirements in circumstances where they did not make sense and failing to consider industry arguments that exceptions should be made resulted in business perceptions of regulatory unreasonableness and unresponsiveness.[58] To industry managers, it did not make sense for the government to prescribe a single technology for a problem when plants were so different. For example, there were sixteen major copper smelters in the United States and almost as many different copper smelting processes.[59] To apply one occupational health standard to these different cases seemed ridiculous. Applying for a variance was difficult and time-consuming. The application criteria were very stringent. The firm could not deal with the individual inspector but had to appeal to a higher supervisory level.

Inspectors had to view their jobs in terms of violations, formal prosecutions, and penalties, and not in terms of advice-giving and problem-solving.[60] The effects of the legalistic approach were major reductions in fatalities in some industries. The mining industry, for example, after passage of the 1969 Federal Coal Mine Health and Safety Act, experienced a reduction in fatalities.[61] However, rule-bound inspection officials, insisting on the concrete detail of the requirements, often could miss the real issues.[62] They were not effective in preventing a major accident (the DC-10 crash in 1979), for example.[63] Often they did not receive honest and informative communications from industry because of a fear of self-incrimination. The attention of rule-bound officials was focused on superficial matters rather than on an open-ended search for the important problems. According to Bardach and Kagan, "Regulatory toughness in its legalistic manifestation creates resentment and resistance, undermines attitude and information sharing practices that could otherwise be cooperative and constructive, and diverts energies of both sides into pointless and dispiriting legal routines and conflicts."[64]

To cope with enforcement challenges, firms had to be prepared. Their facilities and their people had to be ready when enforcement officials came. They had to be cooperative, but they could not be so open as to put their companies in unnecessary jeopardy.[65]

Employees had to know what company policies were, and plant managers had to be intimately involved in the inspection process. The company and its employees had a responsibility to be informed about the regulatory process and the specific requirements individual programs placed on it. A firm had to restrain itself from overreacting when fined or when found in noncompliance. It had to learn how to work with the system, not fight it, because standards and inspection officials could be managed. Managing them meant understanding something about the technical details of due process and administrative proceedings. It meant understanding bargaining and negotiating, and making trades of reduced fines for declarations of good faith, when necessary.[66]

Organizational Units for Compliance

Many companies decided to establish special organizational units to deal with compliance requirements. Some hired full-time legal and public relations specialists to keep up with these requirements and to devise "programs to keep the company out of trouble."[67] Others trained safety and other experts whom they placed at their plants. Compliance specialists often moved to higher levels of responsibility in the corporation. They had considerable influence with the board of directors, the top level of management, and line officials.[68] They often received support for expensive technological changes and initiated a broad range of anticipatory actions.

The type of units created by companies to cope with new compliance requirements varied a great deal from company to company. Marc Roberts and J. S. Bluhm found these different organizational forms among the utility companies they examined:

• A permanent integrating or planning unit

• A semi-permanent project team

• An ad hoc committee or task force

• A formal or informal top management group

• A permanent intergroup team[69]

Roberts and Bluhm believed that none of these organizational forms or techniques was best.[70] An organization's performance was heavily dependent on "the attitudes and abilities of those in pivotal integrator roles."[71] Extensive top management involvement in decision making and a well-defined hierarchy, typical of organizations operating in stable, low-stress environments, were characteristics of the "most responsive organizations."[72]

"Positive responsiveness," according to Roberts and Bluhm, was the result of:

• a conscious strategy to anticipate future demands in current decision making

• an organization that supported such a policy

• a role for public relations, law, *and* environmental engineering

• policies that motivated mid-level managers to implement the strategy.[73]

However, Roberts and Bluhm qualified their findings by admitting that they might be limited to electric utilities, which operate in a regulated environment.[74] The main focus of the utilities was not on competition but production. In a crisis, moreover, formal organization was not that relevant. Hierarchy broke down and informal networks operated. Finally, Roberts and Bluhm emphasized that lower-level integrating units were as necessary as the upper-level units.[75]

Roberts and Bluhm concluded that there was no right way to organize the compliance function.[76] Strong managers, who encouraged "a certain amount of questioning and dissent," were necessary; and responsive organizations needed to include people with diverse backgrounds who had the character trait of flexibility.[77]

UNCERTAINTY AND DISCRETION IN COMPLIANCE

Compliance allowed considerable room for discretion.[78] According to Ackerman, responding typically followed the pattern of an issue's development.[79] The right to collective bargaining in the United States demonstrates the cycle that an issue may pass through. Originally, the issue was not on the public agenda. However, as interest developed and was sustained, the issue passed through a period of increasing awareness, growing expectation, demand for action, and ultimately enforcement. At the end of the enforcement period, which was measured in decades, it ceased to be a matter of active public concern.[80]

The life cycle of public issues involves major uncertainties for managers.[81] Activists and the causes they champion are subject to change. Some issues become enduring facets of business operations, while others fall by the wayside. Acceptable standards of behavior, which are difficult to determine, change over time. Appropriate and effective methods of response may not exist or may be unknown when demands are first made. Technologies may have to be developed and new sources of skilled employees identified. Moreover, the complete costs of compliance are not likely to be known. Only after considerable experience with requirements are their full cost implications apparent.

Uncertainties provide opportunities for discretion.[82] Managers may have more discretion early in the issue life cycle, when uncertainty is greatest, and less discretion later, when uncertainty is reduced. During the life cycle of a public issue, managers have a variety of options for approaching impending compliance, but ultimately these options are narrowed or even eliminated as a new standard of behavior becomes more generally accepted and is enforced through regulatory means and sanctions.

As enforcement and implementation replace political controversy, discretion is reduced. This reduction in discretion does not mean that managers are ever without influence. Even when an issue appears closed, controversy can be rekindled, and managers can create a new zone of discretion.

Available options open to managers that have to comply with new social regulations have been characterized in terms of the degree of "lead or lag" in responsiveness.[83] Roberts and Bluhm give several reasons why managers would want to lead rather than lag:

- The company can escape more severe demands and disruptive requirements that otherwise might develop.
- It gains control over the timing, extent and nature of compliance.
- It reduces future uncertainties.
- It prevents unforeseen regulatory roadblocks from developing.[84]

By complying early, managers accept the burden of acting under conditions of greater uncertainty as to the eventual dimensions of the issue and the appropriate means for dealing with it. They also absorb costs when the costs appear less burdensome and are more voluntary.

Major patterns of response that may be distinguished are opportunism and stonewalling.[85] Opportunism is responding early to preserve flexibility. Stonewalling is responding late to avoid uncertainty. These strategies, separately and in combination, are preferable to policy drift.

Opportunism

Opportunism can be illustrated through an examination of Dow Chemical Company's response to the pollution control issue. Herbert Doan, former president of Dow Chemical and currently a member of the board of directors, called pollution control "an opportunity to profit."[86] Opportunism as defined by Doan is the effort to transform regulatory constraints into business opportunities.[87]

Dow tried in three ways to make pollution control profitable.[88] First, it sold the pollution control products and services it developed to others in need of help in controlling their pollution; that is, Dow made its technology available to those who did not have the size or experience to solve pollution control problems on their own. Dow, for instance, acquired a subsidiary, Hydrosciences Associates, Inc. Hydrosciences was in the environmental consulting business and was trying to help other manufacturers meet pollution control deadlines.[89]

Second, Dow sold its expertise and equipment to government agencies. It created an Environmental Testing Advisory Board, which studied the specific impact of various products on the environment for the government; and it had contracts with local governments, such as the city of Detroit, to install sewage treatment plants.

Third, Dow reduced its waste by developing new uses for manufacturing by-products; that is, it recycled waste materials.[90] It looked at waste problems in its manufacturing processes, and tried to convert these losses to saleable products. By doing so, it avoided having to eliminate waste materials, while at the same time gaining new products to sell.

Stonewalling

Dow took steps to convert pollution control requirements into opportunities for gain. In contrast, Reserve Mining Corporation's activities illustrate a stonewalling approach.[91] Stonewalling is using the legal and administrative process to buffer the corporation from the uncertainties of changing government sanctions and requirements. It is resisting the tide by responding slowly to government expectations. In an uncertain environment, the legal process may offer a measure of certainty and predictability which is preferable to the uncertainty of changing government requirements. Stonewalling is resorting to the legal process to protect the corporation from expensive and unnecessary changes.

In the 1970s, Reserve Mining adhered steadfastly to legal procedure to delay the implementation of a ban on direct dumping of taconite wastes, an iron ore by-product which is believed to cause cancer. Reserve's legal strategy was to dispute the precise nature of the discharge, its biological effects, and the eventual destination of the discharged wastes. In 1974 the district court judge ultimately ordered an end to all dumping into Lake Superior despite the case made by Reserve's lawyers, but the company appealed, and the court of appeals extended a stay of injunction. On the question of public health, the court of appeals was unsure that adequate evidence was available to determine proof of substantial health hazard. The Reserve Mining case shows the ability of corporations to use the legal and administrative processes to maintain their present practices in spite of changing government requirements.

The Pitfalls of Opportunism

Opportunism and stonewalling have their pitfalls. By planning to manufacture and sell air bags, Eaton, like Dow, was trying to take advantage of government regulations to achieve corporate profits. It was being opportunistic, but the company ran into trouble because of the uncertainties of the political process and the "untidiness" of democratic decision making.[92] Courts overturned rules that promised Eaton gain from regulation and Congress and the White House reversed decisions that would have allowed Eaton to profit from the air bag business. In California, the Air Resources Board mandated a device to remove nitrogen oxides from the air, but the potential market collapsed when the legislation permitted exceptions. In cases where the government changes the proposed regulations from which companies had expected to profit, companies may have to sue the government and argue that a mandate to install the required devices was an implied contract. Mandated markets for pollution control and auto safety equipment are insecure for three reasons.[93] First, although the public may be concerned about safety and environmental protection, it also is concerned about basic freedoms that requirements for safety and environmental protection may violate. Motorcycle helmet requirements are a splendid example. Second, the possibility of endless lawsuits, which helps stonewalling companies, hurts opportunistic firms. For instance, air bags, which are designed for frontal collisions, are likely to have been the source of endless litigation, as accident victims would try to prove that the bags should have inflated when cars were hit from another angle. Third, opportunistic firms may have decisions reversed by competing federal and local institutions. Congress, for instance, legislated the auto safety interlock system out of existence, and the Department of Transportion and EPA delayed the introduction of air bags.[94]

The Dynamic Features of the Corporate Response

A strict division of corporate response into the two patterns, opportunism and stonewalling, moreover, ignores the dynamic features of actual corporate response, such as simultaneous stonewalling and opportunism or, depending on the issue, movement from stonewalling to opportunism. Both GM and Union Carbide, like Reserve Mining, began to stonewall when first confronted with some of the new social regulations.[95] They looked for legal remedies and refused to comply, based on their belief that such regulations would not be of permanent significance. These two firms, however, unlike Reserve Mining, did not adhere to a stonewalling strategy in perpetuity. Over time, they adjusted their response and moved from one stance to another. The evolutionary pattern of their response, in retrospect, appears appropriate. In both cases, critical events led to a reexamination of priorities. GM replaced non-compliance with an overall business reorientation, while Union Carbide replaced non-compliance with changes in organization and increased public relations.

General Motors

For GM, no single event, but rather a series of events, contributed to a reexamination of prior policies.[96] These events included: (1) declining market share in comparison with the Japanese manufacturers; (2) the Arab oil embargo; (3) recognition that GM autos at one time had the worst average gas mileage among U.S. automakers—a dismal 12 miles per gallon in 1973; (4) government-mandated mile-per-gallon increases—to a 27.5 mile-per-gallon fleet average by 1985; (5) criticism of its pollution control and safety record; and (6) failure to communicate with labor, and labor unrest generally, which ultimately affected product quality.

GM's first response to these issues was to drift, as noted earlier. Then, it began to stonewall, to delay changes impinging from the outside through legal and administrative maneuvers. However, gradually the company tried to transform its problems into managerial and technological challenges. It resorted to the classic mechanisms of good management: planning, strategy making, and reorganization.[97]

First, the corporation brought new influences to bear on the planning process. It created a public policy committee staffed with university professors who were responsible for dealing with labor and environmental protection problems, and it created an energy task force responsible for dealing with the energy issue.

Second, these two groups played a role in the planning process and helped devise the now famous *downsizing strategy*. This strategy was clearly opportunistic, an effort to deal aggressively and constructively with the challenges of the new situation and new regulations. The downsizing strategy was supposed to enable the corporation to recapture greater market share by appealing to a broader public.

Third, after adopting the new marketing strategy, the company reorganized its operations. It brought in new, younger executives to manage the changes it was making, and used the project center concept to implement the innovations it was trying to carry out.

Planning, strategy making, and reorganizing in response to external events were designed to turn the company around—to move it from its drift and stonewalling, from its insular and inner-directed posture to a more positive and dynamic opportunism—an outer-directed, strategic orientation.[98] The company could no longer expect that delay through legal negotiation would preserve the earlier equilibrium where it had achieved unquestioned market dominance. It had to do what was possible to take advantage of the new situation—to accept uncertainty and the need for greater flexibility. By 1977, GM's average MPG (17.8) became the best among the Big Three automakers, and its market share rebounded to 46 percent.[99] Its strategy enjoyed an apparent short-term success. The company also gained a public relations advantage. It improved its image from that of an antisocial company opposed to environmental and energy realities to an innovator adapting to new conditions.

Union Carbide

Union Carbide also moved from a stonewalling posture to a more opportunistic stance in the 1970s, but it ended up in a somewhat different place.[100]

It became a public relations activist organization willing to comply when necessary as long as compliance was reasonable. Events that occurred in West Virginia in the late 1960s and early 1970s were the catalysts for change in the company. At that time, Union Carbide made efforts to delay public and government attempts to clean up its plants. Its strategy was to block efforts to secure compliance through judicial proceedings. The court cases earned the company the reputation of being opposed to environmental progress. A bad reputation, followed by a sudden jump in energy prices and intensified government efforts to regulate the energy business, put Union Carbide in a defensive position. Top managers felt that it was not good for the company to be perceived as resistant to change.[101] They realized that the days were gone when it could protect itself from such changes by quietly dealing with a few "power-brokers" at the federal and state level. The issues that affected the company had a broader front. The company's reputation, earned by its strategy of delay, was a liability, and efforts were needed to overcome it.

Union Carbide responded by reorganizing its public affairs activities under the leadership of a single person and centralizing policy formulation in key areas such as energy, environment, taxation, and safety. It also decided to publicly speak out on the issues. In its public affairs messages it presented itself not as a strident advocate, as companies such as Mobil did, but as a company that believed in "reasoning together."[102] The philosophy of reasoning together involved "fair-mindedness."[103] For example, when the company opposed government efforts to have industry pay more for energy, it also advocated supplementary income devices for the poor. By appearing reasonable, it moved form the rigid stance it had adopted earlier, to this more flexible response.

Both Union Carbide and GM moved from trying to preserve the *status quo ante* through delay to efforts at managing compliance for profit and respectability. Critical events led to changes in policy. Company policy often changes over time in response to critical events over which a company has little control. Flexibility can be maintained if the company is opportunistic, if it takes risks and takes the lead in responding to new requirements. However, the pitfalls of opportunism demonstrate that strategy needs to be balanced between too much risk and too much rigidity.

AN APPROACH TO COMPLIANCE

Compliance varies among firms and industries. Roberts and Bluhm, for example, found considerable variation among the utilities they examined.[104] Surprisingly, private companies were more responsive to public demands than government-owned utilities. Both types of institutions became more responsive as "social and regulatory pressures" increased "in scope and intensity."[105] Studies of pollution control in the paper industry also have suggested that some companies comply earlier than others.[106] Other studies have shown comparable variations among steel companies.[107]

Bardach and Kagan divide regulated companies into the "good" and "bad" apples.[108] They estimate that at least 80 percent of companies are good apples. The good apples are not willing to sacrifice long-term and intangible benefits in exchange for short-term cost cutting. They are capable of sustaining an interest in an issue; concerned about maintaining their reputation and avoiding lawsuits; and unwilling to trade off the costs of compliance against the costs of a fine. According to Bardach and Kagan, the "best apples" have the strongest internal control systems.[109] "Reasonably good apples" exist as well. Only about 20 percent of the firms regulated by a particular agency are truly bad apples that are guided by short-term and narrowly conceived financial considerations.[110] There are many reasons why any firm might seek to avoid compliance, among them: managerial motivations; financial conditions that make broader and more far-sighted vision impossible; costs and inconveniences associated with complying; and perhaps a perception that standards are unreasonable. Compliance decisions then are the result of many factors, including:

- the size of the firm
- the size of its problem
- government discretion
- company inclination to bargain
- the firm's strategic position
- the political setting[111]

Size of the Firm

Political scientists disagree about which firms are more likely to comply with regulations. Bernstein maintains that small firms are more likely to comply, while Wilson argues that large firms are more likely to do so. Bernstein reasons that "the relative inability of the small firm to sustain and finance long, drawn out hearings . . . highlight[s] the unfortunate position of small business subject to regulation. These firms are weak in resources, skills, and experience in dealing with regulatory agencies and the government. Moreover, they are less competent than larger firms in securing political support."[112] Wilson, on the other hand, argues that "when noncompliance is easily concealed in ways that confer an economic advantage, compliance will be greatest among the largest firms and least among the smallest. A few large firms are easier to inspect than many small ones."[113] While Bernstein suggests that large firms have the resources to resist regulation, Wilson stresses that small firms can ignore and more easily conceal their violations.

Size of the Problem

In the case of EPA's smokestack emissions program, which was examined by Marcus, firms with insignificant problems and firms with major problems escaped control, while firms with medium size problems were more likely to comply.[114] The crucial variable was not the size of the firm, but the magnitude of the problem.

Average emissions was used to measure the magnitude of the problem. When compliance was plotted against average emissions, it showed that small emitters in the under 100-ton per year category escaped effective control, as did very large emitters in the over 7,000-ton category; only middle size emitters in the 300- to 500-ton category were effectively controlled. Small problems and large problems were not effectively contained by the government, while medium size problems were more amenable to government control.

Government Discretion

EPA chose to concentrate on the close to 25,000 large (more than 100 tons of particulates and sulfur dioxide per year) pollutors. The more than 200,000 small emitters (less than 100 tons of particulates and sulfur dioxide) included small industrial, commercial, and residential sources that contributed 15 percent of total nationwide emissions.[115] They made a significant contribution to the problem, but no reduction in emissions was required of them.

The non-compliance of these small emitters was entirely the result of government discretion. Agency officials, who were delegated broad powers, decided not to control firms that emitted less than 100 tons of pollutant per year. The officials had limited resources for enforcement. From their perspective, it was reasonable to exclude the small pollutors.

Company Bargaining

The non-compliance of large emitters was related to company bargaining.[116] Non-compliers, for the most part, took legal action to negotiate their actual reduction. When the 1970 Clean Air Act was passed, they asked local pollution control boards for variances (exemptions from compliance). In 1975, when the law said that their right to these exemptions ran out, many agreed, after negotiations in and out of court, to schedules that designated "increments of progress" that they had to achieve over time. United States Steel, for example, agreed to a compliance schedule for its Clariton, Pennsylvania, works only after being brought to court by local officials and an environmental group and after the media made its case into a cause célèbre.

The norms of managers, not economic or technical issues, may determine whether a company bargains.[117] Air pollution regulations are likely to lack legitimacy in the eyes of many of the delaying managers, who may not believe the data the government generates to support its standards, and may come from an old school of rugged individualists who view "any infringement on their freedom of choice as intolerable." Their opposition to regulation may be both philosophic, attitudinal, and practical.

Strategic Position

The strategic position of a company also may influence compliance. Complying firms may be smaller, in more competitive industries, and growing.[118] Their pollution problems are of less magnitude than the pollution problems of non-complying firms, because their plant and equipment are newer. They may lack legal resources and sophistication and generally will have neither the patience nor the desire for long, drawn-out judicial proceedings. They are likely to believe that "whatever is required, let it be done with." Managers of complying firms may also be motivated by conscience or a desire to conform to local values and community norms. However, many are likely to be opportunists. They will try to take advantage of requirements by recycling saleable or usable materials, saving energy, or gaining market share at the expense of competitors.

In contrast, non-complying firms may be larger companies operating in oligopolistic or monopolistic industries, which are growing less rapidly or declining because of factors such as foreign competition or dwindling resource availability. Their regulatory problems may be major and difficult to take care of cheaply because plants and equipment are old. Moreover, these companies are likely to possess a well-developed legal capability, "a standing army of attorneys," who have long experience in dealing with the courts and regulatory agencies. Non-complying firms therefore will refuse to invest in what they consider to be nonproductive innovations. Their managers may believe that stalling makes more sense than overhauling outmoded plants and equipment, which are doomed to extinction within a short time period. Compliance, if it occurs among these firms, generally means shutting down plants or closing facilities, not rebuilding or modernizing them.

Political Setting

The political setting is also likely to affect the response. The key political actors include trade associations, regulatory agencies, and outside experts. They in turn affect the response of Congress, public opinion, the media, the White House, and appointed officials.

Trade Associations. They can speak for an industry as a whole. Concerned about industry survival and viability, they will focus on key factors such as overall industry sales and employment. They are also likely to articulate the industry plight in terms of the general public interest by making arguments such as the following: If the demand for regulatory relief is not met, the net result will be unemployment, social disruption, and increased reliance on foreign products. They are also likely to argue that standards are too strict and could be relaxed without endangering public health or other sacred values. Trade associations will emphasize how much the industry already has done and how much money it already has spent in complying and achieving standards.

Regulatory Agencies. Regulatory agencies may be divided into groups or units concerned with enforcement and groups or units concerned with economic consequences. Often the former will consist of lawyers, while the latter will consist of economists or policy analysts.[119] The director of enforcement generally will be upset at the lack of industry compliance, for example, the fact that over 80 percent of processes are not in compliance with air pollution requirements for the steel industry. Although suspicious of company motives, enforcement officers require company cooperation to move ahead with their efforts. Enforcement officers, therefore, need to be complementary to companies that have already complied and cooperated with regulatory authorities. The economic analysis division, on the other hand, is in the position where it has to defend the agency against charges made by the trade association and industry that costs of compliance are exorbitant. It therefore will care less about the percentage of firms complying than about evidence that can be gathered to defend the agency against charges that it is bankrupting industry.

Outside Experts. They are also likely to be divided. Some will take the side of the agency and argue that industry cost estimates are exaggerated because they ignore, for example, special funding from local and state government, which may make up for the expense of compliance. These experts may maintain that as technologies improve, the costs of compliance will decline. They also may argue that the benefits from the agency's programs outweigh costs, and therefore are justified, even if costs are high. Other experts are likely to take the side of industry and will support a trade association's position that costs are excessive, that standards are too strict, and that the public health can be protected at lower cost. It is also likely that they will hold it to be unreasonable to remove the remaining small percentage of pollution needed to get down to agency specifications. They will argue that the last five percentage points of compliance tend to be the most expensive.[120]

Decision points generally are in (1) judicial and semi-judicial proceedings where industry may push the case to compel the agency to review the health criteria on which standards are based; (2) state and local governments, which have to submit and carry out implementation plans; and (3) Congress, where laws may be revised, amended, and perhaps eliminated.

Typical outcomes are increased compliance over time, perhaps even a doubling in firms that comply. Many other firms will be put on compliance schedules, but nothing approaching total compliance will occur. Outcomes may be influenced by "experiments" tried by innovative companies for strategic and opportunistic reasons. Also, experts who may contend that industry is not as responsible as the agency believes may be important in influencing outcomes.

Compromises can involve not only increased compliance, but also the introduction of innovative compliance methods, such as the EPA initiatives that were taken during the Carter administration (see chapter 10).[121] Policy analysts in an agency may promote these measures because they promise to lower costs, while the enforcement specialists may be skeptical, lest innovations in cost saving become vehicles for delay.

Compromises can lead to a division within an industry, between companies that possess modern equipment and practices and are in a good position to take advantage of innovative compliance mechanisms, and companies that possess less advanced equipment and practices and are not in a position to take advantage of innovative methods. Final determinations often depend on factors such as public opinion, the will of Congress and the bureaucracy, and the strategic considerations of the companies involved.

10 | Overcoming Resistance to Reform

In the case of the old economic regulation, reform generally connotes deregulation—doing away with the price-fixing and entry-permitting authority of the government and returning to marketlike conditions. Deregulation in the case of the old economic regulation generally has meant the elimination of requirements affecting such industries as the airlines, railroads, natural gas producers, and truckers. However, hardly anyone, even the staunchest of free market economists, has argued for the elimination of the new social requirements. Reform's meaning with respect to this regulation is less obvious, and evaluation has been less effective in changing the way regulation is practiced.

For the new social regulation, many types of reform have been proposed, because of a general recognition that the economic and enforcement burden is large, but relatively few reforms have actually been implemented. Businesses, government agencies, congressional committees, and environmental groups are accustomed to the existing system and have been uncertain about the significance of proposed changes—especially about who would be the winners and losers in the process. Suspicion often exists that needed reforms mean weakening hard-won legal enactments and caving in to business pressures in the name of economic efficiency.

Nonetheless, some reform measures have been put into practice. Executive orders issued by the White House have required regulatory agencies to choose alternatives that show the least net cost to society. And regulatory reform at the EPA has tried to increase efficiency while maintaining environmental quality goals. In this chapter, ways of reforming the new social regulation are described, reforms that have been implemented are discussed, and lessons about overcoming resistance to reform are derived.

REFORM MEASURES

Numerous reform measures have been advocated at one time or another by Congress, the White House, the bureaucracy, special interest groups, and various professional associations (for example, the American Bar Association).[1] Particular reform measures vary, but most start with a concern about the economic costs of the new regulation. Economists, for example, have assessed the effects of environmental regulation on the economy as a whole, and have found various negative impacts. The Bureau of Economic Analysis estimated that industry spent $55.7 billion on pollution control activities in 1980.[2] This sum represented 2 percent of gross national product.[3] A study of paper industry productivity by Arthur D. Little demonstrated that by 1983 the average paper price at the mill level would be about 6 percent higher than the 1975 price as a result of air and water pollution control regulations.[4] Twenty-seven of 556 U.S. pulp and paper mills would close. Industries faced severe capital shortages because of large pollution control expenditure requirements that limited their capacity to grow. It was also argued by economists that the costs of pollution control were escalating greatly as the required amount of pollution reduction increased.[5] The Council on Economic Quality (CEQ) estimated that compliance with the Clean Air Act cost $22 billion in 1979, but that compliance costs would increase 38 percent between 1979 and 1988.[6] The last percentage points of reduction would be the most costly.

Changing the Locus of Power

Structural proposals that would change the formal locus of accountability in regulatory decision making included presidential intervention, the legislative veto (since declared unconstitutional), judicial review, the science court, and the sunset approach.[7] The presidential intervention proposal, originally suggested in a 1975 *Yale Law Review* article by Lloyd Cutler and David Johnson, addressed the fact that agencies rarely produced policies that would have been produced by the formally accountable branches of government, that is, Congress and the president.[8] These decisions were political, not technical. They involved the balance of power between competing interests—"which economic and social goals to pursue, how far, and at what economic and social cost."[9] Agency officials were making these political judgments without adequate supervision from the politicians who were officially accountable.

Cutler and Johnson believed that their proposal, greater presidential supervision, would increase the extent to which economic costs, economic growth, and related factors, such as energy generation and consumption, would be taken into account in decision making. However, this proposal had limitations.[10] For one thing, it did not take into account the burden that greater presidential supervision would have on the White House staff. Presidential assistants, not the president, would exercise the new supervisory powers. Moreover, the White House might be biased or single-minded, due to powerful pressures, and might deal only with the economic issues involved. Finally, additional White House review would add time and might cause delay.

Another proposal put forth by critics of regulation was the legislative veto. After major rules were promulgated, but before they took effect, one or both houses of Congress would have the chance to overturn them. This change would shift the locus of accountability to the legislative branch. Several bills were proposed during the 96th Congress for complete veto authority. Congress already had this authority in certain areas. For example, pesticide and FTC regulations could be overturned within sixty days of issuance.

However, the legislative veto had many drawbacks. It gave special interests a second chance to defeat regulations.[11] Rules considered for veto would have been those that affected special interests. These would attract the most attention from powerful congressmen. Moreover, the constitutionality of the legislative veto was questioned. Every recent administration, both Democratic and Republican, has regarded the veto as unconstitutional, and the courts until 1983 had been split on how they have viewed the issue. In 1983, the Supreme Court decided against the constitutionality of the veto.

Judicial review was meant to shift the locus of decision making to the courts. Senator Dale Bumpers of Arkansas, in an amendment bearing his name, argued that the courts should examine regulations with greater care. Their role should not be limited to determining if regulations are arbitrary or within the bounds of the legal statute. They should be directed to make no initial presumption of the validity of the facts underlying agency decisions. Agencies then would have to show greater care in preparing a record in defense of their actions, and judges would have to learn more about the scientific and technical facts and the reasoning used in regulatory decisions.

The drawbacks to this proposal included the fact that judges do not ordinarily have the competence, the time, or the resources to examine agency decisions in detail.[12] From the perspective of the business community, the effects of such a change were uncertain. Increased judicial supervision could lead to greater delay, and in licensing decisions such delays could be very expensive. Judicial review also could result in expanded regulatory scope.

Given the difficulties agencies and courts have in carrying out and evaluating technical analyses, some critics have argued for special technical arrangements. B. Ackerman and associates, for instance, called for a board of technical advisers to act as experts for judges and agencies.[13] A. Kantrowitz called for a science court to decide the relevant facts in policy controversies.[14] However, there are numerous problems with these proposals. The questions of who will serve, how they will reach their results, how they will separate fact from value, and many other issues remain unsolved.[15]

Another structural reform that has been considered is sunset legislation. An agency would cease to exist unless Congress enacted legislation extending its life. Agencies would be reformed on a case-by-case basis as they came under congressional scrutiny. Congress, however, would have to have very specific criteria by which to judge the agencies. The problem with this approach is that there is nothing to guarantee that Congress would take its reform responsibilities seriously.[16] It might simply reenact the old program automatically after a routine and inadequate investigation, or it might arbitrarily eliminate programs subject to political controversy without rigorous examination of actual advantages and disadvantages.

According to Breyer, structural proposals miss the fact that regulatory defects are embedded in statutes and programs and that increased supervision alone cannot eliminate such defects unless the statutes and programs are changed.[17] Breyer calls for substantive changes, not structural changes. The Delaney Amendment, for example, requires that the FDA ban any suspected carcinogen without consideration for cost. The Clean Air Act similarly excludes cost-benefit considerations from many determinations. Breyer argues that increased supervisory authority by various institutions or institutional representatives only makes sense in the context of substantive statutory and programmatic changes.

Substantive changes that could be made include the use of cost-benefit analysis; the use of incentives, rather than directives; increased reliance on information disclosure; increased tailoring of regulations to fit industrial diversity; the use of regulatory mediation; and "one-stop" permitting. The advantages of these proposals may be substantial, but disadvantages persist, as the analysis that follows indicates.

Cost-Benefit Analysis

One method for dealing with the excessive costs of regulation is to require that agencies do cost-benefit analysis. The purpose is to subject them to quantitative constraints like those that apply in the private sector. After cost-benefit analysis, proposed actions can be ranked and compared and rational choices among the alternatives made. The advantages of using cost-benefit analysis are that

- marginal costs and benefits resulting from the actions can be ascertained.
- the point at which the added costs outweigh the added benefits can be computed.
- regulatory actions then can be based on alternatives that generate more benefits than costs.
- alternatives that generate more costs than benefits can be excluded.

At a general level, advocacy of cost-benefit approaches is noncontroversial, but ironing out the practical details can be very difficult.[18] For example, intangibles often are involved in cost-benefit calculations. A forest, for instance, cannot be valued simply in terms of the value of its timber. Estimating its beauty and its value as a wildlife habitat makes simple measurements of impacts impossible. Moreover, the worth of a human life is not objectively measurable. The measure often used by the courts in tort cases, loss of anticipated earnings, is inherently problematic. It suggests significantly different values based on people's education, professional achievement, and existing wealth and health.

Without reliable quantitative measures that apply to all the items in a cost-benefit analysis, agency decision makers are faced with difficult choices. Another operational difficulty in doing cost-benefit analyses is choosing an appropriate discount rate. The impact of a proposed regulation usually extends beyond the present moment. Future costs and benefits are worth less than present costs and benefits, but by how much?

The purpose of cost-benefit analysis is to get administrators to use methods that more accurately and explicitly assess the risks and advantages of decisions. Nonetheless, problems in comparing costs and benefits are significant. Conflicts may exist between jobs and money on the one side and safety and environmental protection on the other. For a company, costs of compliance can approach hundreds of millions of dollars and might add to already high inflationary costs. Closing a facility would mean the loss of jobs, the end to corporate tax payments, and the elimination of company purchases of goods and services in a community. Sometimes spending the money for cleanup or closing a facility are the only alternatives. If the company does not comply, its actions may cause higher rates of death or injury to persons in the community. There is no simple way to compare in monetary terms the costs to society of non-compliance with the benefits of jobs saved and an economy maintained, as there is no good way to compare jobs and income with loss of human life and other forms of damage.

Cost-benefit calculations suffer from serious methodological uncertainties: (1) the causal relationship between a particular chemical—arsenic or saccharin, for instance—and human disease is often uncertain; (2) moreover, the synergistic effect of many chemicals and pollutants working at once against the human body's defenses is not known; (3) in addition, if a product is banned or a factory goes out of business, what is to assure that what replaces the banned product or closed factory will be more benign? Efforts to do cost-benefit analysis reveal the complexities of new social regulatory issues. For example, another issue when computing costs is whether industries, which have a vested interest in exaggerating costs, take into account the learning curve, the fact that costs of compliance may go down after industries have become accustomed to new pollution control practices.

Incentives Rather Than Directives

Another argument is that the new social regulation is problematic, not because of its ends, but because of its means. Its goals are correct, but the methods of reaching these goals result in excessive costs. Economist Charles Schultze, for example, has argued that the government can interfere in private market activities to achieve regulatory objectives in two ways: by grafting a "specific command-and-control module" onto the system of private enterprise, and by modifying "the information flow, institutional structure, and incentive pattern" of the private system. The first manner of control he calls direct regulation; the second, he refers to as the use of incentives. According to Schultze, the use of incentives to achieve regulatory objectives has the following advantages: minimization of coercion and emotional appeals to obtain compliance; reduction in the need to obtain hard-to-get information from companies; flexibility of company response to changing economic circumstances; increased production efficiency; and the ability to direct innovation into socially desirable directions.[19]

Under incentive schemes, society may decide how much damage pollution causes and how much pollution it will allow, and then let market mechanisms—the hidden hand of the price system rather than the heavy hand of government regulation—provide signals that will induce desired industry behavior. Let us take the example of a smelter in Tacoma, Washington. The market, if all pollution costs were taken into account, might dictate its closing. The factory is old and inefficient, and the demand for copper weak. The social costs of its production in a densely populated urban area are very high. If these "externalities" are "internalized," the smelter, influenced by market forces, might be forced to shut down. The hidden hand of the price system and not the heavy hand of government regulation would provide signals that would induce a change in industry behavior. There would be immense local disruption, and high costs to the area and to groups of individuals, but shutting down the smelter through market incentives would promote overall social welfare.

The market is designed to guarantee overall welfare, such as efficiency, increases in growth, or productivity, but it lacks mechanisms that pay attention to the plight of individuals or communities. Direct regulation may tend to perpetuate stable social patterns, however inefficient the present distribution may be.[20] To prevent the full unleashing of market forces, it may protect unprofitable corporate undertakings even when their survival threatens overall welfare. Regulation provides for due process before changes are made and for ample opportunity for bargaining and appeal. The hypothetical Tacoma smelter, like the case of Reserve Mining under direct regulation, has the right to use the legal system for the purposes of gaining a just hearing. It has, in effect, the right to delay.

Using incentives in this way as opposed to the legal system to change corporate behavior is equivalent to saying that any company that introduced risks into society would be taxed. The tax essentially would pay for medical care and compensate for other losses incurred. For example, manufacturers of cigarettes would have to pay an increased tax per cigarette, which would be enough to pay for the social costs of cigarette smoking (hospital costs, fire hazards, reduced working time). Other taxes—five cents per bottle of diet soda—might be imposed, and would have to be accompanied by a tax of five cents on other sodas as well to prevent people from switching to sugar-based soda.

The issue in question is how high these taxes should be, and the answer in some cases might depend on how much a human life is worth. How difficult it is to make this determination already has been indicated. The critics of direct regulation argue that, whether risks are explicitly quantified or not, decisions about such risks occur and are necessary. Individuals make these decisions and politicians make them for citizens on a larger scale. On one level, the critics admit that life is priceless, death is final, that these issues of life and death and ultimate meaning are beyond the reach of law and government. On a different level, they hold that society must affix a value to these matters and does so all the time: for additional millions of dollars any high-risk industrial activity could be made accident-proof and environmentally harmless. However, in a difficult balance, society decides how much safety and environmental protection it can or cannot afford.

Information Disclosure

A related criticism of the new regulation is that government has assumed an overly paternalistic role and has denied individuals free choice. Some critics, such as George Stigler, find traces of authoritarianism in regulatory command and control.[21] Ronald Reagan has made this point: "I believe that government's principal function is to protect us from each other, not from ourselves. We get into dangerous ground when we allow government to decide what is good for us."[22] Rather than establishing and enforcing specific standards, an alternative is for the government to facilitate informed individual choice. Cigarette consumption is an example. Warning labels have been put on cigarette packages. A similar approach with respect to auto-mobile safety might mean that the government would require air bags as an optional feature, but not as a mandatory one, and that it would provide information relevant to the choice about whether to purchase this feature.

The appeal of such an approach is that it flows naturally from the ethos that emphasizes individual freedom. It fits the free market model, since Adam Smith argues that the government role should be minimal and that an effec-tive market requires substantial knowledge on the part of consumers. It also dovetails with fear of overly centralized power. Government no longer has to make decisions for the public and define its best interest.

However, there are fundamental problems with this approach. A basic question is how far, even assuming the availability of considerable informa-tion, one is willing to go with the notion that free choice is paramount. Another problem is the diffficulty of communicating accurately and yet with appropriate power the possible effects of using a particular product or service. The consequences of the fact that a substance has been found to cause some disease in animal experiments may be difficult to translate to the general public. Moreover, the type of technical jargon that must be used to convey accurately what scientists have found may not be conducive to public understanding. Accordingly, conveying information, and conveying it accurately, is no minor task.

Another problem is that few choices are purely individual ones. Most arise in a social context. Thus, Reagan has urged that any motorcycle rider should have the privilege of not using a helmet.[23] However, the rider will need public ambulances and police assistance if he or she is involved in an accident. The accident will probably affect the speed and movement of other vehicles. The person, if injured seriously, will have to rely heavily on relatives, become a ward of the state, or use large amounts of insurance benefits.

A final, and by no means insignificant, concern is determining the best interest of those who are not yet in a position to exercise independent judgment: for example, children. The purchase of cigarettes by parents is probably related to adolescent and preadolescent use and growing habituation to cigarettes. To take another example, with respect to using a safety belt, it is unclear how much authority a child should have in making this decision.

Tailoring Government Responses to Industrial Diversity

One reason for the perception of high regulatory costs is that regulations often apply uniformly to firms of different size with different technologies. EPA is an example of an agency that has used industry-specific and size-related regulations. The agency has taken into account the number of em-ployees and has used types of production processes as an indicator of the type of regulation needed. It also has looked at the economic impact of proposed regulations, and has considered such factors as compliance data and record-keeping requirements in setting permissible levels from different sources.

Uniform across-the-board procedural and substantive requirements often exact a heavier toll on small companies than on large ones. In fact, some studies have indicated that costs of compliance can run seven to ten times higher for smaller businesses than for large ones.[24] The unintended side effect is reduced competition. When small businesses constitute a large portion of the overall problem, the government may tailor its response to the diverse situations of the small firms. Achievement of the regulatory goal may require individual treatment rather than inflexible general rules.

Accordingly, the basic considerations in tailoring a response to a specific firm may be (1) the total costs of uniform compliance, and (2) the relative share of the problem caused by different sized entities. Specifically, there needs to be some determination of what qualifies as a small firm and what firms should be less regulated. Relevant considerations in this regard include the number of employees, market share, and assets. An additional factor affecting the feasibility of tailored responses is the magnitude of anticipated harm. If this harm is potentially great, laxness toward smaller entities is neither possible nor justified.

Regulatory Mediation

Disillusionment with the regulatory process is associated with overreliance on costly and time-consuming litigation as a means of dispute resolution. As indicated, opposing interests perceive of themselves as adversaries, prepare to litigate almost from the outset, and therefore fail to provide input or reach consensus during the stage of promulgation. The current system is topsy-turvy; the type of debate and resolution that occurs at the end of the process should be occurring at an earlier phase. Regulatory mediation essentially facilitates consensus building at an earlier stage through the establishment of forums composed of representatives from various constituencies. (The Coal Policy Project described in chapter 8 is an example of this approach.) The mediator is a pivotal actor in a consensus-building process. The expense, delay, confusion, and regulatory burdens that result from a litigation-oriented solution are reduced.

However, there remain significant problems with regulatory mediation. First, the discussants must be genuinely representative of the major affected interests; otherwise any agreements they reach will have limited impact. Also, all major interests must be represented, or again the decision will be of limited binding force. Furthermore, mechanisms of effective negotiation have to be ironed out for each case, as there are no fail-safe negotiating principles.

One-Stop Permitting

Often, especially with respect to land use and environmental issues, the applicant for permits can become entangled in a web of agencies with overlapping and largely uncoordinated responsibilities. As a result, work is duplicated and complete information is not obtained by any of the administering bodies. For example, an applicant in California may have to deal with, among other agencies, the State Resources Board, the Air Resources Board, and the California Coastal Commission. Most projects will encounter permit requirements from local, state, and federal governments.

In addition to being bothersome, these duplications in permitting requirements can be time-consuming and costly. The maze of administering agencies presents problems for both decision makers and applicants. For decision makers, there are overlaps, as well as gray areas of uncertain authority. There is also in some instances a rather patchwork division of labor. For the applicant, it is confusing to face this divided authority. It may also cause unnecessary expense in terms of paperwork and procedural requirements.

These problems present strong reasons for the coordination of permitting requirements. Coordinated permitting means, at the minimum, some central authority to identify required permits and coordinate application forms. It also may involve the use of a master application. A single administering agency would then have the burden of distributing information to other concerned agencies.[25] The other agencies might, if necessary, require additional information from the applicant. (This information would be put in appendices in the master application.)

The process could involve the use of a joint hearing examiner. The examiner would administer the coordinated hearing process. One person would be ultimately responsible for maintaining the permit register, processing the master applications, sending them to appropriate permitting agencies, and scheduling hearings. A time requirement for agency decision making might be set up to provide for some generally applicable deadlines. The deadlines would expedite processing, with resulting savings to industry and government.

The government gains from this system a central repository of information and increased coordination. The applicant probably saves time, money, and paperwork. President Carter suggested this approach when he called for the creation of an Energy Mobilization Board (see chapter 4). To varying extents, and in different combinations, the one-stop permit has been tried in such locations as Dade County, Florida, Fairfax County, Virginia, and Los Angeles. In many areas, the verdict is still out; it is not clear whether the system is effective, whether it facilitates and hastens decision making, or whether it adds further complications and contributes to delay. One problem has been arriving at agreement among agencies, which may differ in their missions and in their perceived constituencies. There also has been difficulty in insuring that master applications suit the needs of various agencies without being extremely cumbersome.

EXECUTIVE ORDERS FOR COST-BENEFIT ANALYSIS

Substantive changes that have been carried out include executive orders issued by the White House requiring the use of cost-benefit analysis, and EPA reform initiatives that replace direct regulation with the use of incentives. The slow and gradual process by which these reforms have been implemented demonstrates some of the difficulties in reforming the new regulation.

Trade associations and firms have challenged the government to show that net benefits of regulations exceed net costs. The White House, in addition, has understood that the president's overall popularity depends on economic indicators such as inflation and employment (the "misery" index). Presidents Nixon, Ford, Carter, and Reagan therefore established cost reduction as a major regulatory objective.[26] They issued executive orders that required agencies to establish programs for cost-benefit analysis. President Ford's 1974 executive order required that "major" proposals be accompanied by an inflationary impact evaluation. Costs to consumers and businesses, effects on productivity, and effects on competition had to be considered. The Council on Wage and Price Stability (COWPS), which had a major role in administering the program, interpreted this requirement to mean cost-benefit analysis. The program ran through 1976 and was extended by President Carter in 1977 under the title "Economic Impact Statement Program."

It was generally conceded that the effects of the Ford program were disappointing.[27] Generally, in the analyses that were done more attention was given to costs than to benefits and little attention was paid to alternatives. Costs were often computed in a casual manner. There were no uniform rules for evaluating intangibles, assessing risk, or establishing a discount rate. The term *major*, which triggered an inflation analysis, was never systematically defined. The analyses were often done by outside consultants who had little impact on agency actions. OSHA, which had virtually no internal economic staff, contracted its work out to these private consultants. EPA had to develop a cadre of in-house economists to defend itself against charges that its regulations were costly and inefficient, but this cadre of economists was separate from the program offices that developed the regulations and had only marginal impact. Nonetheless, one of the main effects of the Ford program was to strengthen the position of economists within agencies. Substantive changes were less significant. Independent commissions did not comply with the requirement that they prepare regulatory analyses, and the Council on Wage and Price Stability, whose recommendations were advisory, had little overall power or authority. Its influence depended on its ability to persuade through reasoned argument.

In response to these problems, President Carter in 1978 established the Regulatory Analysis Review Group (RARG). The group was composed of representatives from the major executive branch agencies and was chaired by the Council of Economic Advisers. The President's 1977 executive order called for a semi-annual agenda of "significant" regulations under development or review by all agencies and the preparation of cost-benefit analyses. COWPS continued to provide staff support in doing regulatory analyses and in reviewing analyses done by the agencies. Significant regulations were defined as those resulting in an annual effect on the economy of $100 million or more. A separate Regulatory Council, composed of major department and agency heads and chaired by the EPA administrator, prepared the regulatory agenda and promoted the use of cost-effective and other innovative analytical techniques.

The analyses done under Carter's plan had to include the economic consequences of alternatives rather than just cost impact. Each analysis had to contain a succinct statement of the problem, a description of the major alternatives considered by the agency, an analysis of the economic consequences of these alternatives, and an explanation of why an alternative was chosen over others. Agencies that participated were supposed to examine costs and benefits of alternatives and choose cost-effective solutions whenever possible. Agency heads were supposed to monitor the process and remand or remove flawed or unnecessary proposals before they emerged publicly. One of the purposes of Carter's plan was to get the agency administrators more involved in regulatory oversight.

RARG was to review and comment on about ten or twenty analyses which were prepared by the agencies each year. However, the regulatory analysis requirement was only partially implemented. Between 1978 and 1981, 109 regulatory analyses were prepared by executive agencies, but only 19 were reviewed by RARG. OMB sponsored a conference and worked closely with some of the agencies to improve the quantity and quality of their analyses.[28] Some agencies completed numerous regulatory analyses, but others, particularly the independent commissions, were less willing to comply, as it was doubtful whether they were legally required to do so.

Some agencies, such as OSHA, began to consider costs more frequently in regulatory determinations. However, OSHA's discussion of benefits often consisted of an enumeration of reasons why it was difficult to estimate benefits. Moreover, agency heads had trouble monitoring the details of emerging regulations. Because they had to defend the legitimacy of the agency's actions and support its mission, they also often had little interest in balanced evaluations. They tended to agree with the career officials and were reluctant to challenge their findings. The analytical work, therefore, was often devoted to arguing in favor of the options that the agency intended to adopt and not to a balanced assessment of the alternatives.

RARG review covered a broad range of topics and strained the technical expertise of the relatively small (five to six member) staff assembled for the task.[29] The staff was rarely able to collect original data, prepare position papers, or write formal reports in the limited time available. Moreover, RARG staff could not challenge the statutes, but had to decide how to develop the "best" regulations given the constraints in the statutes.

In some cases, RARG reports were rejected by the agencies, especially when they asked agencies to rethink their positions. For example, the Building Energy Performance Standards were attacked by RARG. It asked that Congress postpone the date of final promulgation and undertake a comprehensive reassessment of the desirability of the program. The assistant secretary for Conservation and Solar Energy questioned the RARG report and complained that it had gone beyond the scope of its authority. However, not all RARG reports resulted in such controversy. Some supported standards that were stricter than agency standards (the acrylonitrile standard, for example); some were positive and supportive of agency efforts to use cost-benefit techniques; some reports were pedagogical, attempting to instruct agency personnel in the use of these techniques; and some agencies willingly changed requirements or proposed different standards because of RARG review. The overall effect, nonetheless, was regulatory delay. More comprehensive and careful documentation and lengthening of both preparation times and intervals between proposal and final promulgation slackened the pace for adoption of new requirements.[30]

The Reagan program began in 1981 when the president established a Task Force on Regulatory Relief with Vice President Bush as chairman. The purpose was to have OMB review all major regulatory proposals and assess existing regulations. Reagan's executive order attempted to centralize review of all major regulations in the Executive Office of the President.[31] It took power away from agency heads and established new rules for decision making: (1) decisions had to be based on adequate information concerning the need for and consequence of the action; and (2) the alternative invoking the least net cost to society had to be chosen. Agencies were to describe the potential benefits and costs of a proposed rule, including specific benefits and costs that could not be quantified in monetary terms; and they had to identify principal winners and losers from each rule. They were to describe alternative approaches that could achieve the same goal at less cost and explain why such alternatives had not been adopted.

Reagan's executive order was more specific about the kind of information that had to be contained in a regulatory analysis. Unlike the Carter order, it explicitly required a simple cost-benefit test.[32] While Carter shifted working control of the analyses from program offices to agency heads, Reagan shifted oversight from agency heads to the Office of Management and Budget—an external reviewer that historically had been suspicious of regulation. OMB had more influence under Reagan, but it still did not have the formal power to overturn a regulation because of a regulatory analysis.

It is significant that OMB under Reagan received substantially more regulatory analyses to review than the White House did under Carter. In the first half of 1981 alone, OMB received over 800 regulations to review and sent over 50 regulations back to the agencies because they violated the president's executive order.[33] In that year OMB intended, with a relatively small staff, to review an additional 100 regulations.[34] It estimated that the savings would be $15.5 to $18 billion on a one-time basis, or approximately $6 billion annually.[35] Whatever the actual savings, the new controls—in combination with budget cuts and the president's regulatory appointments—slowed the pace of rulemaking. They officially diverted the path and extended the total number of days needed for promulgation. The average monthly number of proposed and final rules, accordingly, declined significantly.[36]

The implementation of the Reagan reforms can be attributed to the gradual building of economic capabilities in the White House and in the agencies during the course of three administrations.[37] Key staff in the Council on Wage and Price Stability and in other White House offices became experienced with cost-benefit analysis. As Eads comments, "The Reagan initiatives are . . . a logical but significant extension of the process of experimentation" begun earlier and carried on by the president's predecessors.[38] "The form this experimentation has taken in each administration reflects each president's character, his views about the value of regulation, and his attitudes toward the regulatory bureaucracy."[39] The cost-benefit reforms initiated by the presidents did not begin suddenly, have a major impact, and then dissipate. They evolved slowly and matured gradually. Each successive executive order was more specific and explicit in stating objectives and establishing procedures. Each built on the experience of the last.

The White House efforts to apply cost-benefit analysis, however, were attacked in the courts. The Supreme Court decided in 1981 in the cotton dust case that cost-benefit analysis by OSHA "is not required by the Act, because feasibility analysis is."[40] According to the Court, if Congress had intended cost-benefit analysis to be performed it would have been clearly indicated in the original 1970 clean air statute. Instead, this statute explicitly required criteria related to "technological and economic feasibility."[41] The Court decided that "technological and economic feasibility" meant that industry as a whole had to have the ability to comply, but that some marginal companies might have to go out of business. It also decided that OSHA could be technology-forcing. This decision was a setback for the White House and for the twelve cotton textile manufacturers and the American Textile Manufacturers Institute, who contended that OSHA had to show a "reasonable relationship" between risk reduction and costs.

EPA INITIATIVES

Most economists, as indicated, have advocated replacing direct regulation with incentives.[42] In 1978, the Environmental Protection Agency announced a regulatory reform program to replace regulations with alternative strategies that make use of economic incentives.[43] Partially under authority granted to it by the 1977 Clean Air Amendments and partially in response to initiatives taken by its administrator, Douglas Costle, the agency began a series of experiments in regulatory reform. The experiments tried to "use elements of the private market, and not the government, to allocate the costs to society of controlling pollution."[44] The purpose, in Costle's words, was to unite "the equity of public administration with the efficiency of private enterprise."[45]

However, EPA only partially converted the idea advocated by economists to action. Putting an idea such as the use of economic incentives into action requires taking concepts—rational abstractions offered by academic experts —and building them into programs so that they are part of government's ongoing activities. Between the creation of the idea and the realization of its practical significance lie distinct stages, such as awareness and interest, and testing and evaluation. The stages have hurdles. They function as checkpoints or gatekeepers that stand between the idea and its realization. At each stage, the idea must prove compatibility with the existing program and situation; technical superiority; and political feasibility.[46] Compatibility refers to the "goodness of fit" between the idea and the existing program and situation; technical superiority refers to the relative advantage the idea appears to have over other ideas and the status quo; and political feasibility refers to the political support the idea receives from relevant participants. If the idea does not prove its compatibility, technical superiority, and political feasibility, it will be altered or rejected. If it is authorized, it will be authorized with the expectation that the commitment made to it can be retracted. It may be divided into numerous units, and many scaled-down versions may be tested and evaluated.[47] If change occurs, it will be partial. Part of the idea will be accommodated in a reduced and administratively tested form.

At the EPA, only a scaled-down version of the incentives notion survived. Versions of the idea that were more compatible with existing programs, technically acceptable, and politically feasible, rather than the pure concept, emerged. In the remaining sections of this chapter, some of the schemes economists proposed for reducing pollution, some of the notions actually carried out by EPA, and some of the reasons EPA reforms overcame resistance to change are discussed.

The Economists' Schemes

Economists maintained that air pollution regulations were not cost-effective: that is, they abated pollution at higher costs than were necessary.[48] For example, most states regulated the steel industry and the paper industry similarly despite evidence that marginal cleanup costs were higher in the steel industry than in the paper industry. Additionally, the states treated major steel industry processes uniformly in spite of widely varying marginal cleanup costs across different industries and processes. As a result, society was paying more for a given amount of pollution reduction than was required.

To overcome such added costs, economists advocated a number of different incentive schemes. Effluent charges were generally considered to be the optimal method.[49] The underlying logic—the "pollutor pays" principle, was simple and compelling.[50] The government would determine the damage caused by different emissions and the pollutor would pay for the damage. However, the damage function was difficult to determine. The exact harm caused by pollution could not be determined in the precise quantitative terms needed. Therefore, the economist J. H. Dales advocated setting up markets in pollution rights.[51] The government would set an upper limit to the amount of pollution that the environment of a particular region could absorb, and would then issue pollution rights, or licenses, based on this limit, and put them up for sale, requiring anyone that discharged in the area to hold these rights. The rights would command a positive price and a continuous market would develop in response to competition among buyers and sellers.

Cooperatives, less frequently mentioned in the economic literature than effluent charges or marketable permits, were an extension of the idea of treating a number of pollution sources as one source and setting a single limit for each pollutant from this source. Doing so would encourage pollutors to devise ways to meet standards so as to minimize the cost of abatement. Successful cooperatives were operating in the Ruhr River valley of Germany, where the government established area-wide pollution control goals and companies cooperated to allocate pollution control burdens to reduce total costs. The cooperative idea was very attractive. Potential savings from setting up a cooperative in the Chicago area, according to an EPA study, were on the order of 80 percent.[52]

Technical Problems

Technical problems, overlooked by the economists who wrote about the advantages of incentives, prevented implementation of the economists' proposals. The technical problems are summarized below.

Monitoring. Although a pricing scheme abolishes the need to establish specific emissions standards, it does not eliminate the need for monitoring emissions. The task of keeping track of the discharges from a multitude of factories and government operations is still very complicated.[53]

Assigning prices to pollution damage. To achieve economic efficiency under the pollution charge scheme, an administrative body would have to determine the dollar value of all pollution harms. Assessing these harms is extremely difficult, if not impossible.[54] The scientific information that connects a given level of pollution to specific health effects is too imprecise.

Achieving quality goals. If the fees are determined not as a means of internalizing precisely calculated damages, but rather as a means of achieving a fixed standard, pricing schemes suffer from another problem. Theoretically, the schedule of fees can be adjusted upward or downward to achieve any level of quality, but the connection between the fees and achievement of a specific quality level is uncertain.

Allocating permits. If permits are given to existing firms, they would possess a windfall which might discourage entry of new competitors. On the other hand, auctioning them might entail large payments by firms to continue existing production.

Policing the market. If a market for permits developed, states would have to review sales for ambient effects, assure that the same permits were sold only once, and carry out smooth permit transfers without cumbersome and prohibitive transfer procedures. The administrative burden on state agencies was likely to be great.

Legal and constitutional issues. The legality of the government's selling rights to private users on a basis other than cost to the government has not been determined.

Designing equivalency for permits. In protecting the public welfare, it is necessary to insure that the trading of permits between different forms of pollutants are equivalent. The effects of emissions of different pollutants and of air pollutants in different locations of the country, however, is not the same. In addition, the detrimental effects of emissions may not be at a constant level over time.

Equity. In an open market, small businesses, given the potential for large business to monopolize the trading of permits, may be at a disadvantage. An effluent charge or marketable permit scheme can harm small firms which are not able to bid against large businesses for the right to acquire permits.

Inducing firms to participate. This may be the most difficult obstacle with cooperatives. While it may be in the collective interest for all firms to participate, each firm may stand to gain a particular advantage if it refuses to join. If a firm's costs of control are lower than those of its competitors, then the firm may want to legitimize the existing regulatory scheme and not a cooperative alternative to gain competitive advantage. Firms may wish to join and exclude other potential cooperative members because such exclusion would result in competitive advantage.

Administration and operation. There are likely to be enforcement problems if the cooperatives do not achieve required pollution reductions in a timely manner. Who should be held responsible—the individual firms that do not accomplish their particular goal or the cooperative as a whole?

Financial arrangements. How would the expected savings from cooperative arrangements be allocated among the members? Is the company that has to change its processes or install new pollution control equipment to be rewarded for the hassle it has to endure? Or should this company be expected to contribute extra funds to the common treasury because it has had the opportunity to modernize its plant and equipment at the expense of the cooperative?

Thus, although economists urged the use of economic incentives because of increased efficiency, the economist's prescription was theoretical and suffered because it lacked concrete solutions to implementation problems. Without demonstration that one system was technically superior to another, proponents of change could not convincingly argue for a radical departure from the status quo.

Political Problems

Given these technical problems, it was not surprising that the idea of using economic incentives received only lukewarm support and sporadic attention from the relevant political entities, including business, Congress, environmentalists, the EPA, and the White House.

Business. The business community was ambivalent about the idea of using economic incentives to control pollution.[55] On the one hand, the idea fit well into the rhetoric of business pronouncements. The notion that business should be allowed to decide, that it knows best, was appealing. On the other hand, when actual proposals to use economic incentives surfaced, parts of the business community vigorously opposed their use. They had a stake in the existing system and did not want to see changes that might alter the status quo.[56]

How can the reaction of the business community be understood? Michael Levin argues that incentives increased industry uncertainty: "current problems were minor annoyances compared to the investments needed to learn a wholly new system."[57] Steven Kelman, in interviews with policy participants, found that trade association people were not only among the most critical toward effluent charges, but "also, as a group, the least informed about charges."[58] They had fewer sources of information about policy alternatives, and were more likely to be concerned about the stringency of a particular requirement affecting their industry.

Together, these circumstances suggest a picture of trade association lobbyists in a defensive posture, not so concerned with new ideas or policy alternatives as with warding off encroachments, and too dependent on member firms to take policy initiatives in these areas. Indeed, a number of industry respondents stated as much—that industry mainly tended to react to the proposals of others. They didn't think up new proposals themselves (and they probably wished that others wouldn't either).[59]

According to Kelman, many industry respondents viewed charges as "just another tax" that the state could use for the purpose of generating revenue.[60] Those who supported the charges proposal (the Chamber of Commerce, for example) did so for ideological reasons without understanding its practical implications.

Congress. In opposing the use of economic incentives, the business community had an unusual ally—Congress. Senators William Proxmire (Democrat, Wisconsin) and Gary Hart (Democrat, Colorado) were the leading spokespersons within Congress for a system of effluent charges. However, until 1980 Senator Edmund Muskie (Democrat, Maine) and Representative Henry Waxman (Democrat, California) held vital positions as chairmen of the Senate and House pollution control subcommittees, and opposed any change in the existing system. One of their main concerns was that the adoption of incentives schemes would be interpreted as a failure of programs they helped author.[61]

In interviews with congressional staff, Kelman discovered that ideological issues were very important in explaining congressional opposition and that the efficiency argument made little impression.[62] Democratic staffers were hostile to effluent charges, and Republican staffers endorsed them, but the main reasons of both groups were ideological ("less bureaucracy," "use of the market," "appeals to self-interest").[63] Democrats were worried about "giving pollutors a right to pollute" and the political difficulties of setting the charges high enough given declining support for the environment; while Republican staffers were concerned about various technical details.[64] The key Muskie staff person, Leon Billings, commented, "There is a basic philosophical difference between regulatory people and economists. Economists don't really care whether you achieve a reduction in pollution, but we really care."[65] The key staff person for the House subcommittee commented that health "is a moral issue, and I'm afraid of putting the fox in charge of the chicken coop by leaving this to the judgment of the private sector."[66] According to Kelman, Senator Hart endorsed the charges proposal for ideological, not efficiency, reasons.[67] According to Hart's aides, charges were a way "to have your environmental cake" and to still be able to respond to "concerns about government interference."[68]

Environmentalists. Giving business the ability to pay for pollution, in the eyes of many environmentalists, was akin to giving it a "license to pollute."[69] Environmentalists feared that changing a system of direct regulation, which incorporated many of their goals and values, for an incentives system might lead to less pollution reduction. Levin holds that environmental groups supported the Clean Air Act not just to clean the air, "but to punish."[70] In Kelman's interviews, concern about the need to stigmatize pollutors surfaced.[71] A full 76 percent of the respondents had "a basically positive attitude toward use of the word 'criminal'" to describe polluting industries.[72] According to many of the respondents, the use of charges rather than standards would do away with the social statement that pollution was "wrong." In addition, it would open the situation for the "rich" to pay their fines, while the "poor" suffered.[73]

However, Kelman also found substantial knowledge about, and support for, incentives among the environmentalists.[74] Over 30 percent were familiar with the efficiency arguments, in comparison with 0 percent among industrial respondents and 10 percent among congressional staffers.[75] He explains this support as generational.[76] Many people came into the environmental movement as a result of their 1960s' political concerns. It was a natural evolution for those who had been involved in the civil rights and anti-draft movements. These people were critical of many aspects of society, including the government, and therefore were willing to consider reliance on self-interest rather than government intervention.

The EPA. Agency officals were divided in their attitudes about the use of economic incentives. Organizationally, the agency had a policy planning office, an enforcement office, a number of program offices, and a research office.[77] Professionally, it was composed of economists, lawyers, scientists, and engineers. Career-wise, it has contained appointed officials and permanent civil servants. The idea of using incentives received some support from the policy planning office, from the economists in the agency, and from some of the appointed officials, particularly the former administrator, Douglas Costle, and the former assistant administrator for planning, William Drayton. However, support and interest from these quarters were tempered by opposition from program managers and career bureaucrats and by inevitable preoccupations with shorter-term problems. Opposition to the incentives idea came from the program offices, from lawyers with a penchant for enforcement, and from career civil servants closely identified with specific programs.

The White House. On the surface, the Carter White House was a forceful and ardent proponent of regulatory reform, but underneath the symbolic demonstrations of White House support there was a lack of substantive backing for the economic incentive idea. There were at least three relevant entities in the Carter White House: the Council of Economic Advisers (CEA), the Council on Environmental Quality (CEQ), and the Office of Management and Budget (OMB). CEA favored the introduction of incentives because of pollution control impacts on macroeconomic matters like inflation and productivity, but CEA was small organizationally and was preoccupied with managing larger economic issues. It was not in a position where it could implement a regulatory reform scheme. CEQ also favored the notion of incentives, but CEQ was not influential with the president and had little operational authority. OMB was the White House office that had the programmatic authority for regulatory reform. However, OMB tended to stress reducing red tape and paperwork requirements as much as substantive reforms such as economic incentives. Thus, within the White House there was no solid backer of the proposal.

Proposals Carried out by EPA

The proposals put into practice by EPA were not the effluent charges, markets, or cooperative mechanisms, but reforms known as *bubbles, netting, offsets, emissions banking,* and *non-compliance penalties.*[78] These schemes, developed by government officials, differed substantially from what had been promoted by the economists. They were developed by officials in the course of carrying out their specific administrative responsibilities, not by economists in the course of theorizing about the optimal method of abatement.

Under the *bubble* policy, firms could construct an imaginary bubble over two or more existing sources and adjust the emissions between sources as long as total emissions were the same. "Stack by stack" rules were replaced with a single limit that applied to a whole industrial complex. By operating under the imaginary bubble, plant engineers had the flexibility to find the most cost-effective mix of pollution controls.

Netting involved the use of a bubble when a plant was undergoing modifications. The plant could avoid having to install the best available control technology or having to achieve the lowest available emission rate, if it could demonstrate that there would be no significant increase in overall plantwide emissions from the alteration.

Offsets were designed to allow industrial growth in areas that had not attained national ambient air quality standards (the so-called nonattainment areas). New sources in these areas had to meet stringent technological standards and had to achieve an overall reduction in emissions. They could do so by offsetting their emissions with reduced emissions from another source that the same or a different company owned in the area. Credits for reduced amounts of air pollution then could be *banked* and *traded*. EPA imagined that government or private industry would operate a clearinghouse for the buying and selling of emissions reduction credits. The system would include a register of such credits and a set of rules governing their use or sale.

The final scheme, *non-compliance penalties*, was also the work of EPA officials trying to achieve a feasible solution to an immediate problem.[79] The problem was non-achievement of air quality goals because of non-compliance by regulated industries, particularly industries that made the largest contributions to the total amount of air pollution emitted. The economic theory that justified the use of economic incentives, however, did not justify the use of non-compliance penalties. Penalties maximized goal achievement, not overall efficiency.

The author analyzed EPA's reform initiatives in the spring of 1979 and discussed them with thirteen EPA officials in Washington, D.C.[80] EPA officials admitted that the reform efforts lacked coherence. The pieces were "looking for a structure." They had not reached a "critical mass" in regard to their development. Commitment to them was only provisional. It could be retracted if further analysis and practice demonstrated that the reforms were not worth pursuing. Bubbles showed the most promise. Indeed, as of January 1, 1983, EPA had approved 33 bubbles, saving their users more than $120 million over the cost of conventional pollution controls.[81] Another 100 bubbles, averaging over $2 million each in savings, were under review at the state or federal level.[82]

Other EPA reform initiatives were not as successfully carried out, and encountered White House resistance. Anne Burford, the agency's first administrator during the Reagan administration, believed that regulatory reform meant reducing EPA's staff and budget and adopting a more solicitous attitude toward industry. These efforts did not emphasize the implementation of cost-effective alternatives. Moreover, despite all the attention paid to reform ideas, businesses on the whole were slow to adopt them. One reason for this was that suits brought by environmentalists limited their use. In *ASARCO v. EPA* and *NRDC v. Gorsuch*, the courts decided that netting could not be used to avoid the basic technology standard that was applicable to all new sources, and that it could not be used to avoid achieving the lowest achievable emission rate in nonattainment areas.[83]

Offsets were also limited, not by the courts, but by the business community, which failed to take advantage of them. Only a small percentage of offsets involved trades between firms. As of September 1981, 90 percent of the 1,500 documented cases had taken place within the same company.[84] EPA reported that more than half the inter-company offsets were state-generated.[85]

Although EPA promoted the banking concept by holding seminars throughout the country, only a few areas had approved banks (including Puget Sound in Washington; the San Francisco Bay area in California; Allegheny County in Pennsylvania; and the Louisville area in Kentucky). Oregon's banking and trading rules were approved in August 1982, but the formal banking program was slow in starting. Companies did not invest in pollution reductions so as to bank or trade the resulting emission credits. Credits banked were incidental by-products of innovations or plant closings. In short, legal and practical problems plagued EPA's reform program. Uncertainties and unresolved disputes prevented the wider adoption of offsets, netting, and banking.

Overcoming Resistance

Why did the bubble policy survive the process of testing and evaluation, while compatibility, technical, and political problems plagued the other proposals? The bureaucrats took the basic rationale—that more pollution reduction could be achieved for less expense by joint action—and applied it to actual program needs under the 1970 Clean Air Act.[86] The bubble policy succeeded because it fit in with existing pollution control programs that were based almost entirely on direct regulatory measures.

The existing air pollution law seemed to pose many barriers. For example, it was based on state implementation plans (SIPs). The plans had "short deadlines, backed by severe penalties, for SIP submittal and approval."[87] The Clean Air Act implied that any emission change had to be processed as a SIP change, with notice, comment, hearing, and review at both the state and federal levels.

However, the strategy that overcame resistance in the case of the bubble policy fit in well with the existing system.[88] According to Levin,

1. It offered concrete benefits to key participants, rather than relying on abstract efficiency claims.
2. It started small and grew as it overcame constraints and broadened its appeal.
3. It was marketed so that it would be easily understood and used.
4. It produced short-run successes for specific firms that others in industry tried to copy.
5. It was backed by organizational changes within EPA.
6. It built a constituency outside the agency.[89]

The bubble approach also had industry backing. It started during the Nixon administration, when smelters asked that their plants be treated as a single source. In 1978, EPA set up a task force to examine the legal and technical feasibility of this policy. The main impetus behind the task force was the financial difficulties of the steel industry. The steel industry was represented by Armco, Inc. Armco had the reputation in the EPA of being a "good actor." It did detailed studies of the engineering and economic benefits of setting up bubbles at its plants.

The EPA task force recommended that the bubble policy be adopted. However, it stated that bubbles could not allow air quality to deteriorate and that there had to be certain procedural safeguards, including the prohibition of trades between toxic and nontoxic pollutants and between stacks and vents. Numerous firms responded by saying that in principle the policy was a good idea but that the safeguards and other procedural constraints had to be lifted. Armco, in particular, argued that it had to be allowed to trade smokestack emissions for open dust in order to secure the requisite financial advantages.

EPA then formed a regulatory reform staff within the Office of Policy and Management.[90] The staff held numerous workshops and conferences with regional personnel, state officials, and industry representatives to explain the bubble concept. It made many speeches before trade associations, development groups, and air pollution professionals; developed documents, ranging from the elementary to the technical, to explain the policy; and cultivated key press and trade journal contacts. By 1980, many bubbles (forty) were being applied for, but industry still complained that the procedural "hoops" were too complex and the burden of proof too difficult.[91]

The regulatory reform staff convened a national conference to resolve this issue. Ultimately, in 1981, just before Reagan's nomination as the Republican presidential candidate, policy was liberalized and a new generic rule was adopted that decreased delays and increased industry certainty. After adoption of the generic rule, over ninety bubbles were under development.[92] They averaged $2 million in savings over conventional controls.[93] After much trial and error, the bubble policy was implemented more fully, but it won acceptance only after much effort had been expended to refine and explain it.

PRACTICAL PRESCRIPTIONS

For effluent charges, markets, cooperatives, and other incentive approaches to gain acceptance, a strategy is required. The strategy would have three objectives: to gain the support of critical political actors, to demonstrate technical superiority, and to plan an orderly transition.

Gain the support of critical political actors. Support for the idea of using economic incentives needs to be increased. Elements in the business community, the environmental community, Congress, the EPA, and the White House have favored its use, but other elements have opposed it. The idea needs an ardent advocate willing to build support for the notion by bringing together the disparate elements that favor it into a coherent coalition. If brought together, these elements would constitute a formidable power bloc. A coalition could be created if a single-minded zealot, a young and energetic policy entrepreneur—attached to Congress, the bureaucracy, the White House, an environmental group, or even business—could effectively promote the idea.[94] Ralph Nader, an independent critic working closely with and against various congressional committees, proved to be an effective publicizer of auto safety, pollution control, and many other issues. Stephen Breyer, a staff member of Senator Edward Kennedy's Administrative Practices Subcommittee, played a similar role with respect to airline deregulation (see chapter 7). George Gilder, Arthur Laffer, and others forged links with politicians such as Jack Kemp to gain acceptance for supply-side economics.

The policy entrepreneur, though, needs a forum for publicizing the idea. The congressional hearing, carefully planned to receive maximum publicity, may be an ideal place to focus attention on the issue. However, the chairmen of the Senate and House pollution control subcommittees do not welcome such hearings, because they have vested interests in the present system of direct regulation. The policy entrepreneur therefore might have to persuade other congressmen, whose committees have broad jurisdiction, to hold the hearings. The government operations committees of the Senate and House are possibilities. Another possibility is to persuade congressmen with energy concerns. However, the committee chairman who agreed to hold these hearings would have to bear the almost certain wrath of the existing pollution control subcommittee chairman, particularly if the planned hearings were critical of the current programs.

Demonstrate technical superiority. Before hearings were actually held, a popular book in muckraking style which avoids the jargon of economists would need to be written. This book would try to lay the foundations for hearings by demonstrating the unequivocal technical superiority of the idea. Demonstrating unequivocal technical superiority requires showing the failings of the current programs—the money wasted, the negative impact on the economy, and the breakdown in business-government relations. Then, to clinch the argument, the proponents of incentives need to vividly demonstrate the advantages of using the idea. Examples of effectively functioning incentive systems would be helpful. The contrast between inexpensive unregulated airline fares in the intrastate market and expensive regulated fares in the interstate market provided the advocates of airline deregulation with the symbolically significant evidence to support their case.[95] An effectively functioning charge of market scheme, which could be contrasted with the current system of ineffective direct regulation, is the kind of evidence that the advocates of incentives need.

Plan an orderly transition. The current system is entrenched, and dismantling it without caution could yield undesired setbacks in pollution control efforts. Charles Schultze believes that "market-like instruments can supplant current command-and-control techniques only gradually. But not much thought has been devoted to dynamic strategies that, step by step, mesh a dwindling reliance on regulations with a cautiously expanding use of market instruments."[96] Alfred Kahn used his powers as CAB commissioner to accomplish an orderly transition to airline deregulation. A figure with similar clout and convictions is needed to plan EPA's and other agencies' transition from direct regulation to incentives.

If political support could be mustered and convincing technical arguments made that would shift the burden of proof from the proponents of change to the opponents of change, then the conditions which breed incremental change might be reversed and a broad, redrafted Regulatory Experiments bill might be passed. Such a bill, carefully composed to mitigate environmental critics, would be essential for an orderly transition to a new system.

Reforming the new social regulation is not as clear-cut as reforming the old economic regulation because it deals with fundamentally difficult value conflicts centering around issues of assigning a value to damages and subjecting industry to reduced market opportunities.[97] The new social regulation often involves the allocation of scarce resources among competing ends in which fundamentally agonizing trade-offs have to be made. One good thing has to be sacrificed for another: the health of one group for the health of another (for example, Three Mile Island residents versus coal miners); and the jobs and prosperity of an area for the health and safety of its citizens (for example, the prosperity of smelter manufacturers versus the long-term health of local citizens). These issues involve tragic and unfair choices in which suffering of some kind for someone is inevitable.[98]

11 | Managing Regulation

The strategic approach, which has been developed in this book, signifies that managers need to be aware of the competitive and financial implications of proposed regulations. However, they also need to track and monitor government decision making and implementation. Companies need to establish a position for a liaison officer; make an effort to understand government agendas and participants; and build coalitions and exercise power through the granting of approval and legitimacy for some policies and the promotion of alternatives to other policies. They have to combine economic analysis with political action. To make political choices, managers need to be sophisticated about the regulatory politics. The intricacies of regulatory politics, however, defy simple theorizing. It is unwise to jump at every regulatory opportunity or to stall using every legal maneuver; careful evaluation of regulatory situations and settings is required. Factors that may be important are a firm's size, the extent of its regulatory problem, the policies of government officials, the attitudes of managers, and a company's expected growth and competitive position. Along with a knowledge of the political environment, this knowledge of strategic factors can improve regulatory management. In this chapter, some of the theoretical and practical implications for managers who must cope with the opportunities and constraints of regulation are discussed.

THE MANAGERIAL APPROACH

Corporations can manage and gain from regulation, as has been suggested. Firms can take advantage of entrepreneurial opportunities provided by regulatory problems. By manufacturing safety equipment or marketing expertise needed to solve regulation-induced dilemmas, they stand to profit from regulation.[1] They can recover raw materials from waste. The Dow Chemical Company, for instance, has reaped savings from pollution cleanup process changes that have resulted in recovery of chemicals from waste.

Moreover, firms can gain competitive advantage. Regulation may erect entry barriers to new competitors and new or competing technologies. A regulatory tax on oleomargarine, for example, once protected the dairy industry against competition from a substitute product.[2] As Leone has noted, "almost always some plants, companies, or geographic areas experience higher cost changes than do others because of regulation."[3] An example is water pollution controls in the metal finishing industry. Mandatory pollution control standards increase economies of scale by "at least a factor of five."[4] Increases in scale are barriers to entry that may favor large existing operators over small firms and new entrants.

Firms can receive direct subsidies from regulatory agencies. Mitnick provides the examples of the Federal Maritime Commission (FMC) and the old Atomic Energy Commission (AEC), which were given statutory authority to promote regulated industries "through direct subsidy, research and development services, or other means."[5] Firms may also benefit from price fixing.[6] Mitnick observes that "the ICC and CAB once rigidly regulated the rates charged by subject industries, thus both ensuring stability in the respective industries and, often, rate structures higher than the unregulated market would establish."[7]

Firms can cushion themselves from rapid social change, for "it is well known that free market economies are subject not merely to the greater or lesser periodic booms and busts of the various cycles of macro-economic activity, but also to sudden and total dislocation of a particular micro-sector as a result of shifts in technology and demand. The free market is, in a word, risky."[8] Regulation can also protect firms from legal challenge. As Leone comments, "Advances in epidemiology (the study of the causes and control of diseases in large populations) have made industry . . . vulnerable to legal action and possibly . . . costly class action suits."[9] Regulation, at the cost of some efficiency and some progressivity, may provide substantial benefits by protecting companies and citizens from both economic and legal risks they otherwise would have to bear.[10]

The Participants

The managerial approach focuses on the participants that gain and seek advantage from regulation.[11] Public interest activity may be analyzed from this perspective as well as business activity. The success of public interest groups often depends on what they can gain from regulation. The characteristics of the groups favoring reform—their size, funding, and incentives—

as well as their perceptions of the advantages and disadvantages of regulation are important.[12] As Mitnick points out, the managerial approach
emphasizes the following questions: (1) What are the characteristics (size,
structure, composition, resources) of the groups seeking advantage from
regulation? and (2) What are their strategic orientation, tactics, methods of
advocacy, and routes of access to government?[13]

While earlier theories emphasized outcomes favorable to businesses and
accused them of being "villains who capture or manipulate regulation," the
managerial approach developed in this book emphasizes the open-ended
character of regulatory outcomes (see chapter 2). It focuses on stages in the
policymaking cycle. As a policy moves from stage to stage, preferences
change, positions are altered, and outcomes vary.

Relevant questions at different stages include:

Formation

1. How do coalitions and broad movements for reform come into existence, and get
   issues on the public agenda?
2. How do businesses, public interest associations, and others influence government
   decision making?
3. How is legislation that is passed transformed into government programs?

Implementation

1. How do government officials interpret and administer these programs?
2. How do they respond to the pressures from external parties?
3. How do the programs impact the external groups and interests?

Evaluation

1. What coalitions form favoring or opposing regulatory innovation?
2. What obstacles hinder the institutionalization of such changes?
3. What actions can be taken to overcome these obstacles?

Formation

According to Wilson, free market economists and Marxists both believe
that the government regulates with the support of business.[14] The arguments
presented in this book, however, suggests a more complicated pattern of
regulatory formation:

1. The old economic agencies were not necessarily formed to protect business. Some
   of the agencies were created over the objections of business. Almost all of the
   new social agencies were created despite business opposition. That many
   agencies, both old and new, were created without the cooperation of business
   contradicts the theory that, if given the chance, any business would jump at the
   opportunity to be regulated.

2. Proconsumer sentiment was important in the formation of many of the old economic agencies. Broad popular movements, anti-business sentiment, and the support of progressive politicians played a role. The involvement of public-spirited individuals and their participation in broad popular movements contradicts the notion that business protection is the only factor explaining regulatory origins.

3. The business community is not monolithic in regard to regulation. Small firms and large, profitable firms and unprofitable ones, react differently to the constraints and opportunities offered by regulation. Business power theories do not take into account significant divisions within the business community which arise during regulatory creation. The 1916 Shipping Act, for example, was passed despite the opposition of the carriers that were to be regulated, but with the support of other businesses whom the act was supposed to aid.[15] The Federal Trade Commission, likewise, had support from a significant element in the business community: small firms that hoped that the new agency would restrict the activities of the large industrial giants. Business power theories tend to treat business as a monolith and to ignore important divisions within the business community. There is no business interest, only the interest of individual firms and companies. As seen in the CAB/airlines case, where United Airlines broke off from the industry coalition, divisions within the business community have an important role in determining whether regulatory change takes place.

4. The power of different parts of the business community waxes and wanes in response to various events of national importance and the public's perception of these events. During periods of equilibrium in American politics, when social reform movements are weak, businesses on the whole are in a better position to take advantage of regulation; but during periods of instability, when new forces challenge the status quo, the powers of business decline. During these periods business leaders react by attempting to regroup and reorganize in order to regain powers they feel they have lost. A business domination theory fails to take into account the cyclical character of politics.

5. Even in cases of agencies created with the explicit intent of promoting particular businesses (the FCC to aid the communications industry; the CAB to aid the airlines), there was also broad public sentiment in favor of promoting the industry. Businesses need and often have broad public support for their positions, especially during hard economic times such as depressions or recessions. For example, during the Depression, when government involvement in the economy was common, the public was supportive of the notion that the airlines and the communications industry should develop and prosper and that therefore it was legitimate to subsidize these sectors; only subsequently were members of the public moved by events or individuals to reevaluate this position.

6. Finally, the importance of scandals (such as the thalidomide disaster), crises (such as a large oil spill), and congressional investigations (into matters such as traffic safety) is ignored by simple theories of business dominance. Factors such as these are often needed to stimulate the creation of regulatory bodies. These factors also may bring about agency decline, but are not taken into account by analysts who explain regulation only with reference to business power. Important events and public spectacles, which create broad public reactions because of media coverage, have a role in regulatory change. Symbols play as much of a role as substance.

A business domination theory of regulatory origins is too narrow. It ignores the fact that businesses do not, in each and every instance, seek regulation. It implies wrongly that a firm should perpetuate regulation whenever possible. Instead, the managerial theory holds a firm must carefully assess regulatory situations for their potential impact and evolve distinct strategies for dealing with different situations.

Implementation

A liberal critic of business domination theories, Marver Bernstein, argues that, at best, if agencies are not created to serve businesses, they end up doing so.[16] Periods of youthful enthusiasm dissipate into "senility," as agencies are captured by those they are supposed to control.[17] In the case of the old economic regulatory agencies, their behavior is likely to change over time; however, the change is not necessarily as Bernstein would have predicted. Laws originally designed to promote business development may begin to serve broader social goals not connected to business profit. New appointments, legislative amendments, policies, and court cases may alter the way agencies, supposedly captured by business, actually behave. The FCC, for example, which before the 1960s was often perceived as being industry-serving, was by 1975 no longer perceived in this manner. At that time the industry became interested in deregulation.

Agencies do not necessarily lose their vigor during the implementation process. In some cases, businesses have no alternative but to retreat. In the FCC case, the broadcast industry achieved a strategic retreat by using some of the following tactics:

- conceding on a lesser point to prevent a greater evil
- having government incorporate existing industry standards
- insisting on case-by-case rulemaking as opposed to general standards
- appealing to other decision-making bodies
- resigning itself to defeat on certain key issues

The notion of inevitable capture during implementation does not apply to the new social agencies. Instead, most firms face costly compliance decisions in vital areas of their operation, such as personnel administration, product development, selling and marketing, and design and operation of production. Regulation can have adverse long-term consequences in terms of declining managerial autonomy, red tape, or a need for unachievable economies of scale. Higher prices and a decline in productivity also may be associated with the requirements of the new social regulation. Economic dislocations, with substantial impacts on particular sectors, technical difficulties, and operational uncertainties, are the challenges that implementation of the new social regulation bring to management.

In response to these challenges, managers have to decide whether to lead or lag, whether to respond early to preserve flexibility or respond late to avoid uncertainty. Stonewalling eliminates flexibility. When a firm ultimately decides to respond, it may have little choice but to comply under conditions of duress and under terms defined by others. Opportunism, on the other hand, is an uncertain strategy because of possible changes in public perceptions and policies. Regulations from which firms expect to profit can be abolished. A changeable public, endless lawsuits, and decisions by competing institutions make efforts to profit from government regulation inherently uncertain.

Many firms, therefore, refuse to make the stark choice between a stonewalling strategy and an opportunistic one. Rather, many refuse to choose at all, falling into drift and letting critical events evoke a gradual accommodation from them. In response to critical changes in its environment, a firm may reorient its business, as GM did when it decided to downsize its automobiles. Another response may be increased public relations activism, like that initiated by Union Carbide after environmental and energy issues put it in a defensive posture. Factors responsible for varying responses by firms include the size of the firm, the size of the problem, control of markets, discretion by government officials, managerial attitudes, a company's growth and age, and the general political climate.

The evidence on implementation, therefore, does not show a pattern of strict industry-serving behavior on the part of regulatory agencies, but rather patterns such as increasing pressures on businesses as older regulatory agencies mature, and constant pressures on them by new agencies. How businesses respond to these pressures varies a great deal and depends on different strategic adaptations.

Evaluation

Agencies often pass through a cycle, but not the cycle of inevitable decay. The cycle is more likely to be cybernetic in that in response to feedback there is change and adjustment. Agencies are created; they implement new laws, and they have their performance evaluated and their statutes revised in accordance with new perceptions of their functions, capabilities, and performance. This process can occur several times in an agency's existence.

New proposals for regulatory change are generated and considered for many reasons: changes in technology or the economy generate public interest group activity; the national media take notice of specific issues; newly appointed heads of agencies seek to be perceived as innovators; congressional staffwork and committee investigation stir controversies; and policy entrepreneurs bring together key participants for dramatic confrontations that receive extensive public discussion.

An important factor in developing ideas and getting them on the agenda is changes in the pattern of academic education. For example, younger public officials may have opinions about regulation that are different from those held by their predecessors.[18] A student in college or law school in the 1930s or 1940s probably had been taught that government regulation was desirable and that applying neutral administrative expertise to the management of economic enterprise was feasible. By contrast, in the 1960s college and law students were told that regulatory agencies were captured by industry and that commissions went through life cycles that inevitably led to their decay. The 1960s students when they entered government service were influenced by these academic arguments. They believed that agencies should be designed to prevent their capture. The EPA, for example, had a single administrator and was governed by standards and deadlines which afforded minimal opportunity for the exercise of discretion favorable to business.

Intellectual descriptions and criticisms of institutional arrangements have had practical consequences. However, only some of the ideas proposed by academics and other researchers actually have been adopted. Barriers to the adoption of theoretically sound ideas include their incompatibility with the existing situation and political and technical implementation problems. For instance, the notion that incentives should be used to reduce pollution is an academic idea taught in universities that has gained general acceptance, but it has not seen widespread adoption. Innovative pollution control suggestions carried out by the government were developed by officials in the course of carrying out their duties, not by economists who theorized about optimal methods of abatement.

Changes in regulatory practice are not always to businesses' liking. They may try to prevent reform. On the whole, they have had no interest in the idea of using incentives for pollution control. In addition, not all businesses have supported deregulation of the old agencies, and many have since argued for reregulation.

Regulated firms may oppose changes and make an effort to prevent them, but they may be unable to do so. The ICC-trucking, FPC-natural gas, CAB-airlines, and ICC-railroads cases do not conform to a simple business domination theory. When industries are divided and the public is aroused to support changes through the activities of policy entrepreneurs, business's power may be limited. In the airlines case, industry was not united, and opposition to regulatory change was overcome by a policy entrepreneur who galvanized broad support for regulatory change through media coverage of congressional hearings.

The power of business, judging from the evidence examined in this book, is as limited as the power of other interested parties. Many cases end in stalemate with no winners or losers and the economy as a whole suffering. Firms most capable of thriving in a regulatory environment are those that best manage regulation. Nonetheless, public interest pressure is likely to be substantial, and businesses may be divided into competing factions. Regulatory agencies, at some point in their existence, are likely to impose substantial burdens on business, but regulatory agencies themselves change. They have to accommodate new conditions in their environment, and are neither consistently anti-business or pro-business, as if business's interest and the public's interest were always in opposition.

A Modified Public Interest Theory

The theory and empirical research that support the notion that businesses join together to maximize their self-interest through regulation have significant weaknesses.[19] This book suggests that a modified public interest approach may be more appropriate. A simple public interest theory holds that regulation remedies inefficiencies and inequities in the operation of the market. However, as Posner points out, regulation is not imposed mainly in highly concentrated industries where the danger of monopoly is greatest or in industries that generate substantial external costs.[20]

A modified public interest theory accepts that the activities of government are not costless and predictable, especially with respect to market behavior. In fact, government activities may generate substantial uncertainties. Sound regulatory goals may combine with weaknesses in administration. As Posner remarks, whether agencies are created for bona fide public interest purposes is not as important as that they cannot be managed so that their purposes, whatever they may be, are consistently achieved. Although socially desirable results may be sought by groups influencing the enactment of regulatory legislation, the important point is that the typical agency does not operate with reasonable efficiency to achieve either socially beneficial or socially harmful goals. For one thing, agencies often rely on case-by-case decision making, rather than comprehensive and rational planning, to make policy. Moreover, they cannot predict the future or know the results of regulatory standards and enforcement. Failures of regulation in the public interest, therefore, may be as much a result of bureaucratic incapacities as they are of legislative mistakes. Regulation often may be an authentic but flawed method to promote the public interest. Posner notes that "some policies are adopted because they conform to the public interest—as conceived by politicians."[21] However, the intractable character of many of the tasks that have been assigned to regulatory agencies and the lack of necessary instruments of measurement and control mean that agencies are often asked to do what they are not able to do, and in the end they fail.

Nonetheless, a modified public interest theory does not accept the notion that over time agencies inevitably are dominated by the industries they regulate. The interactions between regulatory agency and firm cannot be characterized by the "metaphor of conquest."[22] Regulatory legislation is the product of negotiation among legislators. An increasing workload means that they delegate much work to regulatory agencies and exercise progressively less control. When other problems come before them, they have trouble monitoring the agencies they have created. Implementation involves bargaining among agencies and regulated firms, with consumer and public interest groups having an interest in the outcome and attempting to capture the agency just as much as regulated firms. The absence of a consistent pattern of domination is notable. As Posner maintains, when a single agency like the ICC regulates separate industries (truckers, railroads, and barge lines) that have conflicting interests, it is uncertain which of these industries the ICC is likely to favor. Moreover, there are competing groups in most industries. With regard to CAB regulation, the interests of the trunk lines have not been identical to those of the regional or local service lines.

Regulation does not simply serve the interests of politically active businesses. Firms often do not know their interests or do not advance them rationally. One would suppose, in the regulatory sphere, that it would be in the interest of politically active firms to coordinate their efforts to obtain favorable regulation. The smaller the number of firms the less problems there would be in joining together for collective action. However, as Posner points out, many industries that have obtained favorable regulation lack this characteristic.[23] Posner gives these reasons: (1) the demand for regulation may be greater among some industries, as they lack a suitable substitute, such as cartelization; (2) the intervention of the political process means that some industries may be able to influence outcomes at lower cost than other industries; and (3) industry members for whom regulation is a significant advantage may overcome almost single-handedly obstacles to forming effective coalitions.

In political settings, regulatory legislation is passed by the vote of the elected representatives of the people. Large numbers have voting power. Geographic concentrations of people and voting blocs are important. The role of presidential initiative and legislative process in forming policy cannot be ignored. Public opinion is influential. Public interest considerations play a role. Posner argues that a number of standard features of public utility and common carrier regulation have public interest characteristics.

Particular outcomes are hard to interpret, particular effects are hard to trace, and empirical research has been largely limited to case studies. Practically all observations can be reconciled with the existing studies. The case studies are not necessarily typical, and counter-examples exist. The new regulation and the resurgence of previously "lethargic" agencies, moreover, do not conform to simple business domination models. Sometimes public interest rationales have plausibility. Their immediate rejection is questionable. As Posner remarks, for such reasons "it may be possible to revive the public-interest-miscarried theory."[24]

BUSINESS POWER

A managerial theory rests not only on different ideas of the public interest but also on different ideas about business power and regulatory change. As Wilson argues, the power of business depends on the perceived costs and benefits of a policy.[25] If costs and benefits are perceived to be widely distributed, then *majoritarian politics* is likely to prevail. Everybody stands to gain, and everybody may have to pay. Specific industry groups do not have special incentives to organize, because they do not capture a dispro-portionate share of the benefits or suffer a disproportionate share of the burdens. When benefits and costs are perceived as widely distributed, neither specific business opposition nor specific business support is likely. Popular sentiment and elite opinion are more likely to affect outcomes.

On the other hand, when both costs and benefits are perceived as narrow and concentrated, the conditions are ripe for the involvement of specific *interested parties* such as business firms and industries. A subsidy such as a price control or entry restriction will benefit one firm or industry at the expense of another. Specific business interests, therefore, will have a strong reason to organize to try to exercise influence. When both costs and benefits are narrowly concentrated, specific business groups and other economically interested parties can dominate because the general public does not seem to be directly affected. Although one economic interest may prevail over another, the situation is dynamic. The other business interest can recapture power and prevail at another point in time. Thus, regulatory laws are amended at different times to suit the different parties to a conflict.

Specific businesses are likely to gain greatest advantage when benefits are perceived as concentrated and costs as widely distributed. Wilson calls this situation *client politics*.[26] In these situations the specific businesses enjoy an advantage over the general public. Most directly affected, they are also fewer than the general public and more easily organized. They have a powerful incentive to mobilize their political resources and to lobby for favorable policies. If the costs of measures they advocate are distributed at a low per capita rate over a large number of people, no one has much to lose and therefore little public organization or opposition can be expected. Hence, while particular firms or industries have a strong incentive to support the measure, average citizens have neither the will nor the organiza-tion to oppose it. Businesses in this situation are likely to dominate. However, the political advantages of business are often countered by the emergence of watchdogs or public interest associations, and by mass media attention, scandal, and congressional investigation that temporarily mobilize and organize people not directly affected by the policy. When the so-called public interest is organized and articulated through ideological appeals and persuasion and the use of other purposive incentives, supposedly "cozy" relationships among specific business sectors, government agents, and politicans are not likely to remain stable.

A final case is where the benefits of regulation are perceived as general and the costs as concentrated. Regulation in this instance should not take place. The incentives to organize for those who bear the costs are large, while the incentives to organize for those who reap the benefits are weak. In these cases, if there is to be regulation, it is necessary for entrepreneurs to "mobilize latent public sentiment by revealing a scandal, capitalizing on a crisis, and putting the opponents of regulation clearly on the defensive."[27] Such entrepreneurs need to win the support of "third parties" in the media, members of congressional committees, and heads of voluntary associations, and they have to build winning coalitions to defeat the concentrated power of specific businesses.

REGULATORY PERSPECTIVES

Once created, agencies can be viewed as coalitions of officials with different perspectives.[28] Elements in their governing coalition may include career bureaucrats, politicians, and professionals. Each may have different motives. "Careerists" have tenure in the agency, and therefore may be most threatened by the prospect of a crisis or a scandal. They may work to minimize the chances that the agency will be vulnerable to forces which would use such occurrences as a political weapon. The maintenance of the agency and their position in it is of paramount concern. "Politicians," on the other hand, are likely to seek future elective or appointed positions outside the agency. They hope to move on to better and more important offices. They are concerned about the enhancement of their careers outside the agency. Finally, "professionals" are interested in esteem from organized members of their occupation and most likely will seek to display technical competence. They perform tasks that only individuals trained and certified by an external institution can perform, and have distinctive ways of thinking.

Lawyers, for example, are accustomed to think in terms of two-party adversary proceedings conducted by advocates who use evidence to support their respective cases. As Wilson notes, they have professional reasons for wanting to investigate thoroughly and prosecute vigorously. EPA was dominated in the early 1970s by lawyers.[29] Economists in the agency, however, maintained that the rules established by the lawyers did not adequately take into account costs and benefits. Scientists argued that the lawyers did not provide an adequate scientific basis to support their regulations. Outside groups hired scientists and economists to challenge EPA's decisions. Whichever professional group dominated EPA's decision making—lawyers, economists, or scientists—had an important bearing on regulatory outcomes.

Bureaucratic perspectives that influence regulatory change include the policy perspective, the research perspective, and the program perspective.[30] Those with a policy perspective feel that they have to defend the agency against charges that its actions are contributing to unemployment, inflation, and/or energy dependence. They are accountable to national policy concerns that are of importance to the White House. Those with a program perspective are mostly career civil servants tied to specific laws, functions, and appropriations. They take their cues from Congress, and reflect the fragmented nature of the legislative branch, which passes separate laws and amends them according to different principles. Those with program and policy perspectives have to engage in immediate practical activity; for example, they issue regulations, make economic determinations, and try to achieve statutory deadlines. In contrast, those with a research perspective enjoy the so-called luxury of an ivory tower. They have a different time orientation. They may see their purpose as expanding the state of the art and making contributions that will have a long-term impact.

When officials in appointed positions dominate, a policy perspective is more likely to prevail. When professionals dominate, a research orientation is more likely to be prominent. Careerists and middle-level managers, on the other hand, are likely to maintain a program perspective, doing what they have to because it is dictated by law. The policy perspective is oriented toward changes in public opinion and national policy. The program perspective is task-oriented. The research perspective, on the other hand, means that little is done until more research is carried out.

BUSINESS POLITICS

In the 1970s, businesses became increasingly political. As late as 1977, it was maintained that they fought a defensive action against other interest groups and they usually failed.[31] Corporate political power had reached its zenith in the nineteenth century and had gradually ebbed.[32] Businesses in the late 1970s, however, entered in a new way the arena in which public policy was developed. They took positions and endeavored to get their message across to citizens and government officals by involving high-ranking managers. A company's chief executive officer was often its chief lobbyist. Political action committees (PACs) were formed, as companies tried to mobilize their employees and stockholders in order to provide votes and funds for candidates. In 1982, PACs contributed $83 million to House and Senate candidates as compared with $8 million in 1972.[33] The Reagan administration provided businesses with many opportunities for promoting favorable policies. Pro-business appointees headed OSHA, the ICC, and, for a time, the EPA. As activists in the adversary process, businesses tried to maintain markets, protect subsidies, and gain new benefits, such as various forms of trade protection.[34]

In many American corporations, the public affairs/government relations function became increasingly important. It was expanded and upgraded in terms of both its resources and the rank of responsible officials.[35] No longer the sole province of the public relations department, it often involved a corporate executive who was linked to the strategic planning process. Public affairs became a conduit to top management and a part of strategic planning. Businesses tried to improve their ability to anticipate issues and tried to become better organized and more skillful at using the political process. Executives recognized the importance of business politics and expressed a desire to expand it. Subjects such as cost/benefit analysis of regulation, the theory of regulatory agency behavior, and political strategy became increasingly important.[36] Firms in industries particularly threatened by regulation—the automotive, chemical, energy, and metals industries— were among the quickest to upgrade the public affairs function and to emphasize its strategic importance.[37]

The public, in contrast to corporate executives, may have wanted to see less business involvement.[38] According to Steven Brenner: "The message is clear and unmistakable. Society does not share business leaders' confidence in the long-term benefits resulting from corporate political activities."[39] In the early 1980s, businesses may have been too responsive. Executives from the high-tech industries and fast-growing companies centered around the American Business Conference. Traditional Wall Street and corporate interests had access to the president through special business advisory boards. Many business people came to power with the president, including his "kitchen cabinet" of California friends.[40] While the Business Roundtable in the 1970s promoted passage of general interest legislation including the hazardous waste superfund, civil service reform, and the prohibition of firms from participating in the Arab boycott of Israel, the results of business activities in the early 1980s appeared more purely self-serving.[41]

Corporate officials may not have been in touch with the wishes of the broad public. For example, polls consistently showed that over 90 percent of Americans accepted abstract concepts of free competition and private enterprise.[42] While individual executives may have believed in a libertarian ideology, in their role as corporate executives they tended to favor corporatist solutions.[43] As James O'Toole comments: "As individuals, executives favor laissez faire, but collectively their companies stake out positions that advocate 'competition for thee, and bailout, subsidies, antitrust exemptions, and tariff protection for me.' Perhaps such incon- sistency may contribute to the inability of corporations to answer their critics effectively."[44]

Over-responsiveness was a negative factor because of the inevitable limi- tations on the time of chief executives and other top corporate officials.[45] Frequently, these officials had to free themselves from their other duties to concentrate on political activities. They were involved in the company's internal affairs only if there were unfortunate mistakes or incidents.[46] The preoccupation with external concerns often meant that they did not have enough time for making important strategic decisions, such as which tech- nologies to concentrate on or whether to expand, retrench, acquire, or divest. These were the important decisions upon which the future of their companies and the economy depended. As Peter Drucker argues, management must have the time and energy for public activism, but it also must give consideration to "crucial strategic decisions in a time of uncertainty."[47]

Moreover, business political successes may not be attributable to business political skill. They may be largely the result of ideological changes, especially the marked shift to the right in the late 1970s that has been noted by many commentators.[48] This shift is connected to factors such as the changing attitude among American intellectuals toward capitalism; fear of the Soviet Union; longing for religion, family, and a simpler morality; and disenchantment with liberal solutions to the problems of an ailing economy. Business politics, on the other hand, have been plagued by many problems, including an incapacity to deal with issues in other than "black and white" terms; a tendency to be ill prepared; too much dependence on individual politicians; and an inability to deal with legislative staffs or to promote general ideas that are attractive to the broader public.[49]

Theories of simple business interest fail to comprehend the full implications of regulatory politics. Businesses and other organizations are only sometimes able to recognize their interest, and only sometimes able to achieve what they seek, even when their goals are clear. The political system, as Wilson maintains, differs from markets in at least three ways: (1) political settings do not allow for comparison of preferences in monetary or quantitative terms alone; (2) political coalitions, unlike business deals, may commit others not subject to the deal; and (3) political preferences can be changed.[50] The implications are that:

1. In politics, unlike economics, decisions need justification, and beliefs are as important as interests.[51]
2. The actions businesses take are public and must be justified in terms other than self-interest. Business advocates, who have a stake in an outcome, must convince those who do not have a stake or who have a different one.
3. Businesses need to build support for their viewpoints by appealing to broad constituencies and using ideas. Even in cases where economic factors dominate, political participants need to assemble broad coalitions, appeal to the beliefs of broad constituencies, and win support for their ideas.

AN END TO ADVERSARY RELATIONS?

Aimed at reducing adversary relations between business and government, an industrial policy would try to improve America's international competitive position by fostering the growth of specific industries.[52] Under an industrial policy, additional government bailouts, subsidies, and special tax treatment for particular industries are likely. It is possible that at some point a department of international trade and industry will be formed to protect American industry from foreign competition, to foster the export of

American goods, and to purchase natural resources from foreign cartels through a united front. If a Democratic administration is in office, national planning with five- and ten-year goals and tax incentives for conformance to these goals is possible. A highly centralized financial-investment structure may develop in which the Federal Reserve, commercial banks, and corporations work together to finance industrial expansion. Perhaps under a Republican administration the form of industrial policy will be limited to reductions in corporate income taxes.

These proposals are aimed at creating a new business-government harmony based on less zealous application of federal requirements. However, the proposed "cease-fire" between business and government leaves major issues unresolved. Stakeholders still will present their positions in polarized terms to establish leverage in bargaining. The issues, to be sure, may be quite different and revolve around which firms to subsidize and around which technologies, regions, and specialties deserve special government investment. However, neither the U.S. economy nor any major developed economy (with the possible exception of Japan) is suddenly going to move toward industrial harmony. Stalemate and mutually unsatisfactory compromises are likely to continue to hinder growth. Complex, developed societies have built-in conflicts that make it difficult to alter their basic structures rapidly.[53]

Moreover, it is unlikely that there will be a *single* industrial policy. Rather, industrial development policies of all kinds will be formulated in countless separate bargaining arenas at the state and local levels, and they will be administered haphazardly with little coordination.[54] In a decentralized system, it is easy for declining industries and firms to impose costs on those who are not represented.[55] Consumers and emerging industries may have to bear the brunt of the additional burdens. Troubled smokestack companies have an interest in protectionist policies, while new, emerging industries tend to favor free trade. The new and emerging industries are generally smaller. Although they offer greater potential for sustaining jobs in the future, they offer less immediate openings. In political terms, they are not likely to wield the same power as the declining industries, which have had cities and regions dependent on them for years.

Old, troubled industries are most interested in subsidies. They are likely to be preoccupied with politics—mobilizing suppliers, contractors, distributors, employees, and stockholders to maintain survival through legal protection and regulatory change. Small and emerging companies, on the other hand, are likely to be busy developing new products and markets. They will have little time for exerting political pressure and little reason to do so because they offer greater promise for the future and can raise capital with less trouble. Business and government may strike a different balance in the remainder of the 1980s, but an adversary system of discord, paradox, and contradiction will persist.

Notes

CHAPTER 1

1. John F. Mahon and Edwin A. Murray, "Deregulation and Strategic Transformation," *Journal of Contemporary Business* 9 (1980): 123-38; see the discussion in Joseph A. Raelin, "A Discriminant Analysis of Strategic Regulatory Response" (Paper delivered at Institute for Public Service, School of Management, Boston College, October 25, 1982).

2. John R. Meyer, "Transportation Deregulation: Possibilities and Prospects," *Journal of Contemporary Business* 9 (1980): 69-85; as cited by Raelin.

3. Mahon and Murray, "Deregulation"; as cited by Raelin, p. 6.

4. Robert Leone, "The Real Costs of Regulation," *Harvard Business Review* 55 (November/December 1977); see also "Pollution and Profit: Do They Correlate?" *Economic Priorities Report* (June-July 1971): 15-17.

5. Keith Davis and Robert Blomstrom, *Business and Society*, 3d ed. (New York: McGraw-Hill, 1975), pp. 85-86.

6. See James E. Post, *Corporate Behavior and Social Change* (Reston, Va.: Reston, 1978), pp. 167-85.

7. Elizabeth Gatewood and Archie B. Carroll, "The Anatomy of Corporate Social Response: The Rely, Firestone 500, and Pinto Cases," *Business Horizons* 24 (September/October 1981): 9-16.

8. Ibid.

9. See Jeffrey A. Sonnenfeld, *Corporate Views of the Public Interest* (Boston: Auburn House, 1981), pp. 27-64.

10. See Post, *Corporate Behavior*, p. 27.

11. Quoted in Charles G. Burck, "There's Big Business in All That Garbage," *Fortune*, April 7, 1980, pp. 106-112.

12. Ibid.

13. See Michael G. Royston, "Making Pollution Prevention Pay," *Harvard Business Review* 58 (November/December 1980): 6-10.

14. Ibid.

15. Post, *Corporate Behavior*, p. 27.

16. Sonnenfeld, *Corporate Views*, pp. 127-42.

17. Post, *Corporate Behavior*, pp. 3-21.

18. Ibid. On different corporate response strategies see also S. Prakash Sethi, "Dimensions of Corporate Social Responsibility," *California Management Review* 17, no. 3 (1975): 58-64.

19. See Alfred A. Marcus, "Command and Control: An Assessment of Smokestack Emission Regulation," in John Brigham and Don Brown, eds., *Policy Implementation: Penalties or Incentives?* (Beverly Hills, Calif.: Sage, 1980); and Roland J. Cole and Paul Sommers, "Business and Government Regulation: A Theory of Compliance Decisions," *Journal of Contemporary Business* 10, no. 1 (1981): 143-53.

20. See Donald D. Holt, "Why Eaton Got Out of the Air-Bag Business," *Fortune*, March 12, 1979, pp. 146-49.

21. Gatewood and Carroll, pp. 10-12.

22. Ibid.

23. Ibid.

24. Ibid.

25. See Post, *Corporate Behavior*, p. 18.

26. L. S. Sproull, "Responses to Regulation: An Organizational Process Framework," *Administration and Society* 12, no. 4 (1980): 447-70. Sproull focuses on information processing and decision making. Other organizational models exist in the literature.

27. As cited by Sonnenfeld, *Corporate Views*, p. 3.

28. Peter Drucker, "Coping with Those Extra Burdens," *Wall Street Journal*, May 2, 1979, p. 22.

29. J. P. Kotter, "Managing External Dependence," *Academy of Management Review* 4 (1979): 87-92; as cited by Sonnenfeld.

30. Jeffrey Pfeffer and Gerald R. Salancik, *The External Control of Organizations* (New York: Harper and Row, 1978); as cited by Sonnenfeld, p. 32.

31. Talcott Parsons, *Structures and Process in Modern Societies* (New York: Free Press, 1960); as cited by Sonnenfield, p. 12.

32. Sonnenfeld, *Corporate Views*, pp. 51-61.

33. Ibid.

34. Ibid.

35. Ibid.

36. Ibid.

37. J. D. Thompson, *Organizations in Action* (New York: McGraw-Hill, 1967); as cited by Sonnenfeld, p. 40.

38. See Sonnenfeld, *Corporate Views*, p. 40.

39. S. L. Holmes, "Corporate Social Performance: Past and Present Areas of Commitment," *Academy of Management Journal* 20 (1977): 433-38; as cited by Sonnenfeld. See also Alvin F. Zander, *Groups at Work* (San Francisco: Jossey-Bass, 1977), pp. 122-24, and James Post et al., "The Public Affairs Function in American Corporations," *Long Range Planning* 15 (1982): 12-21.

40. See Sonnenfeld, *Corporate Views*, pp. 27-44. During the recent recession, corporate public affairs staffs were cut severly, although not as much as planning departments.

41. Ibid.

42. Ibid.

43. Ibid.

44. Pfeffer and Salancik, *External Control*, p. 271.

45. See J. Woodward, "Management and Technology," in D. S. Pugh, ed., *Organization Theory* (London: Penguin, 1971), pp. 56-71.

46. See Leone, "Real Costs," pp. 61-66.

47. As cited by Raelin, p. 5.

48. Arthur Gerstenfeld, "Government Regulation Effects on the Direction of Innovation: A Focus on Performance Standards," *The Institute of Electronic and Electrical Engineers Transactions on Engineering Management*, EM-24 (1977), pp. 82-86.

49. See Murray L. Weidenbaum, *The Future of Business Regulation* (New York: Amacom, 1979); and Barry Mitnick, "The Strategic Uses of Regulation and Deregulation," *Business Horizons* 24 (March 1981): 71-83; as cited by Raelin.

50. Joseph A. Raelin and Betty B. Sokol, "Rethinking the Relationship between Regulation and R&D Lag," *Business Forum* 7 (1982): 11-13; as cited by Raelin, p. 3.

51. Raelin, "A Discriminant Analysis," pp. 12-16.

52. Ibid.

53. Ibid., p. 12.

54. Ibid., p. 13.

55. See Erwin G. Krasnow and Lawrence D. Longley, *The Politics of Broadcast Regulation*, 2d ed. (New York: St. Martin's Press, 1978), pp. 150-80.

56. See Leone, "Real Costs," p. 65.

57. Ibid.

58. Bruce Owen and Ronald Braeutigam, *The Regulation Game* (Cambridge, Mass.: Ballinger, 1978), p. 7.

59. Ibid.

60. See Barry Mitnick, "Taking Advantage of Regulation and Deregulation," Working Paper Series (WP-391), Graduate School of Business, University of Pittsburgh, 1980, p. 9.

61. Ibid.

62. Owen and Braeutigam, *Regulation Game*, p. 5.

63. B. Peter Pashigian, "The Political Economy of the Clean Air Act: Regional Self-interest in Environmental Regulation," publication of the Center for the Study of American Business, Washington University, St. Louis, 1982, no. 51, as cited in the 1982 Annual Report.

CHAPTER 2

1. For a discussion of the participants in regulation, see Paul Joskow, "Inflation and Environmental Concern: Structural Change in the Process of Public Utility Price Regulation," *Journal of Law and Economics* (October 1974): 296.

2. E. A. Grefe, *Fighting to Win: Business Political Power* (New York: Harcourt Brace Jovanovich, 1981), p. x.

3. Ibid.

4. Anne Strick, "What's Wrong with the Adversary System: Paranoia, Hatred, and Suspicion," *Washington Monthly* 8 (January 1977): 19-28.

5. Roger W. Mullin, Jr., "The Adversary Society," in Lewis Benton, ed., *Private Management and Public Policy* (Lexington, Mass.: Lexington Books, 1980), pp. 131-45.

6. Ibid.

7. Ibid.

8. Ibid.

9. Ibid.

10. Ibid.

11. Ibid.

12. See John T. Dunlop et al., "Business and Public Policy," *Harvard Business Review* 57 (November/December 1979): 85-101.

13. Ibid.

14. See Grefe, *Fighting to Win*, p. 13.

15. Dunlop et al., "Business and Public Policy," p. 93.

16. Ibid.

17. Ibid.

18. Mancur Olson, "Stagflation and the Political Economy of the Decline in Productivity," *American Economic Review* 72 (May 1982): 143-48.

19. Ibid.

20. Ibid.

21. Dunlop et al., p. 95.

22. Ibid., p. 98.

23. Ibid.

24. Thorsten Veblen, *The Theory of the Business Enterprise* (New York: Mentor, 1958), p. 36.

25. Ibid.

26. See Joskow, "Inflation," p. 296.

27. William R. Dill, "Business Organizations," in James G. March, ed., *Handbook of Organizations* (Chicago: Rand McNally, 1965), pp. 1071-1114.

28. Ibid.

29. See M. H. Spencer and L. Siegelman, *Managerial Economics* (Homewood, Ill.: Irwin, 1959); as cited by Dill, p. 1073.

30. N. W. Chamberlain, *The Firm: Microeconomic Planning and Action* (New York: McGraw-Hill, 1962), as cited by Dill, p. 1074.

31. R. Marris, "A Model of the 'Managerial' Enterprise," *Quarterly Journal of Economics* 77 (1963): 185-209; as cited by Dill.

32. See J. G. March and H. A. Simon, *Organizations* (New York: Wiley, 1958).

33. Edwin A. Murray, Jr., "Strategic Choice as a Negotiated Outcome," *Management Science* 24 (May 1978): 960-72.

34. Ibid., p. 965.

35. Ibid., p. 960.

36. See R. M. Cyert and J. G. March, *A Behavioral Theory of the Firm* (Englewood Cliffs, N.J.: Prentice-Hall, 1963).

37. Anthony J. Parisi, "The Men Who Rule Exxon," *New York Times Magazine*, August 3, 1980, pp. 19-25.

38. Ibid.

39. As cited in Murray, "Strategic Choice," p. 961.

40. John Kenneth Galbraith, *The Affluent Society* (Boston: Houghton Mifflin, 1958); as cited by Dill, p. 1082.

41. Grefe, *Fighting to Win*, p. 13.

42. Jeffrey Pfeffer and Gerald R. Salancik, *The External Control of Organizations* (New York: Harper and Row, 1978).

43. See Philip Selznick, *Leadership in Administration* (New York: Harper and Row, 1957); Graham T. Allison, *Essence of Decision: Explaining the Cuban Missile Crisis* (Boston: Little, Brown, 1971); and Richard Neustadt, *Presidential Power* (New York: Wiley, 1960), as cited by Murray, "Strategic Choice," p. 962.

44. Charles E. Lindblom, "The Science of 'Muddling Through,'" in Jay Shafritz and Albert C. Hyde, eds., *Classics of Public Administration* (Oak Park, Ill.: Moore Publishing, 1978), pp. 202-14. See also James Bryan Quinn, *Strategies for Change: Logical Incrementalism* (Homewood, Ill.: Irwin, 1980).

45. Henry Mintzberg, D. Raisinghani, and A. Theoret, "The Structure of Unstructured Decision Processes," *Administrative Science Quarterly* 21 (June 1976): 246-75.

46. Ibid.

47. Ibid.

48. See James Q. Wilson, "The Politics of Regulation," in James W. McKie, ed., *Social Responsibility and the Business Predicament* (Washington, D.C.: Brookings Institution, 1974), pp. 135-69.

49. James Q. Wilson, ed., *The Politics of Regulation* (New York: Basic Books, 1980).

50. Ibid.

51. Bruce Owen and Ronald Braeutigam, *The Regulation Game* (Cambridge, Mass.: Ballinger, 1978), p. 14.

52. Joskow, "Inflation," p. 296.

53. See Theodore Lowi, *The End of Liberalism* (New York: Norton, 1969); and Alfred A. Marcus, "The Environmental Protection Agency," in Wilson, *Politics of Regulation*, pp. 267-304.

54. Joskow, "Inflation," p. 296.

55. See James F. Anderson, *Public Policy-Making* (New York: Praeger, 1975), p. 10; Alan A. Altshuler and Norman C. Thomas, eds., *The Politics of the Federal Bureaucracy* (New York: Harper and Row, 1977), p. 113; and George C. Edwards and Ira Sharkansky, *The Policy Predicament* (San Francisco: W. H. Freeman, 1978), p. 7.

56. Lindblom, "Muddling Through."

57. Ibid.

58. Ibid.

59. See Alfred A. Marcus, *Promise and Performance: Choosing and Implementing an Environmental Policy* (Westport, Conn.: Greenwood Press, 1980), p. 14.

60. See Michael Lipsky, *Street-level Bureaucracy* (New York: Russell Sage Foundation, 1980).

61. A vast amount of literature on the subject of implementation exists. Some of the more notable works are the following: Jeffrey L. Pressman and Aaron Wildavsky, *Implementation* (Berkeley: University of California Press, 1973); Donald S. Van

Meter and Carl E. Van Horn, "The Policy Implementation Process: A Conceptual Framework," *Administration and Society* 6 (February 1975): 445-87; Eugene Bardach, *The Implementation Game* (Cambridge, Mass.: MIT Press, 1977); Peter W. House and David W. Jones, *Getting It off the Shelf: A Methodology for Implementing Federal Research* (Boulder, Colo.: Westview Press, 1978); James Larson. "When Government Programs Fail" (Paper presented at the American Political Science Association Meeting, September 1979, Washington, D.C.); Richard F. Elmore, "Mapping Backward: Using Implementation Analysis to Structure Policy Decisions" (Paper presented at the American Political Science Association Meeting, September 1979, Washington, D.C.); Paul Sabatier and Daniel Mazmanian, "The Conditions of Effective Implementation: A Guide to Accomplishing Policy Objectives," *Policy Analysis* 5 (Fall 1979): 481-505; *Symposium on Successful Policy Implementation, Policy Studies Journal* 8 (Special #2, 1980); George C. Edwards, *Implementing Public Policy* (Washington, D.C.: Congressional Quarterly, 1980); Robert Nakamura and Frank Smallwood, *The Politics of Policy Implementation* (New York: St. Martin's, 1980).

62. See Todd LaPorte, ed., *Organized Social Complexity: Challenge to Politics and Policy* (Princeton, N.J.: Princeton University Press, 1975).

63. Ibid.

64. Ibid.

65. See Roger Cobb and Charles Elder, *Participation in American Politics: The Dynamics of Agenda-Building* (Baltimore: Johns Hopkins Press, 1972).

66. Wilson, *Politics of Regulation*, pp. 370-71.

67. Allison, *Essence of Decision*.

68. Ibid.

69. See Bardach, *Implementation Game*, pp. 36-58.

70. Ibid., pp. 98-141.

71. Ibid.

72. See Lindblom, "Muddling Through."

73. Ibid.

74. John Steinbruner, *The Cybernetic Theory of Decision* (Princeton, N.J.: Princeton University Press, 1974), p. 146; as cited in Robert F. Coulam, *Illusions of Choice* (Princeton, N.J.; Princeton University Press, 1977).

75. Frederic A. Morris and Alfred A. Marcus, "Institutional Analysis: An Overview," in Frederic A. Morris, Roland J. Cole, and Alfred A. Marcus, eds., *Institutional Analysis for Energy Policy* (Seattle, Wash.: Battelle Human Affairs Research Centers, 1979), p. 30.

76. See Murray L. Weidenbaum, *Business, Government, and the Public* (Englewood Cliffs, N.J.: Prentice-Hall, 1977).

77. See George J. Stigler, *The Citizen and the State: Essays in Regulation* (Chicago: University of Chicago Press, 1975); and Marver H. Bernstein, *Regulating Business by Independent Commission* (Princeton, N.J.: Princeton University Press, 1955). Stigler's theory is that private groups, whether they be industry or consumer interests, dominate the state. He frequently, however, is interpreted as saying that industry protection is the only result.

78. Robert Leone, "The Real Costs of Regulation," *Harvard Business Review* 55 (November/December 1977): 58.

79. Barry Mitnick, "Taking Advantage of Regulation and Deregulation," Working Paper Series (WP-391), Graduate School of Business, University of Pittsburgh, 1980, p. 1.

80. A. Lee Fritschler and Bernard H. Ross, *Executive's Guide to Government* (Cambridge, Mass.: Winthrop, 1980), pp. 109-21.

CHAPTER 3

1. Congressional Quarterly, *Federal Regulatory Directory 1980-81* (Washington, D.C., 1980), p. 11; also see Timothy Clark, "The Public and Private Sectors: The Old Distinctions Grow Fuzzy," *National Journal*, January 19, 1980, pp. 99-104.

2. Ronald J. Penoyer, *Directory of Federal Regulatory Agencies—1982 Update* (St. Louis: Center for the Study of American Business, 1982), p. 1.

3. Ronald J. Penoyer, *Directory of Federal Regulatory Agencies* (St. Louis: Center for the Study of American Business, 1981), p. 6.

4. Penoyer, *1982 Update*, p. 5.

5. A. T. Peacock and J. Wiseman, *The Growth of Public Expenditures in the United States* (Princeton, N.J.: Princeton University Press, 1961), as cited by Patrick Larkey et al., "Theorizing about the Growth of Government: A Research Assessment," *Journal of Public Policy*, 1, pt. 2 (May 1981): 167.

6. See Bruce D. Porter, "Parkinson's Law Revisited: War and the Growth of American Government," *The Public Interest* (Summer 1980); on the growth of government see also Richard Rose, "What if Anything Is Wrong with Big Government?" *Journal of Public Policy* 1 (February 1981): 5-37.

7. Penoyer, *1982 Update*, p. 4.

8. William Lilley III, and James C. Miller III, "The New Social Regulation," *The Public Interest* (Spring 1977): 49-62.

9. Ibid.

10. Frederick C. Mosher, "The Changing Responsibilities and Tactics of the Federal Government," *Public Administration Review* (November/December 1980): 541-48.

11. Penoyer, *Directory*, p. 4.

12. Lilley and Miller, "New Social Regulation," p. 50. Agencies often also require the creation of state and local government agencies to implement and enforce certain regulations.

13. Congressional Quarterly, *Federal Regulatory Directory*, p. 43.

14. Timothy Clark, "The Costs and Benefits of Regulation: Who Knows How Great They Really Are?" *National Journal*, December 1, 1979, p. 2024.

15. David Vogel, "The Inadequacy of Contemporary Opposition to Business," *Daedalus* (Summer 1980): 49. Also see Mark Green and Norman Waitzman, "Business War on the Law: Analysis of the Benefits of Federal Health/Safety Enforcement," Corporate Accountability Research Group, 1979, as cited by Vogel.

16. Congressional Quarterly, *Federal Regulatory Directory*, p. 47.

17. Ibid.

18. "Commerce Department Measures Antipollution Spending," *Public Utilities Fortnightly*, May 7, 1981, p. 27.

19. Ibid.

20. "Costs of Antipollution Efforts Assessed," *Public Utilities Fortnightly*, November 8, 1979, p. 39. Cost studies ignore transfers and distributional effects. Costs to one party are benefits to another. Cost studies also ignore long-term versus short-term effects. While in the long run pollution control expenditures may be inefficient, in the short run they may stimulate employment and growth.

21. Clark, "The Costs and Benefits of Regulation," p. 2024.

22. Ibid.

23. Lester B. Lave, "An Economist's View," in Robert W. Crandall and Lester B. Lave, eds., *The Scientific Base of Health and Safety Regulation* (Washington, D.C.: Brookings Institution, 1981), p. 275.

24. Ibid.

25. Bernard L. Cohen, "How Much Should We Spend to Save a Life?" *Public Utilities Fortnightly*, November 19, 1982, p. 24.

26. Murray L. Weidenbaum, "The Future of Business/Government Relations in the United States," in Max Ways, ed., *The Future of Business* (New York: Pergamon, 1979), p. 49. Barry Mitnick notes that the Congressional Budget Office counted 33 departments and agencies in 1976; that a Domestic Council study found 90 such agencies or bureaus in 1977; and that the General Accounting Office identified 116 agencies in 1978; see Barry Mitnick, *The Political Economy of Regulation* (New York: Columbia University Press, 1980), p. 18.

27. Penoyer, *1982 Update*, pp. 43-48. Mitnick notes that some of the new regulatory agencies, such as EPA and CPSC, were created in large part through the reorganization of existing units.

28. Lilley and Miller, "New Social Regulation," pp. 49-62.

29. See Christopher DeMuth, "What Regulation Is" (Paper delivered at the Second Annual Research Conference of the Association for Public Policy Analysis and Management, Boston, October 23-25, 1980); also see Mel Dubnick, "Making Regulators Regulate" (Paper presented at the annual meeting of the American Society for Public Administration, Baltimore, Md., April 1-4, 1979).

30. Robert E. Cushman, *The Independent Regulatory Commissions* (New York: Oxford University Press, 1941), as cited by Dubnick.

31. Mitnick, *Political Economy of Regulation*, as cited by Dubnick.

32. Theodore Lowi, "Four Systems of Policy, Politics, and Choice," *Public Administration Review* 32 (July/August 1972): 298-310; as cited by Dubnick.

33. Alfred E. Kahn, *The Economics of Regulation: Principles and Institutions*, 2 vols. (New York: Wiley, 1970), as cited by Dubnick.

34. Harold D. Koontz, "Extent of Administrative Regulation in Economic Affairs," *The Annals* 22 (May 1942), as cited by Dubnick.

35. Roger Noll, *Reforming Regulation: An Evaluation of the Ash Council Proposals* (Washington, D.C.: Brookings Institution, 1971), as cited by Dubnick.

36. Y. Aharoni, *Markets, Planning, and Development: The Private and Public Sectors in Economic Development* (Cambridge, Mass.: Ballinger, 1977), as cited by Larkey et al.

37. DeMuth, "What Regulation Is," p. 4.

38. See Jonathan R. Hughes, *The Governmental Habit: Economic Controls from Colonial Times to the Present* (New York: Basic Books, 1977).

39. See Lilley and Miller, "New Social Regulation," p. 49; and Weidenbaum, "Business/Government Relations," p. 48.

40. Alfred A. Marcus, "The EPA," in James Q. Wilson, ed., *The Politics of Regulation* (New York: Basic Books, 1980).

41. Weidenbaum, "Business/Government Relations," p. 53.

42. Ibid.

43. See A. Grant Jordan, "Iron Triangles, Wooly Corporatism, or Elastic Nets: Images of the Policy Process," *Journal of Public Policy* 1, pt. 1 (February 1981): 95-125.

44. Ibid., p. 96.

45. A. L. Fritschler, *Smoking and Politics* (New York: Appleton-Century-Crofts, 1975), as cited by Jordan.

46. John Dunlop et al., "Business and Public Policy," *Harvard Business Review* 57 (November-December 1979): 93.

47. Paul Weaver, "Regulation, Social Policy, and Class Conflict," *The Public Interest* (Winter 1978): 45-64.

48. As cited in Larkey et al., "Theorizing," p. 116.

49. D. R. Cameron, "The Expansion of the Public Economy: A Comparative Analysis," *American Political Science Review* 72 (1978): 1243-61; as cited by Larkey et al.

50. Alexis de Tocqueville, *Democracy in America* (Oxford: Oxford World Classics, 1835), as cited by Larkey et al.

51. Allan Meltzer and Scott Richard, "A Rational Theory of the Size of Government," *Journal of Political Economy* 89, no. 5 (October 1981): 914-27.

52. See Larkey et al., "Theorizing," p. 170.

53. Ibid., p. 179.

54. James B. Kau and Paul H. Rubin, "The Size of Government," *Public Choice* 37, no. 2 (1981): 261-74.

55. Larkey et al., "Theorizing," p. 186.

56. Ibid., p. 192.

57. James N. Tattersall, "The Crisis of the Public Economy," *Public Affairs Report* (Bulletin of the Institute of Governmental Studies, University of California, Berkeley) 20, no. 1 (February 1979).

58. Robert W. Crandall, "Twilight of Deregulation," *Brookings Bulletin* 18, nos. 3 and 4 (Winter-Spring 1982): 3.

59. Penoyer, *1981 Update*, pp. 15-16.

60. Vogel, "Inadequacy," p. 50. See also A. F. Ehrbar, "A Tax Strategy to Renew the Economy," *Fortune*, March 9, 1981, pp. 42-96; James O'Toole, "What's Ahead for the Business-Government Relationship,"*Harvard Business Review* 79 (March/April 1979): 94-105; and Richard Hudson, "SEC May Be Losing Its Former Toughness Some Observers Think," *Wall Street Journal*, March 22, 1982, p. 1.

61. Penoyer, *1982 Update*, p. 1.

62. Penoyer, *1981 Update*, pp. 16-18.

63. Penoyer, *1982 Update*, introduction.

64. Marvin H. Kosters and Jeffrey A. Eisenbach, "Is Regulatory Relief Enough?" *Regulation* (March/April 1982): 24. The issue of passive restraints reemerged later in the Reagan administration after Elizabeth Dole became secretary of the Department of Transportation.

65. Ibid.

66. Ibid., p. 20.

67. Robert Crandall, *Brookings Bulletin* (Fall 1982): 1.

68. Kosters and Eisenbach, p. 22.

69. Lucien E. Smartt, "Some Effects of Pervasive Regulation," *Public Utilities Fortnightly*, May 7, 1981, p. 7.

70. Robert N. Miller and Jimmy D. Johnson, *Corporate Ambassadors to Washington* (Washington, D.C.: American University, Center for the Study of Private Enterprise, 1970), p. 4; as cited by J. Ronald Fox, *Managing Business-Government Relations* (Homewood, Ill.: Irwin, 1982), p. 310. During the recent recession, the platoons of intermediaries decreased.

71. Fox, pp. 310-11.

72. Robert B. Reich, "Regulation by Confrontation or Negotiation?" *Harvard Business Review* 59 (May-June 1981): 82-92. Reich disagrees about the role of intermediaries, arguing that they create confrontation, not negotiation.

73. John E. Fleming, "Linking Public Affairs with Corporate Planning," *California Management Review* (Winter 1980): 35-43.

74. Kim McQuaid, "The Roundtable: Getting Results in Washington 81," *Harvard Business Review* 59 (May/June 1981): 114-23.

75. Stephen Sansweet, "Political Action Units Are Assailed by Some over Tactics," *Wall Street Journal*, July 24, 1980, p. 1.

76. Ann Matasar, "Corporate Responsibility Gone Away?: The Corporate Political Action Committee" (Paper prepared for delivery at the 1981 Annual Meeting of the American Political Science Association, New York Hilton Hotel, September 3-6, 1981).

77. Maxwell Glen, "The PACs Are Back Richer and Wiser to Finance the 1980 Elections," *National Journal*, December 24, 1979, pp. 1982-84.

78. Richard E. Cohen, "Congressional Democrats Beware—Here Come the Corporate PACs," *National Journal*, August 9, 1980, p. 1305.

79. Fox, *Business-Government Relations*, p. 326.

80. John S. Shockley, "Corporate Spending in the Wake of the Bellotti Decision: National Implications" (Paper prepared for the American Political Science Convention, New York, 1978).

81. Richard E. Cohen, "The Business Lobby Discovers That in Unity There Is Strength," *National Journal*, June 28, 1980, pp. 1050-55.

82. Richard I. Kirkland, Jr., "Fat Days for the Chamber of Commerce," *Fortune*, September 21, 1981, pp. 149-56. The Chamber of Commerce experienced major failures in the 1982 elections and as a result its rapid growth subsided.

83. Fox, *Business-Government Relations*, p. 325.

84. Timothy B. Clark, "After a Decade of Doing Battle Public Interest Groups Show Their Age," *National Journal*, July 12, 1980, pp. 1136-41.

85. James W. Singer, "Liberal Public Interest Law Firms Face Budgetary, Ideological Challenges," *National Journal*, December 8, 1979, pp. 2052-56. During the Reagan administration some public interest associations capitalized on the anti-Reagan mood to make comebacks.

CHAPTER 4

1. Roland Cole et al., "A Theoretical Approach to Analyzing Incentives for Energy Production," in Battelle Pacific Northwest Laboratories, *An Analysis of Federal Incentives Used to Stimulate Energy Production* (Richland, Wash., 1980),

pp. 33-34. Also see Charles Reich, "The New Property," *Yale Law Journal* 73 (1964): 733-86.

2. Cole et al., "A Theoretical Approach," executive summary.

3. Robert D. Hershey, "Energy: Blessing or Boondoggle?" *New York Times*, September 21, 1980, p. 1.

4. Jerry Bishop, "Synfuel: Bonanza for the Synjargonists," *Wall Street Journal*, September 25, 1979, p. 18.

5. See Hershey, "Energy," p. 1.

6. See Walter A. Rosenbaum, *Energy Politics and Public Policy* (Washington, D.C.: Congressional Quarterly Press, 1981), pp. 163-65.

7. Paul Joskow and Robert Pindyck, "Subsidizing Synthetic Energy Production," *Regulation* (September/October 1979): 18-24.

8. See Howard D. Johnson, "Financing Synthetic Fuel Projects: An Overview," *University of Pittsburgh Law Review* 43 (1981): 103.

9. Ibid.

10. Ibid.

11. Joskow and Pindyck, "Subsidizing."

12. Most of these arguments are made by Joskow and Pindyck.

13. See Rosenbaum, *Energy Politics*, pp. 174-75.

14. Ibid., p. 173.

15. See Bill Paul, "Shortage of Energy Engineers Looms, Threatening Delay of U.S. Synfuel Plan," *Wall Street Journal*, July 11, 1980, sec. 2, p. 21.

16. Quoted by Hershey, "Energy," p. 1. See also Peter DeLeon, *Development and Diffusion of the Nuclear Power Reactor: A Comparative Analysis* (Cambridge, Mass.: Ballinger, 1979).

17. See Hershey, "Energy," p. 1.

18. Rosenbaum, *Energy Politics*, p. 168.

19. H. D. Johnson, "Financing Synthetic Fuel," p. 104.

20. Peter Nulty, "Shale Oil Is Braced for a Big Role," *Fortune*, September 24, 1979, pp. 42-50.

21. Ibid.

22. See H. D. Johnson, "Financing Synthetic Fuel," pp. 108-10.

23. Alfred A. Marcus, "Policy Uncertainty and Technological Innovation," *Academy of Management Review* 6 (1981): 443-48.

24. G. Hatsopolous et al., "Capital Investment to Save Energy," *Harvard Business Review* 56 (December 1978): 111-23.

25. H. D. Leonardi, "Draft on Composite Fuels" (memo, The Dravo Corporation) (Pittsburgh, 1978).

26. William A. Johnson, "Why U.S. Energy Policy Has Failed," in W. Kalter and W. Vogely, eds., *Energy Supply and Government Policy* (Ithaca, N.Y.: Cornell University Press, 1976), pp. 280-306.

27. Carnegie-Mellon Institute of Research, *Regional Energy Policy Alternatives: A Study of the Allegheny County Region* (Pittsburgh: Carnegie-Mellon Institute, 1977), executive summary.

28. Kenneth Knight, George Kozmetsky, and Helen Baca, *Industry Views the Role of the Federal Government in Innovation* (Springfield, Ill.: National Science Foundation, 1976).

29. Adapted from A. Myrick Freeman III, Robert Haveman, and Allen V. Kneese, *The Economics of Environmental Policy* (Santa Barbara, Calif.: Wiley, 1973), pp.

21-23. For a similar analysis of barriers in power plant development, see Dennis P. Ward, "The Rules of the Game: Regulations and the Power Plant Design Process," *Public Utilities Fortnightly*, March 26, 1981, pp. 28-34.

30. Subcommittee on Energy Research and Development of the Committee on Energy and Natural Resources, U.S. Senate, *Petroleum Industry Involvement in Alternative Sources of Energy* (prepared at the request of Frank Church) (Washington, D.C.: Government Printing Office, 1977), p. 319.

31. Mining Act of 1866 as amended, 14 Stat. 251.

32. Oil Shale Commercialization Task Force, *Oil Shale Commercialization Strategy, Parts I, II, and III* (draft, 1979), executive summary.

33. Interagency Energy-Environment Research and Development Program, *Oil Shale and the Environment* (Washington, D.C.: U.S. EPA Office of Research and Development, 1977).

34. U.S. Department of the Interior, *Final Environmental Impact Statement for the Prototype Oil Shale Leasing Program* (Washington, D.C.: Government Printing Office, 1973), p. III-13.14.

35. Resource Conservation and Recovery Act of 1976. U.S. Code 1976 Title 42, Sec. 6901 et seq., October 21, 1976, P.L. 94-580, 90 Stat. 2795.

36. 40 C.F.R. 241.100.

37. John J. Schanz and Harry Perry, "Oil Shale—A New Set of Uncertainties," *Natural Resources Journal* 18 (1978): 776; and *Science* 198 (December 9, 1977): 1023, 1027.

38. See Colorado Air Pollution Control Commission, *Ambient Air Standards* (adopted 1970, repealed and readopted April 12, 1979).

39. See Interagency Energy-Environment Research and Development Program, *Compendium Reports on Oil Shale Technology* (Las Vegas, Nev.: U.S. EPA Environmental Monitoring and Support Laboratory, 1979), p. 110.

40. I. Berenblum and R. Shoental, "Carcinogenic Constituents of Shale Oil," *British Journal of Exploratory Pathology* 24 (1943): 232; and I. Berenblum and R. Schoental, "The Difference in Carcinogenicity between Shale Oil and Shale," *British Journal of Exploratory Pathology* 25 (1944): 95.

41. Interagency Energy-Environment Research and Development Program, *Oil Shale and the Environment*, p. 110.

42. Federal Mine Safety and Health Amendments Act of 1977. U.S. Code 1976 Title 5, Secs. 5314, 5315.

43. *Oil Shale Processing Technology*, Report SFT 102 (Los Angeles, Calif.: Fluor Engineers and Constructors, Inc.), p. 2-1.

44. Ibid.

45. Hearing before the Subcommittee on Energy Production and Supply of the Committee on Energy and Natural Resources, U.S. Senate, *Oil Shale Technologies: Part 2* (Washington, D.C.: Government Printing Office, 1978), p. 441.

46. Edward W. Merrow, Stephen W. Chapel, and Christopher Worthing, *A Review of Cost Estimation in New Technologies* (Santa Monica, Calif.: Rand, 1979), p. 98.

47. Henry E. Lippek, Carol A. Kemp, and Theodore Paul Hunter, *Preliminary Notes on Selected Legal and Political Issues Affecting the Development of Oil Shale* (Seattle, Wash.: Battelle, 1979), p. II-2.

48. Assistant Secretary for Environmental Office of Technology Impacts,

Environmental Analysis of Synthetic Liquid Fuels (Washington, D.C.: U.S. Department of Energy, 1979), p. 9.

49. Marcus, "Policy Uncertainty," pp. 443-48.

50. See Hershey, "Energy," p. 1.

51. See "Conferees Close on Mobilization Board, but Waiver Power Unresolved," *Synfuels*, December 21, 1979, p. 3; also see Lawrence Mosher, "A Fast Track for Colorado," *National Journal* (January 2, 1980), p. 1284.

52. "Conferees Close."

53. Rosenbaum, *Energy Politics*, p. 163.

54. See Richard Corrigan, "The Ill-advised Rush to Synfuels," *National Journal*, November 10, 1979, p. 1902; Joskow and Pindyck, "Subsidizing"; Hershey, "Energy"; and Peter Nulty, "The Tortuous Road to Synfuels," *Fortune*, September 8, 1980, pp. 58-64.

55. Nulty, "Tortuous Road," p. 58.

56. Ibid.

57. Rosenbaum, *Energy Politics*, p. 189.

58. Ibid.

59. Nulty, "Tortuous Road," p. 62.

60. Fred J. Cook, "The Costly Sin of Synfuels," *Amicus Journal* (Spring 1982): 9-11.

61. Nulty, "Tortuous Road," p. 60.

62. Wendell Wiser, "Synfuels: Are Goals Hasty and Impractical?" *Christian Science Monitor*, December 3, 1980, p. 18.

63. Ibid.

64. Ibid.

65. Nulty, "Tortuous Road," p. 59.

66. Ibid.

67. Ibid.

68. Andy Pastzor, "Synfuels Work May Be Curbed by White House," *Wall Street Journal*, February 2, 1981, p. 4.

69. H. D. Johnson, "Financing Synthetic Fuels," p. 105.

70. See Bill Paul, "Future of Synthetic Gas from Coal Grows Cloudy as Court Ruling, Lack of Financing Stall a Plant," *Wall Street Journal*, December 10, 1980, p. 48.

71. Ibid.

72. Johnson, "Financing Synthetic Fuels," p. 118.

73. Richard Myers, "Requiem for Synthetic Fuels," *Energy Daily*, January 27, 1982, p. 2.

74. Ibid.

75. See Eleanor Johnson Tracy, "Exxon's Abrupt Exit from Shale," *Fortune*, May 31, 1982, p. 106.

76. Paul, "Future of Synthetic Gas," p. 48.

77. Elena Folkerts-Landau, "The Sinful Cost of Synfuels," *Wall Street Journal*, May 13, 1983, p. 20.

78. Lawrence Mosher, "Synfuels Subsidies—What Some Call 'Insurance,' Others Call a Giveaway," *National Journal*, May 7, 1983, pp. 965-68.

79. See Robert B. Reich, "Making Industrial Policy," *Foreign Affairs* 60 (Spring 1982): 852-81.

CHAPTER 5

1. Barry Cole and Mal Oettinger, *Reluctant Regulators: The FCC and the Broadcast Audience* (Reading, Mass.: Addison-Wesley, 1978), p. 4.

2. Ibid.

3. Marver H. Bernstein, *Regulating Business by Independent Commission* (Princeton, N.J.: Princeton University Press, 1955), pp. 74-95.

4. Ibid., p. 81.

5. Ibid., p. 91.

6. See Barry Mitnick, *The Political Economy of Regulation* (New York: Columbia University Press, 1980), pp. 172-73. On the capture hypothesis, see also Bernstein, *Regulating Business*; Gabriel Kolko, *Railroads and Regulation, 1877-1916* (Princeton, N.J.: Princeton University Press, 1965); Gabriel Kolko, *The Triumph of Conservation* (Glencoe, Ill.: Free Press, 1963); George J. Stigler, "The Theory of Economic Regulation," *Bell Journal of Economics and Management* 2 (1971): 3-21. Criticism and correction of the capture theory begins with: James Q. Wilson, "The Politics of Regulation," in James W. McKie, ed., *Social Responsibility and the Business Predicament* (Washington, D.C.: Brookings Institution, 1974); Richard A. Posner, "Theory of Economic Regulation," *Bell Journal of Economics and Management* 5, no. 2 (1974): 335-58; Sam Peltzman, "Toward a More General Theory of Regulation," *Journal of Law and Economics* (August 1976): 211-41; and Paul Sabatier, "Social Movements and Regulatory Agencies: Toward a More Adequate and Less Pessimistic Theory of Clientele Capture," *Policy Studies* 6 (1976): 302-42. A synthesis is provided by Mitnick, pp. 79-242; see also Paul J. Quirk, *Industry Influence in Federal Regulatory Agencies* (Princeton, N.J.: Princeton University Press, 1981), pp. 3-23.

7. See Stigler, "Theory," p. 3. Stigler's theory is usually associated with business firms. However, in his book *The Citizen and the State* (Chicago: University of Chicago Press, 1975), he broadens it to include all economic interests including consumers. The focus here, however, is primarily on the implications of his theory for business corporations.

8. See Posner, "Economic Regulation," p. 355.

9. Stigler, "Theory," pp. 4-6.

10. Ibid.

11. Ibid.

12. Ibid.

13. Ibid., p. 7.

14. Ibid., p. 5.

15. Ibid., pp. 11-13.

16. Robert E. Cushman, *The Independent Regulatory Commissions* (New York: Oxford University Press, 1941; Repr. Octagon Books, 1972), as cited by Mitnick, *Political Economy*, p. 98.

17. Merle Fainsod and Lincoln Gordon, *Government and the American Economy* (New York: Norton, 1941); as cited by Mitnick, p. 100.

18. Posner, "Economic Regulation," p. 335.

19. John R. Baldwin, *The Regulatory Agency and the Public Corporation: The Canadian Air Transport Industry* (Cambridge, Mass.: Ballinger, 1975), as cited by Mitnick, pp. 142-44.

20. Wilson, "Politics of Regulation," pp. 135-68. There is an obvious difference between the public interest theory being a rationale for regulation and its being a theory that explains regulatory behavior. See chapter 11 for additional discussion of this important point.

21. Peltzman, "General Theory," as cited by Mitnick, pp. 122-25.

22. Barry R. Weingast, "A Positive Model of Public Policy Formation: The Case of Regulatory Agency Behavior," Working Paper No. 25 (Washington University, St. Louis: Center for the Study of American Business, January 1978), as cited by Mitnick, p. 125. Legislators are likely to appeal to the median voter and committees may make decisions based on the position of their constituencies on a broad range of issues.

23. Merle Fainsod, "Some Reflections on the Nature of the Regulatory Process," in *Public Policy*, C. J. Friedrich and Edward S. Mason, eds. (Cambridge, Mass.: Harvard University Press, 1940), vol. 1, pp. 297-323, as cited by Mitnick, p. 154.

24. Ibid.

25. William S. Comanor and Bridger M. Mitchell, "The Costs of Planning: The FCC and Cable Television," *Journal of Law and Economics* 15, no. 1 (April 1972): 177-206, as cited by Mitnick, pp. 107-8.

26. Albro Martin, *Enterprise Denied: Origins of the Decline of American Railroads, 1897-1917* (New York: Columbia University Press, 1971); and "The Troubled Subject of Railroad Regulation in the Gilded Age—A Reappraisal," *Journal of American History* 61, no. 2 (September 1974): 339-71, as cited by Mitnick, p. 184.

27. Mitnick, "Political Economy," pp. 185-204.

28. Ibid.

29. Edward A. Purcell, Jr., "Ideas and Interests: Businessmen and the Interstate Commerce Act," *Journal of American History* 54 (December 1967): 561-78, as cited by Mitnick, p. 178.

30. As quoted by Cole and Oettinger, *Reluctant Regulators*, p. 4.

31. H. Robert Keiser, "The New Regulation of Health and Safety," *Political Science Quarterly* 95 (Fall 1980): 479-91.

32. See Wilson, "Politics of Regulation," pp. 138-46.

33. Posner, "Economic Regulation," p. 342.

34. See Daniel Fiorino and Daniel Metlay, "Theory of Agency Failure, or, Why Regulatory Agencies Continue to Be Unreliable When the Solutions Seem So Obvious" (Paper presented at American Political Science Association meeting, Washington, D.C., September 1977). See also Daniel Metlay, "Error Correction in Bureaucracy" (Ph.D. diss., University of California at Berkeley, 1978).

35. Bruce M. Owen and Ronald Braeutigam, *The Regulation Game* (Cambridge, Mass.: Ballinger, 1978), pp. 14-15.

36. See Edwin M. Epstein, *The Corporation in American Politics* (Englewood Cliffs, N.J.: Prentice-Hall, 1969), p. 15.

37. See Mitnick, "Political Economy," pp. 259-80.

38. See George Getschow, "Some Middle Managers Cut Corners to Achieve High Corporate Goals," *Wall Street Journal*, April 1, 1980, p. 1.

39. Thomas Dye, *Understanding Public Policy* (Englewood Cliffs, N.J.: Prentice-Hall, 1978), pp. 3-18; and James Anderson, *Public Policymaking* (New York: Praeger, 1975), pp. 1-27.

40. See, for example, David B. Truman, *The Governmental Process* (New York: Knopf, 1951), pp. 14-45.

41. See, for example, G. William Domhoff, *The Higher Circles* (New York: Random House, 1970).

42. For a critique of the synoptic theory, see David Braybrooke and Charles E. Lindblom, *A Strategy of Decision* (New York: Free Press, 1970), pp. 21-37.

43. See David Easton, *A Systems Analysis of Political Life* (New York: Wiley, 1965).

44. See John D. Steinbruner, *The Cybernetic Theory of Decision* (Princeton, N.J.: Princeton University Press, 1974), p. 84.

45. Dan H. Fenn, "Finding Where the Power Lies in Government," *Harvard Business Review* 79 (September/October 1979): 145-46; see also J. E. Post et al., "The Public Affairs Function in American Corporations," *Long Range Planning* 15 (1982): 3-11; and Public Affairs Research Group, *Public Affairs Offices and Their Functions* (Boston: School of Management, Boston University, 1981), pp. 1-39.

CHAPTER 6

1. Marver H. Bernstein, *Regulating Business by Independent Commission* (Princeton, N.J.: Princeton University Press, 1955), pp. 74-95. See also Barry Mitnick, *The Political Economy of Regulation* (New York: Columbia University Press, 1980), pp. 34-79.

2. George J. Stigler, "The Theory of Economic Regulation," *Bell Journal of Economics and Management* 2 (1971): 3-21.

3. On the FCC, see Erwin G. Krasnow and Lawrence D. Longley, *The Politics of Broadcast Regulation*, 2d ed. (New York: St. Martin's Press, 1978); Mark Green, ed., *The Monopoly Makers* (New York: Grossman, 1973), pp. 35-103; Roger G. Noll, Merton J. Peck, and John J. McGowan, *Economic Aspects of Television Regulation* (Washington, D.C.: Brookings Institution, 1973); Barry Cole and Mal Oettinger, *Reluctant Regulators: The FCC and the Broadcast Audience* (Reading, Mass.: Addison-Wesley, 1978); and Edward J. Epstein, *News from Nowhere* (New York: Random House, 1973), pp. 44-77. The FCC's involvement in the telecommunications industry is documented in Richard Barke and Alan Stone, "An Incentive-Constraint Theory of Regulation—The Dynamics of Telecommunications Policy," Discussion Paper Series, Center for Public Policy, University of Houston, 1984.

4. Krasnow and Longley, *Broadcast Regulation*, pp. 150-51.

5. See Cole and Oettinger, *Reluctant Regulators*, p. 134.

6. Paul J. Quirk, *Industry Influence in Federal Regulatory Agencies* (Princeton, N.J.: Princeton University Press, 1981), pp. 3-22.

7. Ibid., p. 19. Also see Ross D. Eckert, "The Life Cycle of Regulatory Commissioners," *Journal of Law and Economics* (April 1981): 113-20.

8. See Noll, Peck, and McGowan, *Television Regulation*, pp. 120-28.

9. Krasnow and Longley, *Broadcast Regulation*, p. 10.

10. Ibid., pp. 27-38.

11. Ibid., pp. 107-27.

12. Ibid., p. 37.

13. See Krasnow and Longley, *Broadcast Regulation*, pp. 107-94; Cole and Oettinger, *Reluctant Regulators*, p. 81-319; and Bruce Owen and Ronald

Braeutigam, *The Regulation Game* (Cambridge, Mass.: Ballinger, 1978), pp. 121-57.

14. Mark P. Petracca, "The Regulation and Deregulation of Cable Television: Changes in the Agenda of Public Policy" (Paper prepared for delivery at the 1981 Annual Meeting of the American Political Science Association, September 3-6, 1981, New York City); see also Owen and Braeutigam, *Regulation Game*, pp. 121-57.

15. See Cole and Oettinger, *Reluctant Regulators*, pp. 243-89.

16. Ibid., p. 266.

17. Krasnow and Longley, *Broadcast Regulation*, pp. 94-105.

18. See Cole and Oettinger, *Reluctant Regulators*, pp. 64-68.

19. Krasnow and Longley, *Broadcast Regulation*.

20. Owen and Braeutigam, *Regulation Game*, pp. 131-34; and Petracca, "Regulation and Deregulation," pp. 23-28.

21. Petracca, "Regulation and Deregulation," p. 28.

22. Krasnow and Longley, *Broadcast Regulation*, pp. 100-105.

23. Cole and Oettinger, *Reluctant Regulators*, pp. 277-78.

24. Ibid., p. 279.

25. Ibid., p. 213.

26. Ibid., p. 281.

27. Petracca, "Regulation and Deregulation," p. 26.

28. Ibid.

29. Cole and Oettinger, *Reluctant Regulators*, p. 258.

30. Ibid., p. 262.

31. Gideon Doron, "How Smoking Increased when T.V. Advertising of Cigarettes Was Banned," *Regulation* (March/April 1979): 48-52; also see Eugene Lewitt, Douglas Coate, and Michael Grossman, "The Effects of Government Regulation on Teenage Smoking," *Journal of Law and Economics* (December 1981): 545-69.

32. Doron, "How Smoking Increased."

33. Ibid. Also see Kenneth E. Warner, "Cigarette Smoking in the 1970's: The Impact of the Antismoking Campaign on Consumption," *Science* (February 1981): pp. 729-30.

34. Michael Wines, "FTC under Siege," *National Journal*, January 29, 1983, pp. 221-23; and James W. Singer, "The Federal Trade Commission: Business's Government Enemy No. 1," *National Journal*, October 13, 1979, pp. 1671-80.

35. Mark V. Nadel, *The Politics of Consumer Protection* (Indianapolis: Bobbs-Merrill Company, 1971); and Barry R. Weingast, "The Renaissance of the Federal Trade Commission" (Washington University, St. Louis: Center for the Study of American Business, December 1978), pp. 1-32.

36. Michael Wines, "Doctors, Dairymen Join in Effort to Clip the Talons of the FTC," *National Journal*, September 18, 1982, pp. 1589-94.

37. See Barry R. Weingast and Mark J. Moran, "The Myth of Runaway Bureaucracy" (Washington University, St. Louis: Center for the Study of American Business, August 1982), pp. 1-11; see also Mark J. Moran and Barry R. Weingast, "Congress as the Source of Regulatory Decisions: The Case of the Federal Trade Commission," *American Economic Association Papers and Proceedings* (May 1982), pp. 109-13; and Barry R. Weingast and Mark J. Moran, "Bureaucratic Discretion or Congressional Control: Regulatory Policymaking by the Federal Trade Commission" (Washington University, St. Louis: Center for the Study of American Business, January 1982), pp. 1-68.

38. James W. Singer, "Endangered Species?" *National Journal*, December 1, 1979, p. 2034.

39. See Wines, "FTC under Siege," p. 1590.

40. David M. Welborn and Anthony E. Brown, "State Economic Regulation: Transitions in Environment and Performance" (Paper prepared for the Symposium on Regulatory Policy, Houston, Texas, November 19-20, 1979), p. 6. See also William T. Gormley, Jr., *The Politics of Public Utility Regulation* (Pittsburgh: University of Pittsburgh Press, 1983).

41. Ibid., pp. 8-14.

42. Ibid.

43. Douglas D. Anderson, "State Regulation of Electric Utilities," Working Paper, Graduate School of Business, Harvard University, 1979, pp. 1-64.

44. Krasnow and Longley, *Broadcast Regulation*, pp. 180-94.

45. See Welborn and Brown, "State Economic Regulation," p. 22.

CHAPTER 7

1. Michael Wines, "Verdict Still Out on Deregulation's Impact on U.S. Air Travel System," *National Journal*, March 6, 1982, pp. 404-9.

2. Thomas S. Robertson, Scott Ward, and William M. Caldwell IV, "Deregulation: Surviving the Transition," *Harvard Business Review* 60 (July/August 1982): 20-23; Thomas S. Robertson and Scott Ward, "Management Lessons from Airline Deregulation," *Harvard Business Review* 61 (January/February 1983): 40-44; and Joel A. Bleeke and James W. Goodrich, "Winners and Losers under Deregulation," *Wall Street Journal*, December 7, 1981, p. 23.

3. George J. Stigler, "The Theory of Economic Regulation," *Bell Journal of Economics and Management* 2 (1971): 3-21.

4. See Paul Weaver, "Unlocking the Gilded Cage of Regulation," *Fortune*, February 1977, pp. 179-88; Donald D. Simon, "Senator Kennedy and the Civil Aeronautics Board," Parts I, II, and Sequel, Kennedy School of Government (1977); "The Big Deregulation Battle," *Duns Review* (March 1978): 49-65; Barry Mitnick, "Deregulation as a Process of Organizational Reduction," *Public Administration Review* (July/August 1978): 350-57; Rush Loving, Jr., "How the Airlines Will Cope with Deregulation," *Fortune*, November 20, 1978, pp. 38-41; Charles G. Burck, "Truckers Roll toward Deregulation," *Fortune*, December 18, 1978, pp. 75-85; Alexander Stuart, "A Bad Start on Gas Deregulation," *Fortune*, February 12, 1978, pp. 86-90; Albert R. Carr, "Truck Firms Gear up Major Lobbying Effort to Fight Deregulation," *Wall Street Journal*, July 5, 1979, p. 1; "One Year after Deregulation: The Airlines Hit a Downdraft," *Business Week*, November 5, 1979, pp. 104-12; Rush Loving, Jr., "The Railroads Bad Trip to Deregulation," *Fortune*, August 25, 1980, pp. 45-48; Michael R. Gordon, "Shippers Are Likely to Foot the Bill When Railroad Deregulation Arrives," *National Journal*, September 20, 1980, pp. 1553-55; Barry R. Weingast, "Regulation, Reregulation, and Deregulation: The Political Foundations of Agency-Clientele Relationships" (St. Louis: Center for the Study of American Business, November 1980), 62: 1-58; Fritz R. Kahn, "Motor Carrier Regulatory Reform: Fait Accompli," *Transportation Journal* 19 (Winter 1979): 5-11; W. Glen Harlan, "Airline Deregulation: Antitrust and Safety Considerations," *The Forum* 14 (Summer 1979): 1001-31.

5. See George W. Wilson, "Regulating and Deregulating Business," *Business Horizons* 25 (July/August 1982): 45-52.

6. See Paul J. Quirk and Martha Derthick, "Congressional Support for Pro-competitive Regulatory Reform" (Paper prepared for delivery at the 1981 annual meeting of the American Political Science Association, New York City, September 3-6, 1981), p. 25.

7. Ibid., p. 26.

8. Ibid., p. 6.

9. Irwin M. Stelzer, "Electric Utilities: Next Stop for Deregulators?" *Regulation* (July/August 1982): 29-35.

10. Walter Guzzardi, Jr., "Reagan's Reluctant Deregulators," *Fortune*, March 8, 1982, pp. 34-40.

11. Michael L. King, "Deregulation by ICC Appears to Hold Down Truck-rates Inflation," *Wall Street Journal*, May 9, 1980, pp. 1, 28.

12. Burck, "Truckers Roll," p. 78.

13. Ibid.

14. For a dissenting opinion, see Martin Farris, "The Case against Deregulation in Transportation, Power, and Communication," *ICC Practitioners Journal* (1980): 306-32.

15. See Quirk and Derthick, "Congressional Support," p. 35.

16. Ibid., p. 32.

17. Kahn, "Motor Carrier Regulatory Reform," pp. 5-11.

18. Donald V. Harper, "Consequences of Reform of Federal Economic Regulation of the Motor Trucking Industry," *Transportation Journal* (Summer 1982): 35-58.

19. Ibid.

20. Michael Wines, "If You Thought the Battle over Truck Deregulation Was Ended, Look Again," *National Journal*, September 5, 1981, pp. 1577-82.

21. Ibid.

22. See S. David Freeman, *Energy: The New Era* (New York: Walker and Co., 1974), pp. 170-71; Stephen Breyer and Paul W. MacAvoy, "Regulating Natural Gas Producers," in Robert J. Kalter and William A. Vogely, eds., *Energy Supply and Government Policy* (Ithaca, N.Y.: Cornell University Press, 1976), pp. 161-93; David Howard Davis, *Energy Politics*, 2d ed. (New York: St. Martin's, 1978), pp. 16-42; and Alexander Stuart, "The Blazing Battle to Free Natural Gas," *Fortune*, October 19, 1981, pp. 152-67.

23. See Stephen Breyer, *Regulation and Its Reform* (Cambridge, Mass.: Harvard University Press, 1982), p. 240.

24. Ibid.

25. Ibid., p. 243.

26. Ibid., p. 241.

27. Ibid.

28. Ibid.

29. Ibid., p.. 244.

30. Ibid.

31. Ibid.

32. Ibid.

33. See Pietro Nivola, "Energy Policy and the Congress: The Politics of the Natural Gas Policy Act of 1978," *Public Policy* 28 (Fall 1980): 491-543.

34. Stuart, "Blazing Battle," pp. 154-56.

35. Ibid.

36. Ibid.

37. Ibid.

38. Ibid.

39. Ibid.

40. See Richard A. Posner, "Theory of Economic Regulation," *Bell Journal of Economics and Management* 5 (Autumn 1974): 335-58.

41. See Nivola, "Energy Policy," pp. 491-543.

42. Lawrence Mosher, "Rising Natural Gas Prices: A Hard Lesson in Regulatory Miscalculation," *National Journal*, January 1, 1983, pp. 24-26; Victor A. Canto and Kevin A. Melich, "Natural Gas Decontrol: The Road to Lower Energy Prices," *Public Utilities Fortnightly*, October 28, 1982, pp. 31-40.

43. Arlon R. Tussing and Connie C. Barlow, "A Survival Strategy for Gas Companies in the Post-OPEC Era," *Public Utilities Fortnightly*, February 3, 1983, pp. 13-18; Eugene H. Luntey, "Where Was the Gas Industry in 1982?" *Public Utilities Fortnightly*, October 28, 1982, pp. 15-24; Mitch Betts, "White House: Decontrol Bill Will Cut Natural Gas Prices," *Energy User News*, March 7, 1983, pp. 1, 13.

44. As cited by Harlan, "Airline Deregulation," pp. 1001-30.

45. Ibid.

46. See Breyer, *Regulation*, pp. 201-5.

47. Ibid.

48. Ibid.

49. Ibid., pp. 205-9.

50. Richard Caves, *Air Transport and Its Regulators* (Cambridge, Mass.: Harvard University Press, 1962).

51. Breyer, *Regulation*, p. 325.

52. Ibid., p. 317.

53. Ibid., pp. 317-40.

54. Ibid., pp. 324-27.

55. See J. Ronald Fox, *Managing Business-Government Relations* (Homewood, Ill.: Irwin, 1982), pp. 166-89.

56. Breyer, *Regulation,* pp. 335-36.

57. Ibid., p. 336.

58. See Simon, "Senator Kennedy," pp. 36-38.

59. See Breyer, *Regulation*, p. 337.

60. See James C. Miller, "Is Airline Deregulation Working?" *Wall Street Journal*, March 26, 1980, p. 405.

61. Ibid.

62. Ibid.

63. Wines, "Verdict Still Out," p. 405.

64. "One Year after Deregulation," pp. 104-12.

65. Ibid. In 1983, with the end of the recession, profits began to increase and discounts began to decrease.

66. Roy J. Harris, Jr., "Stalled Jetliner Makers May Not Rise Steeply Even if the Airlines Do," *Wall Street Journal*, December 9, 1981, p. 1.

67. Loving, "Railroads Bad Trip"; see also Ronald D. Anderson, Roger E. Jerman, and James A. Constantin, "Railroad versus Motor Carriers Viewpoints on Regulatory Issues," *ICC Practitioners Journal* (1980): 294-305.

68. Robert J. Samuelson, "Congress Stops, Looks and Listens to Railroad Deregulation Complaints," *National Journal*, November 3, 1979, pp. 1844-48.

69. John D. Williams, "Rail-rate Increases Due for Early Arrival Thanks to New Law," *Wall Street Journal*, October 14, 1980, pp. 1, 28.

70. Loving, "Railroads Bad Trip," p. 45.

71. Bleeke and Goodrich, "Winners and Losers," p. 23; see also Marvin S. Cohen, "Airline Deregulation: A Model for the 80s"; Wesley G. Kaldahl, "Airline Trends under Deregulation"; and John F. Mahon and Edwin A. Murray, "Deregulation and Strategic Transformation"; all found in *Journal of Contemporary Business* 9, no. 2 (1980).

72. Bleeke and Goodrich, "Winners and Losers," p. 23.

CHAPTER 8

1. Charles E. Lindblom, *Politics and Markets* (New York: Basic Books, 1977), pp. 170-89. See also Charles E. Lindblom, "Why Government Must Cater to Business," *Business and Society Review* (Fall 1978): 4-6.

2. Lindblom, "Why Government," p. 5.

3. Ibid.

4. Ibid.

5. Ibid.

6. *The Federalist* (New York: G. P. Putnam's Sons, 1888).

7. James Q. Wilson and Patricia Rachal, "Can the Government Regulate Itself?" *The Public Interest* (Spring 1977).

8. See Murray L. Weidenbaum, "The Future of Business/Government Relations in the United States," in Max Ways, ed., *The Future of Business* (New York: Pergamon, 1979), p. 53.

9. Ibid.

10. Ibid., p. 48.

11. Ibid., p. 50.

12. See Lawrence Mosher, "Big Steel Says It Can't Afford to Make the Nation's Air Pure," *National Journal*, July 5, 1980, pp. 1088-92.

13. Weidenbaum, "Business/Government Relations," p. 52.

14. As cited in John Walsh, "Is R&D the Key to the Productivity Problem?" *Science* 211 (February 13, 1981); also see Edward Meadows, "A Close-up Look at the Productivity Lag," *Fortune*, December 4, 1978, pp. 83-90; George P. Schultz, "Keep This Rerun in the Can," *Wall Street Journal*, May 29, 1979, p. 22; Richard Nelson, "Research on Productivity Growth and Productivity Differences: Dead Ends and New Departures," *Journal of Economic Literature* 19 (September 1981): 1029-64; and Jordan D. Lewis, "Technology, Enterprise, and American Growth," *Science* 215 (March 5, 1982): 1204-11.

15. Walsh, "Is R&D the Key?" pp. 685-88.

16. Ibid.

17. See Alfred A. Marcus, "Public Interest Leaders: Whom Do They Represent?" *Business Horizons* 22 (August 1979): 84-88.

18. E. E. Schattschneider, *The Semisovereign People* (New York: Holt, Rinehart and Winston, 1960), as cited by Marcus, "Public Interest Leaders," p. 84.

19. As cited by Marcus, "Public Interest Leaders," p. 84. See also Andrew S. McFarland, *Public Interest Lobbies: Decision Making on Energy* (Washington, D.C.:

American Enterprise Institute, 1976), pp. 1-25; B. Weisbrod et al., *Public Interest Law* (Berkeley, Calif.: University of California Press, 1978); Mark V. Nadel, *The Politics of Consumer Protection* (Indianapolis: Bobbs-Merrill, 1971); and Paul N. Bloom and Stephen A. Greyser, "The Maturing of Consumerism," *Harvard Business Review* 59 (November/December 1981): 130-39. On the incentives that motivate public interest leaders, see James Q. Wilson, *Political Organizations* (New York: Basic Books, 1973), pp. 30-56.

20. See Jeffrey M. Berry, *Lobbying for the People* (Princeton, N.J.: Princeton University Press, 1977), p. 13.

21. Ibid., pp. 18-45.

22. Ibid., pp. 24-25.

23. Ibid., p. 85.

24. Ibid., pp. 93-94.

25. Ibid., p. 28.

26. Ibid.

27. Ibid., p. 72.

28. Ibid.

29. Ibid., p. 60.

30. Ibid.

31. Ibid., pp. 79-84.

32. Ibid., pp. 96-99.

33. Robert Leone, "The Real Costs of Regulation," *Harvard Business Review* 55 (November/December 1977), p. 60.

34. See Daniel Bell, "Too Much, Too Late: Reactions to Changing Social Values," in Neil H. Jacoby, ed., *The Business-Government Relationships* (Santa Monica, Calif.: Goodyear, 1975), p. 18.

35. Leone, "The Real Costs," p. 60.

36. Bell, "Too Much," p. 18.

37. Ibid.

38. Ibid.

39. Ibid., p. 19. See also Fred Hirsch, *Social Limits to Growth* (Cambridge, Mass.: Harvard University Press, 1976); Mancur Olson and Hans Landsberg, eds., *The No-growth Society* (New York: Norton, 1973); and Lester Thurow, *The Zero-sum Society* (New York: Basic Books, 1970).

40. Bell, "Too Much," p. 19. See also Hirsch, *Social Limits*, p. 62.

41. See James Q. Wilson, "American Politics, Then and Now," *Commentary* (February 1979): 39-46.

42. Ibid.

43. Ibid.

44. Ibid.

45. See Alan Stone, *Regulation and Its Alternatives* (Washington, D.C.: Congressional Quarterly Press, 1982), p. 177.

46. See Eugene Bardach and Robert A. Kagan, *Going by the Book* (Philadelphia: Temple University Press, 1982), p. 224.

47. Murray Edelman, *The Symbolic Uses of Politics* (Urbana, Ill.: University of Illinois Press, 1967), p. 167, as cited by Stone, *Regulation*, p. 186.

48. See Howard Margolis, "The Politics of Auto Emissions," *The Public Interest* 49 (Fall 1977): 3-4; as cited by Stone, p. 187.

49. See Steven Kelman, "Occupational Safety and Health Administration," in

James Q. Wilson, ed., *The Politics of Regulation* (New York: Basic Books, 1980), pp. 236-67.

50. Ibid., p. 241.

51. See Alfred A. Marcus, "Environmental Protection Agency," in Wilson, *Politics of Regulation*, pp. 267-304.

52. *Surface Mining Control and Reclamation Act of 1977*, Hearings before the Senate Subcommittee on Public Lands and Resources (95-7) (Washington, D.C.: Government Printing Office, 1977), p. 203; as cited by Richard Allan Harris, "Towards a Managerial Theory of the Supply and Demand for Regulation: The Political Economy of the Enactment and Implementation of SMCRA" (Paper prepared for delivery at the Fourth Annual Research Conference of the Association for Public Policy Analysis and Management, October 28-30, 1982, Hyatt Regency Hotel, Minneapolis, Minnesota).

53. See Robert Crandall, "Is Government Regulation Crippling Business?" *Saturday Review*, January 20, 1979, pp. 31-34; Bruce A. Ackerman and William T. Hassler, "Beyond the New Deal: Coal and the Clean Air Act," *Yale Law Journal* 89 (July 1980): 1466-1573; and William C. Banks, "EPA Bends to Industry Pressure on Coal NSPS—and Breaks," *Ecology Law Quarterly* 9, no. 67 (1980): 67-117.

54. See William Lilley III and James C. Miller III, "The New 'Social Regulation,'" *The Public Interest* 47 (1977): 58; as cited by Alfred A. Marcus, "The Disproportionate Power of Environmentalists," *Harvard Environmental Law Review* 2 (1977): 582-95.

55. Marcus, "Disproportionate Power," p. 585.

56. Lilley and Miller, "New 'Social Regulation,'" p. 58.

57. James Q. Wilson, "The Dead Hand of Regulation," *The Public Interest* 40 (Fall 1971): 40.

58. Marcus, "Disproportionate Power," p. 585.

59. See Walter Guzzardi, Jr., "Business Is Learning How to Win in Washington," *Fortune*, March 27, 1978, pp. 53-58.

60. See J. Ronald Fox, *Managing Business-Government Relations* (Homewood, Ill.: Irwin, 1982), pp. 458-81.

61. Ibid., p. 467.

62. Ibid.

63. Ibid., p. 470.

64. See Walter Guzzardi, Jr., "A New Public Face for Business," *Fortune*, June 30, 1980, pp. 48-52.

65. Ibid., p. 50.

66. Ibid., p. 49.

67. Ibid., p. 50.

68. Ibid.

CHAPTER 9

1. Eugene Bardach and Robert A. Kagan, *Going by the Book* (Philadelphia: Temple University Press, 1982), p. 52.

2. Ibid.

3. Alfred Marcus, "Command and Control: An Assessment of Smokestack Emission Regulation," in John Brigham and Dan W. Brown, eds., *Policy Implementation: Penalties or Incentives?* (Beverly Hills, Calif.: Sage, 1980), p. 210.

4. See Paul Sabatier and Daniel Mazmanian, "The Implementation of Public Policy: A Framework of Analysis," *Policy Studies Journal* 8 (Special #2, 1980): 538-60.

5. Roland J. Cole and Paul Sommers, "Business and Government Regulation: A Theory of Compliance Decisions," *Journal of Contemporary Business* 10, no. 1 (1981): 143-53; Barry Baron and Philip Baron, "A Regulatory Compliance Model," *Journal of Contemporary Business* 9, no. 2 (1980): 139-51. On the subject of compliance, see also James E. Anderson, *Public Policy-Making* (New York: Praeger, 1975), pp. 120-32; Colin Diver, "The Theory of Regulatory Enforcement," *Public Policy* 28, no. 3 (1980): 257-99; Kathleen Kemp, "Social Responsibility and Coercive Sanctions in Economic Regulation" (Paper prepared for the Symposium on Regulatory Policy, Houston, Texas, November 18 and 19, 1979); and Roland N. McKean, "Enforcement Costs in Environmental and Safety Regulation," *Policy Analysis* 6, no. 3 (1980): 269-89.

6. See Robert W. Ackerman, *The Social Challenge to Business* (Cambridge, Mass.: Harvard University Press, 1975); and Edwin M. Epstein, *The Corporation in American Politics* (Englewood Cliffs, N.J.: Prentice-Hall, 1969).

7. As cited in Ackerman, *Social Challenge*, pp. 8-9.

8. Ibid.

9. Ibid., pp. 12-29.

10. Ibid., p. 23.

11. See Frederick Sturdivant, *Business and Society: A Managerial Approach* (Homewood, Ill.: Irwin, 1977), pp. 233-73.

12. Ibid.

13. Ackerman, *Social Challenge*, p. 17.

14. Alfred A. Marcus, *Promise and Performance: Choosing and Implementing an Environmental Policy* (Westport, Conn.: Greenwood Press, 1980), pp. 165-66. Aggregate employment actually may have increased. GNP was higher in the short run and lower later on.

15. Ibid.

16. Ibid.

17. Ibid.

18. See Timothy B. Clark, "How One Company Lives with Government Regulation," *National Journal*, May 12, 1979, p. 775.

19. Ibid.

20. Ibid.

21. Ibid.

22. Ibid., p. 774.

23. Ibid.

24. See Cole and Sommers, "Business and Government," pp. 147-49.

25. See McKean, "Enforcement Costs," pp. 9-10.

26. Ibid.

27. Ibid.

28. See Clark, "How One Company Lives," p. 778.

29. Ibid., p. 775.

30. As cited by Clark, "How One Company Lives," p. 778.

31. Roberta C. Carter, "The Responses of the American Automobile Industry to Environmental Protection: A Study of Regulatory Experience" (Ph.D. diss., University of Colorado, 1979), p. iii.

32. Ibid., p. 7.

33. Ibid.

34. See Paul Halpern, "The Corvair, the Pinto, and Corporate Behavior: Implications for Regulatory Reform" (Paper prepared for the Symposium on Regulatory Policy, University of Houston and Loyola University of Chicago, Houston, Texas, November 19, 1979), p. 2.

35. Ibid., pp. 3-4.

36. Ibid., p. 4.

37. Ibid.

38. Ibid., p. 5.

39. Ibid.

40. Ibid.

41. Ibid.

42. Ibid., p. 6.

43. Ibid., p. 7.

44. Ibid., pp. 8-9.

45. See Stephen Breyer, *Regulation and Its Reform* (Cambridge, Mass.: Harvard University Press, 1982), p. 96.

46. Ibid., p. 101.

47. Ibid., p. 100.

48. Ibid., p. 117.

49. Ibid., pp. 110-11.

50. Ibid., pp. 103-7.

51. Ibid., p. 110.

52. Ibid., p. 117.

53. Ibid.

54. See Richard J. Tobin, "Federal Regulation of Hazardous Consumer Products" (Paper prepared for the Symposium on Regulatory Policy, University of Houston and Loyola University of Chicago, Houston, Texas, November 19, 1979).

55. See Bardach and Kagan, *Going by the Book*, p. 53.

56. Ibid., p. 52.

57. Ibid., pp. 54-56.

58. Ibid., p. 58.

59. Ibid., p. 59.

60. Ibid., p. 73.

61. Ibid., p. 94.

62. Ibid., p. 101.

63. Ibid.

64. Ibid., p. 119.

65. Arthur W. Hansen, "An FDA Inspection: Preparing for the Inevitable," *Food, Drug, and Cosmetic Law Journal* (December 1981): 641-46.

66. See Paul Danaceau, "Developing Successful Enforcement Programs," in Eugene Bardach and Robert A. Kagan, eds., *Social Regulation* (New Brunswick, N.J.: Transaction Books, 1982), pp. 139-58.

67. See Bardach and Kagan, *Going by the Book*, pp. 217-42.

68. Ibid.

69. See Marc Roberts and J. S. Bluhm, *The Choices of Power* (Cambridge, Mass.: Harvard University Press, 1981), pp. 368-69.

70. Ibid.

71. Ibid., pp. 340-41.

72. Ibid., pp. 325-61.

73. Ibid., pp. 341-43.

74. Ibid.

75. Ibid., pp. 344-45.

76. Ibid., p. 369.

77. Ibid., pp. 346-48.

78. Ibid., p. 339.

79. See Ackerman, *Social Challenge*, p. 31; also see Lee Preston and James Post, *Private Management and Public Policy* (Englewood Cliffs, N.J.: Prentice-Hall, 1975), pp. 75-94.

80. Ackerman, *Social Challenge*, p. 32.

81. Ibid.

82. Ibid., p. 33.

83. Ibid.

84. Roberts and Bluhm, *Choices of Power*, p. 356.

85. See Elizabeth Gatewood and Archie B. Carroll, "The Anatomy of Corporate Social Response: The Rely, Firestone 500, and Pinto Cases," *Business Horizons* 24 (September/October 1981): 9-16. See also Keith Davis and Robert Blomstrom, *Business and Society*, 3d ed. (New York: McGraw-Hill, 1975), pp. 85-86; and Dow Votaw and S. P. Sethi, *The Corporate Dilemma* (Englewood Cliffs, N.J.: Prentice-Hall, 1974), as cited by Gatewood and Carroll.

86. Charles G. Burck, "There's Big Business in All That Garbage," *Fortune*, April 7, 1980, pp. 106-12.

87. Ibid.

88. Ibid.

89. See Michael G. Royston, "Making Pollution Prevention Pay," *Harvard Business Review* 80 (November/December 1980): pp. 6-10.

90. See Burck, "There's Big Business," pp. 106-12. Dow also established a program to monitor the costs of regulatory compliance; see Joseph Bevirt, "The Cost Impact of Federal Government Regulation on the Dow Chemical Company," reprinted from the *1978 Business and Economics Section Proceedings of the American Statistical Association*, pp. 354-58.

91. See James E. Post, *Corporate Behavior and Social Change* (Reston, Va.: Reston, 1978), pp. 167-85. Stonewalling can be a useful tool that buffers the corporation from undesirable changes.

92. See Donald D. Holt, "Why Eaton Got Out of the Air-Bag Business," *Fortune*, March 12, 1979, p. 146.

93. Ibid., p. 148.

94. Ibid.; see also "Is GM Deflating the Air Bag?" *Consumer Reports*, April 1980, pp. 226-27.

95. See Charles G. Burck, "How G.M. Turned Itself Around," *Fortune*, January 16, 1978, pp. 87-100; and Hugh D. Menzies, "Union Carbide Raises Its Voice," *Fortune*, September 25, 1978, pp. 86-90; on the response of the auto industry, see also Carter, "Responses."

96. Burck, "G.M.," pp. 91-95.

97. Ibid.

98. Ibid.

99. Ibid.

100. Menzies, "Union Carbide," pp. 86-90.

101. Ibid.

102. Ibid.

103. Ibid.

104 Roberts and Bluhm, *Choices of Power*, p. 326.

105. Ibid.

106. See Robert Leone, "The Real Costs of Regulation," *Harvard Business Review* 77 (November/December, 1977): 65.

107. Clyde H. Farnsworth, "Study for E.P.A. Finds Rules Are Costly for Steel Industry," *New York Times*, September 26, 1980, p. 25.

108. Bardach and Kagan, *Going by the Book*, pp. 118-19.

109. Ibid.

110. Ibid.

111. See Marcus, "Command and Control," pp. 209-26.

112. See Marver H. Bernstein, *Regulating Business by Independent Commission* (Princeton, N.J.: Princeton University Press, 1955), p. 225.

113. James Q. Wilson, "The Politics of Regulation," in James W. McKie, ed., *Social Responsibility and the Business Predicament* (Washington, D.C.: Brookings Institution, 1974), p. 167.

114. See Marcus, "Command and Control," p. 214.

115. Ibid.

116. Ibid., p. 216.

117. Ibid., pp. 219-20.

118. Ibid., p. 217. Complying firms may be large firms with a great number of small competitors. They may comply as a competitive tool; that is, to legitimate the regulatory scheme, as noted in chapter 1. Their compliance is at least partially designed to put their competitors in a position where they will have relatively higher costs, because it may be difficult for small competitors to comply without greater expense. Small firms in stable or declining industries, like mining, may resist complying because they lack expertise and capital.

119. See Marcus, *Promise and Performance*, pp. 101-19.

120. Ibid., p. 165.

121. See R. Jeffrey Smith, "EPA and Industry Pursue Regulatory Options," *Science* 211 (Feb. 20, 1981): 796-98.

CHAPTER 10

1. The author would like to acknowledge the assistance of Craig Aronson, whose memo, "Regulatory Reform" (Battelle Human Affairs Research Centers, February 23, 1982), was very helpful in drafting this chapter. See, for example, EPA, "Checklist of Regulatory Alternatives" (Washington, D.C.: Office of Planning and Management, July 1980); see also "Guidebook Series on Alternative Regulatory Approaches" (Washington, D.C.: U.S. Regulatory Council, 1981).

2. Mark Nadel, "Regulatory Reform" (concept paper, Battelle Human Affairs Research Centers, Washington, D.C., 1983), p. 12.

3. Ibid.

4. Environmental Protection Agency, *Economic Impacts of Pulp and Paper Industry Compliance with Environmental Regulations* (Washington, D.C.: EPA Office of Planning and Evaluation, 1977), pp. 1-25.

5. See W. I. Watson and R. G. Ridker, "Revising Water Pollution Standards in an Uncertain World," *Land Economics* 10 (1981): 495.

6. See Nadel, "Regulatory Reform," p. 4.

7. See Stephen Breyer, *Regulation and Its Reform* (Cambridge, Mass.: Harvard University Press, 1982).

8. See Lloyd Cutter and David Johnson, "Regulation and the Political Process" (Paper prepared for the President's Advisory Committee on Government Organization), as cited by Breyer, *Regulation*, p. 359.

9. See Breyer, *Regulation*, p. 359.

10. Ibid., pp. 359-60.

11. Ibid., pp. 357-58.

12. Ibid., p. 360.

13. B. Ackerman et al., *The Uncertain Search for Environmental Quality* (New Haven: Yale University, 1974), pp. 147-61; as cited by Breyer, *Regulation*, p. 361.

14. A. Kantrowitz, "Controlling Technology Democratically," *American Scientist* 63 (September-October 1975), p. 505; as cited by Breyer, *Regulation*, pp. 361-62.

15. Breyer, *Regulation*, p. 362.

16. See ibid., pp. 366-67; and Richard E. Cohen, "Sunset Proposals in Congress: Sinking below the Horizon?" *National Journal*, November 24, 1979, pp. 1978-81.

17. Breyer, *Regulation*, p. 361.

18. On regulatory costs, see David A. Gavin and Robert A. Leone, "Regulatory Cost Analysis: An Overview," in *Environmental Impact Assessment Review* 2 (February 1, 1981): 39-62; and Roland N. McKean, "Avoidance and Enforcement Costs in Government Regulation" (Washington University, St. Louis: Center for the Study of American Business, October 1976). On benefits, see Committee on Governmental Affairs, United States Senate, Center for Policy Alternatives at MIT, *Benefits of Environmental, Health, and Safety Regulation* (Washington, D.C.: Government Printing Office, March 25, 1980); and Martin J. Bailey, *Reducing Risks to Life* (Washington, D.C.: American Enterprise Institute, 1980). On some of the problems with cost-benefit analysis, see Nicholas A. Ashford, "The Limits of Cost-Benefit Analysis in Regulatory Decisions," *Technology Review* (May 1980): 70-72. On risk analysis, see Susan Hadden and Jared Hazelton, "Public Policies toward Risk," *Policy Studies Journal* 9 (Autumn 1980): 109-17; Samuel S. Epstein, *The Politics of Cancer* (Garden City, N.Y.: Anchor Books, 1979); Baruch Fischhoff et al., "How Safe Is Safe Enough? A Psychometric Study of Attitudes towards Technological Risks and Benefits," *Policy Sciences* 9 (1978): 127-52; and Subcommittee on Environment and Atmosphere, Congressional Research Service, *Effects of Chronic Exposure to Low-Level Pollutants in the Environment* (Washington, D.C.: Government Printing Office, November 1975).

19. See Charles L. Schultze, "The Public Use of Private Interest," *Regulation* (September/October 1977): 10. Also see the book by Schultze, *The Public Use of Private Interest* (Washington, D.C.: Brookings Institution, 1977).

20. See Bruce M. Owen and Ronald Braeutigam, *The Regulation Game: Strategic Uses of the Administrative Process* (Cambridge, Mass.: Ballinger, 1978), p. 1.

21. George J. Stigler, *The Citizen and the State: Essays in Regulation* (Chicago: University of Chicago Press, 1975), pp. 14-19.

22. Ronald Reagan, Ralph Nader, and Hubert Humphrey, "Government Regulation: What Kind of Reform?" (Washington, D.C.: American Enterprise Institute, 1975), p. 3.

23. Ibid.

24. See *Congressional Record*, August 6, 1980, p. 510936.

25. For more details on how this procedure might work, see Fred Bosselman et al., *The Permit Explosion: Coordination of the Proliferation* (Washington, D.C.: Urban Law Institute, 1978).

26. See Fred Thompson and Larry R. Jones, "Fighting Regulation: The Regulatory Review," *California Management Review* (Winter 1980): 5-19; Patrick J. Hennigan, "Politics of Regulatory Analysis" (Paper prepared for delivery at the annual meeting of the American Political Science Association, New York City, September 4, 1981); David P. McCaffrey, "Executive Orders and the Organization of Regulatory Cost-Benefit Analysis" (Paper presented at Academy of Management National Meetings, New York City, August 1982); and W. Kip Viscusi, "Presidential Oversight: Controlling the Regulators," *Journal of Policy Analysis and Management* 2 (Winter 1983): 157-73.

27. See Thompson and Jones, "Fighting Regulation," pp. 7-9; Hennigan, "Regulatory Analysis," pp. 3-4; and McCaffrey, "Executive Orders," pp. 6-8.

28. See Hennigan, "Regulatory Analysis," p. 12.

29. Ibid., p. 17.

30. See McCaffrey, "Executive Orders," p. 13.

31. Ibid.

32. See George C. Eads, "White House Oversight of Executive Branch Regulation," in Eugene Bardach and Robert A. Kagan, eds., *Social Regulation* (New Brunswick, N.J.: Transaction Books, 1982), pp. 177-200.

33. See Hennigan, "Regulatory Analysis," p. 43.

34. Ibid.

35. McCaffrey, "Executive Orders," p. 13.

36. Ibid.

37. See Eads, "White House Oversight," p. 196.

38. Ibid.

39. Ibid.

40. Neil Sullivan, "The Cotton Dust Decision: The Confusion Continues," *Administrative Law Review* 34, no. 3 (Summer 1982): 483-94.

41. Ibid.

42. See for instance, Larry E. Ruff, "The Economic Common Sense of Pollution," *The Public Interest* (Spring 1970): 69-85; Robert M. Solow, "The Economist's Approach to Pollution and Its Control," *Science* 173 (August 6, 1971): 498-503; Lawrence J. White, "Effluent Charges as a Faster Means of Achieving Pollution Abatement," *Public Policy* (Winter 1976): 645-59; A. Myrick Freeman III, Robert H. Haveman, and Allen V. Kneese, *The Economics of Environmental Policy* (Santa Barbara, Calif.: Wiley, 1973); Allen V. Kneese and Charles L. Schultze, *Pollution, Prices, and Public Policy* (Washington, D.C.: Brookings Institution, 1975); and Tom Alexander, "A Simpler Path to a Cleaner Environment," *Fortune*, May 4, 1981, pp. 234-54.

43. Environmental Protection Agency, *Regulatory Reform Initiatives* (Quarterly Progress Report, December 1978), p. 1. On EPA's program, also see the following: Environmental Protection Agency, ibid.; Environmental Protection Agency, Office of Planning and Management, "Progress Report, October 1979" (Washington, D.C., 1979); Environmental Protection Agency, "Part VII (Bubble Policy): Air Pollution Control; Recommendation for Alternative Emission Reduction Options within State

Implementation Plans" (Policy Statement, *Federal Register* 44, no. 239 (December 11, 1979): 71780-88; John S. Hoffman, "How to Reduce the Costs of Achieving and Maintaining Air Quality Standards in Metropolitan Areas" (Environmental Protection Agency, Office of Planning and Evaluation, Emissions Offsets, Banking and Trading Project, October, 1979); John DiFazio, "Offset Policy Memorandum: Cases to Date" (Environmental Protection Agency, Office of Enforcement, 1978); William H. Foskett, "Emission Offset Policy at Work: A Summary Analysis of Eight Cases" (working paper) (Washington, D.C.: Performance Development Institute, 1979); S. A. Blackman and William J. Baumol, "Modified Fiscal Incentives in Environmental Policy," *Land Economics* 56 (November 1980): 417-31.

44. Environmental Protection Agency, *Regulatory Reform Initiatives*, p. 1.

45. As quoted by Peter Nulty, "A Brave Experiment in Pollution Control," *Fortune*, February 12, 1979, p. 120; also see Bruce Yandle, "The Emerging Market in Air Pollution Rights," *Regulation* (July/August 1978): 21-29.

46. See Gerald Zaltman and Robert Duncan, *Strategies for Planned Change* (New York: Wiley, 1977), p. 14. Also see Jack Rothman, *Planning and Organizing for Social Change* (New York: Columbia University Press, 1974), p. 446; and James D. Sorg, "Implementation of Innovations: A Descriptive Model of the Process" (Paper prepared for delivery at the annual conference of the American Society of Public Administration, Baltimore Civic Center, March 1979).

47. See Zaltman and Duncan, *Strategies*, p. 14.

48. See discussion in Alfred A. Marcus, Paul Sommers, and F. A. Morris, "Alternative Arrangements for Cost Effective Pollution Abatement: The Need for Implementation Analysis," *Policy Studies Review* 3 (1982): 447.

49. Giandomenico Majone, "Choice among Policy Instruments for Pollution Control," *Policy Analysis* (Fall 1976): 597; also see Stephen Linder and Gerry Suchanek, "A Second Best Mechanism for Marketing Emissions Reductions," *Policy Sciences* 13 (1981): 195-203.

50. Majone, "Choice," p. 597.

51. J. H. Dales, *Pollution, Property, and Prices* (Toronto: University of Toronto Press, 1968).

52. See Marcus, Sommers, and Morris, "Alternative Arrangements, p. 479.

53. See Alfred A. Marcus, "Recent Proposals to Improve Environmental Policymaking," *Harvard Environmental Law Review* 1 (1976): 632-45; and Lettie McSpadden Wenner, *One Environmental Law* (Santa Barbara, Calif.: Goodyear, 1976), p. 152.

54. See Rene Dubos, *Man Adapting*, 8th ed. (New Haven, Conn.: Yale University Press, 1972); and Walsh McDermott, "Air Pollution and Public Health," in Paul Ehrlich, John Holdren, and Richard Holm, *Man and Ecosphere* (San Francisco, Calif.: W. H. Freeman, 1971), pp. 137-47.

55. "A Pollution Tax Won't Help Control Pollution," remarks of Daniel W. Cannon, Director of Environmental Affairs, National Association of Manufacturers, before the Environmental Study Conference, United States Congress (Washington, D.C., May 12, 1976).

56. Frederick R. Anderson, Allen V. Kneese, Phillip D. Reed, Serge Taylor, and Russell B. Stevenson, *Environmental Improvement through Economic Incentives* (Baltimore: Johns Hopkins, 1977), p. 158.

57. See Michael H. Levin, "Getting There: Implementing the 'Bubble' Policy," in Bardach and Kagan, *Social Regulation*, p. 65.

58. Steven Kelman, *What Price Incentives?* (Boston: Auburn House, 1981), p. 118.

59. Kelman, *Incentives*, pp. 119-20.

60. Ibid., p. 120.

61. Environment and Natural Resources Policy Division, Congressional Research Service, *Pollution Taxes, Effluent Charges, and Other Alternatives for Pollution Control* (Washington, D.C.: Government Printing Office, May 1977), p. 664.

62. Kelman, *Incentives*, p. 100.

63. Ibid.

64. Ibid.

65. Ibid., p. 102.

66. Ibid., p. 105.

67. Ibid., p. 106.

68. Ibid., p. 107.

69. K. N. Lee, "Options for Environmental Policy," in Environment and Natural Resources Policy Division, Congressional Research Service, *Pollution Taxes*, p. 677.

70. Levin, "Getting There," p. 65.

71. Kelman, *Incentives*, p. 112.

72. Ibid.

73. Ibid., p. 114.

74. Ibid., p. 107.

75. Ibid.

76. Ibid., p. 116.

77. See Alfred A. Marcus, *Promise and Performance* (Westport, Conn.: Greenwood Press, 1980), pp. 101-12.

78. See Nadel, "Regulatory Reform."

79. See David W. Tunderman, "Economic Enforcement Tools for Pollution Control: The Connecticut Plan," reprinted in Environment and Natural Resources Policy Division, Congressional Research Service, *Pollution Taxes*, pp. 835-57. Also see William Drayton, "Comments," in Ann F. Friedlaender, ed., *Approaches for Controlling Air Pollution* (Cambridge, Mass.: MIT Press, 1978), pp. 231-39.

80. See Alfred A. Marcus, "Converting Thought to Action: The Use of Economic Incentives to Reduce Pollution" (Paper prepared for delivery at the annual meeting of the American Political Science Association, Washington Hilton, August 31-September 3, 1979).

81. Nadel, "Regulatory Reform," p. 6.

82. Ibid.

83. Ibid., p. 8.

84. Ibid., p. 7.

85. Ibid.

86. See Nulty, "Brave Experiment," p. 120.

87. See Levin, "Getting There," p. 63.

88. Ibid., p. 66; see also Daniel J. Fiorino, "Implementing Regulatory Reforms— An Agency Perspective" (Paper presented at the Symposium on Strategies for Change in Regulatory Policy, Chicago, Ill., December 3-4, 1979).

89. Levin, "Getting There," pp. 67, 88-89.

90. Ibid., p. 78.

91. Ibid., p. 80.

92. Ibid., p. 84.

93. Ibid.

94. See Donald Simon, "Senator Kennedy and the Civil Aeronautics Board," Part I, Part II, and Sequel (Cambridge, Mass.: Kennedy School of Government, 1977); see also Paul Blustein, "Supply-side Theories Become Federal Policy with Unusual Speed," *Wall Street Journal*, October 8, 1981, p. 1.

95. See Rush Loving, Jr., "The Pros and Cons of Airline Deregulation," *Fortune*, August 1977, pp. 209-17.

96. Schultze, "Public Use," p. 13.

97. See Guido Calabresi and Philip Bobbitt, *Tragic Choices* (New York: W. W. Norton, 1978).

98. Ibid.

CHAPTER 11

1. See Barry Mitnick, "The Strategic Uses of Regulation and Deregulation," *Business Horizons* 24 (March 1981): 71-83.

2. Ibid.

3. Robert Leone, "The Real Costs of Regulation," *Harvard Buisiness Review* 55 (November/December 1977): 62.

4. Ibid.

5. Mitnick, "Strategic Uses," pp. 72-73.

6. Ibid., p. 76.

7. Ibid.

8. Bruce Owen and Ronald Braeutigam, *The Regulation Game* (Cambridge, Mass.: Ballinger, 1978), p. 25.

9. Leone, "Real Costs," p. 60.

10. Owen and Braeutigam, *Regulation Game*, p. 1.

11. Barry Mitnick, "Myths of Creation and Fables of Administration: Explanation and the Strategic Use of Regulation," *Public Administration Review* 40 (May/June 1980): 275-86.

12. Joel F. Handler, *Social Movements and the Legal System* (New York: Academic Press, 1978); as cited by Mitnick.

13. Mitnick, "Strategic Uses."

14. See James Q. Wilson, "The Politics of Regulation," in James Q. Wilson, ed., *The Politics of Regulation* (New York: Basic Books, 1980); also see George J. Stigler, "The Theory of Economic Regulation," *Bell Journal of Economics and Management* 2 (Spring 1971), p. 3.

15. Wilson, "Politics of Regulation," p. 364.

16. See Bernstein, *Regulating Business by Independent Commission* (Princeton, N.J.: Princeton University Press, 1955), pp. 90-95.

17. Ibid.

18. Wilson, "Politics of Regulation," p. 386.

19. Richard A. Posner, "Theory of Economic Regulation," *Bell Journal of Economics and Management* 5 (1974): 335-58.

20. Ibid.

21. Ibid.

22. Ibid.

23. Ibid.

24. Ibid.

25. Wilson, "Politics of Regulation," pp. 364-72.

26. Ibid.

27. Ibid.

28. Ibid., pp. 374-82.

29. Alfred A. Marcus, *Promise and Performance: Choosing and Implementing an Environmental Policy* (Westport, Conn.: Greenwood Press, 1980), pp. 107-12.

30. Ibid.

31. Murray L. Weidenbaum, "The Future of Business: Shock or Stability?" in *The Future of Business Regulation* (New York: Amacom, 1979), p. 3.

32. Ibid.

33. Leslie Wayne, "The New Face of Business Leadership," *New York Times*, May 22, 1983, sec. 3, p. 1.

34. See Paul Morrison, "Playing Political Hardball," *Harvard Business Review* 82 (September/October 1982): 34-40.

35. B. D. Baysinger and R. W. Woodman, "Dimensions of the Public Affairs/Government Relations Function in Major American Corporations," *Strategic Management Journal* 3 (January-March 1982): 27-41.

36. See James O'Toole, "What's Ahead for the Business-Government Relationship," *Harvard Business Review* 57 (March/April 1979): 94-105.

37. See Baysinger and Woodman, "Dimensions," p. 27.

38. Steven N. Brenner, "Business and Politics: An Update," *Harvard Business Review* 57 (November/December 1979): 149-63.

39. Ibid.

40. See Wayne, "New Face."

41. Ibid.

42. O'Toole, "What's Ahead," p. 98.

43. Ibid.

44. Ibid., p. 99.

45. Peter F. Drucker, "Coping with Those Extra Burdens," *Wall Street Journal*, May 2, 1979, p. 22.

46. Ibid.

47. Ibid.

48. As cited by Bruce Bartlett, "The Old Politics of a New Industrial Policy," *Wall Street Journal*, April 19, 1983, p. 28.

49. See Joe D. Waggonner, "Aspects of Legislative Persuasion: Business," *National Tax Journal* 32 (September 1979): 290-95.

50. See Wilson, "Politics of Regulation," pp. 362-63.

51. Ibid.

52. Robert B. Reich, "Making Industrial Policy," *Foreign Affairs* 60 (Spring 1982): 852-81.

53. See O'Toole, "What's Ahead," p. 97.

54. Reich, "Making Industrial Policy," p. 871.

55. Ibid.

Selected Bibliography

THE STRATEGIC APPROACH

Fenn, Dan H. "Finding Where the Power Lies in Government." *Harvard Business Review* 79 (September/October 1979): 144-53.

Fox, J. Ronald. *Managing Business-Government Relations.* Homewood, Ill.: Irwin, 1982.

Fritschler, A. Lee, and Bernard H. Ross. *Executive's Guide to Government.* Cambridge, Mass.: Winthrop, 1980.

Gatewood, Elizabeth, and Archie B. Carroll. "The Anatomy of Corporate Social Response: The Rely, Firestone 500, and Pinto Cases." *Business Horizons* 24 (September/October 1981): 9-16.

Grefe, E. A. *Fighting to Win: Business Political Power.* New York: Harcourt Brace Jovanovich, 1981.

Leone, Robert. "The Real Costs of Regulation." *Harvard Business Review* 77 (November/December 1977): 57-66.

Mitnick, Barry. "The Strategic Uses of Regulation and Deregulation." *Business Horizons* 24 (March 1981): 71-83.

Murray, Edwin A., Jr. "Strategic Choice as a Negotiated Outcome." *Management Science* 24 (May 1978): 960-72.

Owen, Bruce, and Ronald Braeutigam. *The Regulation Game.* Cambridge, Mass.: Ballinger, 1978.

Pfeffer, Jeffrey, and Gerald R. Salancik. *The External Control of Organizations.* New York: Harper and Row, 1978.

Post, James E. *Corporate Behavior and Social Change.* Reston, Va.: Reston, 1978.

Post, James E., E. A. Murray, R. B. Dickie, and J. F. Mahon. "The Public Affairs Function in American Corporations." *Long Range Planning* 15 (1982): 12-21.

Preston, Lee, and James Post. *Private Management and Public Policy*. Englewood Cliffs, N.J.: Prentice-Hall, 1975.

Roberts, Marc, and J. S. Bluhm. *The Choices of Power*. Cambridge, Mass.: Harvard University Press, 1981.

Royston, Michael G. "Making Pollution Prevention Pay." *Harvard Business Review* 80 (November/December 1980): 6-10.

Sethi, S. Prakash. "Dimensions of Corporate Social Responsibility." *California Management Review* 17 (Spring 1975): 58-64.

Sonnenfeld, Jeffrey A. *Corporate Views of the Public Interest*. Boston: Auburn House, 1981.

BUSINESS AND GOVERNMENT

Anderson, James F. *Public Policy-Making*. New York: Praeger, 1975.

Bell, Daniel. "Too Much, Too Late: Reactions to Changing Social Values." In *The Business-Government Relationships*, ed. Neil H. Jacoby, pp. 15-23. Santa Monica, Calif.: Goodyear, 1975.

Berry, Jeffrey M. *Lobbying for the People*. Princeton, N.J.: Princeton University Press, 1977.

Brenner, Steven N. "Business and Politics: An Update." *Harvard Business Review* 79 (November/December 1979): 149-63.

Cyert, R. M., and J. G. March. *A Behavioral Theory of the Firm*. Englewood Cliffs, N.J.: Prentice-Hall, 1963.

Dill, William R. "Business Organizations." In *Handbook of Organizations*, ed. James G. March, pp. 1071-1114. Chicago: Rand McNally, 1965.

Dunlop, John T., Alfred D. Chandler, Jr., George P. Schultz, and Irving S. Shapiro. "Business and Public Policy." *Harvard Business Review* 79 (November/December 1979): 85-101.

Dye, Thomas. *Understanding Public Policy*. Englewood Cliffs, N.J.: Prentice-Hall, 1978.

Epstein, Edwin M. *The Corporation in American Politics*. Englewood Cliffs, N.J.: Prentice-Hall, 1969.

Hirsch, Fred. *Social Limits to Growth*. Cambridge, Mass.: Harvard University Press, 1976.

Jordan, A. Grant. "Iron Triangles, Wooly Corporatism, or Elastic Nets: Images of the Policy Process." *Journal of Public Policy* 1, pt. 1 (February 1981): 95-125.

Joskow, Paul. "Inflation and Environmental Concern: Structural Change in the Process of Public Utility Price Regulation." *Journal of Law and Economics* (October 1974): 291-327.

LaPorte, Todd, ed. *Organized Social Complexity: Challenge to Politics and Policy*. Princeton, N.J.: Princeton University Press, 1975.

Larkey, Patrick, Chandler Stolp, and Mark Wines. "Theorizing about the Growth of Government: A Research Assessment." *Journal of Public Policy* 1, pt. 2 (May 1981): 167.

Lilley, William, III, and James C. Miller III. "The New Social Regulation." *The Public Interest* (Spring 1977): 49-62.

Lindblom, Charles E. "The Science of Muddling Through." *Public Administration Review* 19 (Spring 1959): 79-88.

_____. "Why Government Must Cater to Business." *Business and Society Review* (Fall 1978).

Marcus, Alfred A. "Policy Uncertainty and Technological Innovation." *Academy of Management Review* 6 (1981): 443-48.

_____. "Public Interest Leaders: Whom Do They Represent?" *Business Horizons* 22 (August 1979): 84-88.

Mintzberg, Harry, D. Raisinghani, and A. Theoret. "The Structure of Unstructured Decision Processes." *Administrative Science Quarterly* 21 (June 1976): 246-75.

Mullin, Roger W., Jr. "The Adversary Society." In *Private Management and Public Policy*, ed. Lewis Benton, pp. 131-45. Lexington, Mass.: Lexington Books, 1980.

Olson, Mancur. "Stagflation and the Political Economy of the Decline in Productivity." *American Economic Review* 72 (May 1982): 143-48.

Olson, Mancur, and Hans Landsberg, eds. *The No-growth Society*. New York: Norton, 1973.

O'Toole, James. "What's Ahead for the Business-Government Relationship." *Harvard Business Review* 79 (March/April 1979): 94-105.

Porter, Bruce D. "Parkinson's Law Revisited: War and the Growth of American Government." *The Public Interest* (Summer 1980).

Rainey, Hal, Robert Backoff, and Charles Levine. "Comparing Public and Private Organizations." *Public Administration Review* 36 (March/April 1976): 233-43.

Reich, Robert B. "Making Industrial Policy." *Foreign Affairs* 60 (Spring 1982): 852-81.

Rose, Richard. "What if Anything Is Wrong with Big Government?" *Journal of Public Policy* 1 (February 1981): 5-37.

Sabatier, Paul, and Daniel Mazmanian. "The Implementation of Public Policy: A Framework of Analysis." *Policy Studies Journal* 8 (Special Issue #2, 1980): 538-60.

Schattschneider, E. E. *The Semisovereign People*. New York: Holt, Rinehart and Winston, 1960.

Strick, Anne. "What's Wrong with the Adversary System: Paranoia, Hatred, and Suspicion." *Washington Monthly* 8 (January 1977): 19-28.

Sturdivant, Frederick. *Business and Society: A Managerial Approach*. Homewood, Ill.: Irwin, 1977.

Thurow, Lester. *The Zero-sum Society*. New York: Basic Books, 1980.

Vogel, David. "The Inadequacy of Contemporary Opposition to Business." *Daedalus* 109 (Summer 1980): 49.

Weidenbaum, Murray L. "The Future of Business/Government Relations in the United States." In *The Future of Business*, ed. Max Ways. New York: Pergamon, 1979.

Wilson, James Q., and Patricia Rachal. "Can the Government Regulate Itself?" *The Public Interest* (Spring 1977).

REGULATION AS BUSINESS-GOVERNMENT INTERACTION

Bardach, Eugene, and Robert A. Kagan. *Going by the Book*. Philadelphia: Temple University Press, 1982.

Baron, Barry, and Philip Baron. "A Regulatory Compliance Model." *Journal of Contemporary Business* 9, no. 2 (1981): 139-51.

Bernstein, Marver H. *Regulating Business by Independent Commission*. Princeton, N.J.: Princeton University Press, 1955.

Breyer, Stephen. *Regulation and Its Reform*. Cambridge, Mass.: Harvard University Press, 1982.

Breyer, Stephen, and Paul W. MacAvoy. "Regulating Natural Gas Producers." In *Energy Supply and Government Policy*, ed. Robert J. Kalter and William A. Vogely, pp. 161-93. Ithaca, N.Y.: Cornell University Press, 1976.

Calabresi, Guido, and Philip Bobbitt. *Tragic Choices*. New York: W. W. Norton, 1978.

Cole, Barry, and Mal Oettinger. *Reluctant Regulators: The FCC and the Broadcast Audience*. Reading, Mass.: Addison-Wesley, 1978.

Cole, Roland J., and Paul Sommers. "Business and Government Regulation: A Theory of Compliance Decisions." *Journal of Contemporary Business* 10, no. 1 (1981): 143-53.

Davis, David Howard. *Energy Politics*. 2d ed. New York: St. Martin's, 1978.

DeMuth, Christopher. "What Regulation Is." Paper presented at the Second Annual Research Conference of the Association for Public Policy Analysis and Management, Boston, Massachusetts, October 1980.

Doron, Gideon. "How Smoking Increased When T.V. Advertising of Cigarettes Was Banned." *Regulation* 3 (March/April 1979): 48-52.

Dubnick, Mel. "Making Regulators Regulate." Paper presented at the annual meeting of the American Society for Public Administration, Baltimore, Maryland, April 1979.

Epstein, Edward J. *News from Nowhere*. New York: Random House, 1973.

Fiorino, Daniel J. "Implementing Regulatory Reforms—An Agency Perspective." Paper presented at the Symposium on Strategies for Change in Regulatory Policy, Chicago, Illinois, 1979.

Freeman, David. *Energy: The New Era*. New York: Walker and Co., 1974.

Green, Mark, ed. *The Monopoly Makers*. New York: Grossman, 1973.

Halpern, Paul. "The Corvair, the Pinto, and Corporate Behavior: Implications for Regulatory Reform." Paper prepared for the Symposium on Regulatory Policy, Houston, Texas, November 1979.

Hennigan, Patrick J. "Politics of Regulatory Analysis." Paper prepared for delivery at the annual meeting of the American Political Science Association, New York City, September 4, 1981.

Johnson, W. A. "Why U.S. Energy Policy Has Failed." In *Energy Supply and Government Policy*, ed. W. Kalter and W. Vogely, pp. 280-306. Ithaca, N.Y.: Cornell University Press, 1976.

Joskow, Paul, and Robert Pindyck. "Subsidizing Synthetic Energy Production." *Regulation* (September/October 1979): 18-24.

Kelman, Steven. "Occupational Safety and Health Administration." In *The Politics of Regulation*, ed. James Q. Wilson, pp. 236-67. New York: Basic Books, 1980.

_____. *What Price Incentives?* Boston: Auburn House, 1981.

Kolko, Gabriel. *Railroads and Regulation, 1877-1916*. Princeton, N.J.: Princeton University Press, 1965.

_____. *The Triumph of Conservation*. Glencoe, Ill.: Free Press, 1963.

Krasnow, Erwin G., and Lawrence D. Longley. *The Politics of Broadcast Regulation*. 2d ed. New York: St. Martin's Press, 1978.

Lave, Lester B. "An Economist's View." In *The Scientific Base of Health and Safety Regulation*, ed. Lester B. Lave and Robert W. Crandall, p. 275. Washington, D.C.: Brookings Institution, 1981.

Levin, Michael H. "Getting There: Implementing the 'Bubble' Policy." In *Social Regulation*, ed. Eugene Bardach and Robert A. Kagan, pp. 59-92. New Brunswick, N.J.: Transaction Books, 1982.

Lewitt, Eugene, Douglas Coate, and Michael Grossman. "The Effects of Government Regulation on Teenage Smoking." *Journal of Law and Economics* (December 1981): 545-69.

Linder, Stephen, and Gerry Suchanek. "A Second Best Mechanism for Marketing Emissions Reductions." *Policy Sciences* 13 (1981): 195-203.

McCaffrey, David P. "Executive Orders and the Organization of Regulatory Cost-Benefit Analysis." Paper presented at Academy of Management National Meetings, New York City, August 1982.

McKean, Roland N. "Enforcement Costs in Environmental and Safety Regulation." *Policy Analysis* 6, no. 3 (1980): 269-89.

Majone, Giandomenico. "Choice among Policy Instruments for Pollution Control." *Policy Analysis* (Fall 1976): 597.

Marcus, Alfred A. "Command and Control: An Assessment of Smokestack Emission Regulation." In *Policy Implementation: Penalties or Incentives?*, ed. John Brigham and Don Brown, pp. 209-26. Beverly Hills, Calif.: Sage, 1980.

_____. "Environmental Protection Agency." In *The Politics of Regulation*, ed. James Q. Wilson, pp. 267-304. New York: Basic Books, 1980.

_____. *Promise and Performance: Choosing and Implementing an Environmental Policy*. Westport, Conn.: Greenwood Press, 1980.

Margolis, Howard. "The Politics of Auto Emissions." *The Public Interest* 49 (Fall 1977): 3-4.

Mitnick, Barry. *The Political Economy of Regulation*. New York: Columbia University Press, 1980.

Nadel, Mark V. *The Politics of Consumer Protection*. Indianapolis: Bobbs-Merrill, 1971.

Nivola, Pietro. "Energy Policy and the Congress: The Politics of the Natural Gas Policy Act of 1978." *Public Policy* 28 (Fall 1980): 491-543.

Noll, Roger G., Merton J. Peck, and John J. McGowan. *Economic Aspects of Television Regulation*. Washington, D.C.: Brookings Institution, 1973.

Peltzman, Sam. "Toward a More General Theory of Regulation." *Journal of Law and Economics* 19 (August 1976): 211-41.

Penoyer, Ronald J. *Directory of Federal Regulatory Agencies*. St. Louis: Center for the Study of American Business, 1981.

_____. *Directory of Federal Regulatory Agencies—1982 Update*. St. Louis: Center for the Study of American Business, 1982.

Posner, Richard A. "Theory of Economic Regulation." *Bell Journal of Economics and Management* 5 (1974): 335-58.

Quirk, Paul J. *Industry Influence in Federal Regulatory Agencies*. Princeton, N.J.: Princeton University Press, 1981.

Quirk, Paul J., and Martha Derthick. "Congressional Support for Pro-competitive Regulatory Reform." Paper prepared for delivery at the annual meeting of the American Political Science Association, New York, September 1981.

Rosenbaum, Walter A. *Energy Politics and Public Policy*. Washington, D.C.: Congressional Quarterly Press, 1981.

Rothman, Jack. *Planning and Organizing for Social Change*. New York: Columbia University Press, 1974.

Sabatier, Paul. "Social Movements and Regulatory Agencies: Toward a More Adequate and Less Pessimistic Theory of Clientele Capture." *Policy Studies* 6 (1976): 302-42.

Schultze, Charles L. "The Public Use of Private Interest." *Regulation* (September/October 1977): 10.

_____. *The Public Use of Private Interest*. Washington, D.C.: Brookings Institution, 1977.

Sorg, James D. "Implementation of Innovations: A Descriptive Model of the Process." Paper prepared for delivery at the annual conference of the American Society of Public Administration, Baltimore, March 1979.

Stigler, George J. *The Citizen and the State: Essays in Regulation*. Chicago: University of Chicago Press, 1975.

_____. "The Theory of Economic Regulation." *Bell Journal of Economics and Management* 2 (1971): 3-21.

Stone, Alan. *Regulation and Its Alternatives*. Washington, D.C.: Congressional Quarterly Press, 1982.

Stone, Christopher D. *Where the Law Ends: The Social Control of Corporate Behavior*. New York: Harper and Row, 1975.

Stuart, Alexander. "The Blazing Battle to Free Natural Gas." *Fortune*, October 19, 1981, pp. 152-67.

Thompson, Fred, and Larry R. Jones. "Fighting Regulation: The Regulatory Review." *California Management Review* (Winter 1980): 5-19.

Tobin, Richard J. "Federal Regulation of Hazardous Consumer Products." Paper prepared for the Symposium on Regulatory Policy, Houston, Texas, November 1979.

Viscusi, W. Kip. "Presidential Oversight: Controlling the Regulators." *Journal of Policy Analysis and Management* 2 (Winter 1983): 157-73.

Weaver, Paul. "Regulation, Social Policy, and Class Conflict." *The Public Interest* (Winter 1978).

Weingast, Barry R. "The Renaissance of the Federal Trade Commission." Pamphlet from the Center for the Study of American Business, Washington University, St. Louis, Missouri (December 1978), pp. 1-32.

Wilson, James Q. "The Politics of Regulation." In *Social Responsibility and the Business Predicament*, ed. James W. McKie, pp. 135-69. Washington, D.C.: Brookings Institution, 1974.

Wilson, James Q., ed. *The Politics of Regulation*. New York: Basic Books, 1980.

Zaltman, Gerald, and Robert Duncan. *Strategies for Planned Change*. New York: Wiley, 1977.

Index

About the Author

ALFRED A. MARCUS teaches in the Department of Strategic Management and Organization at the University of Minnesota. From 1979 to 1984 he was a Research Scientist and Policy Analyst at the Battelle Human Affairs Research Centers in Seattle, Washington. He has worked for business and government agencies and has taught business and government courses at the University of Washington. He is the author of *Promise and Performance: Choosing and Implementing an Environmental Policy* (Greenwood Press, 1980), and numerous articles and chapters in publications such as *Government Agencies* (Greenwood Press, 1983), *The Politics of Regulation*, and *The Academy of Management Review*.

 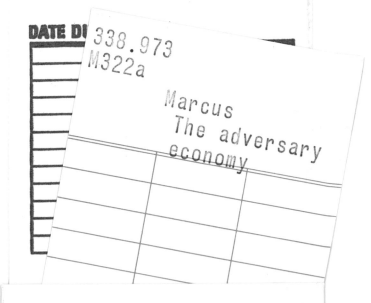